THE
Ms. Money Book

ALSO BY EMILY CARD

Staying Solvent: A Comprehensive Guide to Equal Credit for Women

Consumer Reports Money Book (co-author)

EMILY CARD, Ph.D.

THE Ms. Money Book

E. P. DUTTON   NEW YORK

Published in the United States by E. P. Dutton, a division of Penguin Books USA Inc., 2 Park Avenue, New York, N.Y. 10016.

Published simultaneously in Canada by Fitzhenry and Whiteside, Limited, Toronto.

Library of Congress Cataloging-in-Publication Data
Card, Emily.
The Ms. money book/Emily Card.—1st ed.
Includes index.
p. cm.
ISBN 0-525-24669-X
1. Women—Finance, Personal. 2. Finance, Personal. I. Ms.
II. Title.
HG179.C328   1990
332.024'042—dc20   89-16920
                                         CIP

Designed by Steven N. Stathakis

3 5 7 9 10 8 6 4 2

*This book is dedicated to Melinda Benedek,
Nancy Brown, Betty Friedan, Susan McHenry,
Joan Palevsky, Gloria Steinem,
and Susan Weiss.*

*Each helped in her special way
to teach me to reach for more
and desire less.*

CONTENTS

Part III: Strategies for Success
in the Coming Decade

Conclusion: The Myths and Realities
of Money Management   214

ACKNOWLEDGMENTS

The most important contributors to this books are its characters.
The characters are drawn from actual law and business clients
of mine. Names and geographic identities have been changed,
and, in some cases, aspects of one or more people's financial lives
have been merged to make the example clearer.

The Ms. Money Book involved collaboration with several
members of the extended *Ms.* family. The book has survived the
sale of both the publishing house, E. P. Dutton, and *Ms.* magazine itself. At *Ms.,* the book was born on a summer's day in 1983
in a meeting with Pat Carbine, then *Ms.* publisher, and Gloria
Steinem, *Ms.* founding editor, when they had the idea of turning
my cable network television money series into a book.

I took six years to write the book, no longer based on the
series. In those years, Susan McHenry, then *Ms.* Senior Editor
for Finance, became the book's champion. Susan's commitment
made the book happen and her editing made the book whole. My
hat's off to Susan for her faith, commitment, and concern for the
project and to her continuing friendship during the creative
process.

Suzanne Levine, the *Ms.* Managing Editor, also contributed greatly by her support for both the book and the *Ms.* columns that I wrote during that period. Letty Pogrebin, Joanne Edgar, Mary Thom, and Rosemary Bray all added their support.

The "new *Ms.*" has carried on the tradition, and I must thank Anne Summers for her support.

My literary agent, Denise Marcil, guided me from beginning to end.

The book's research was an enormous effort, which was enhanced and supported by a series of *Ms.* interns, and students from the University of California at Los Angeles, Harvard University, and Stanford University. Thanks are due to Jennifer Megquier, Jennifer Sakuri, Melinda Wong, Kathleen Deming, Kerry Conway, Amy Stirnkorb, Lisa Shorago, Michelle Orecklin, Jill Kessler, Dawn Cymrot, Stephanie McFadden, Joy Selby, Cheryl Conly, Katie Hobin, Michelle Arlene Agulire, Melissa Kester, and Brenda Beardsley.

Several professionals also played a role in research or writing earlier versions of material that was utilized. These included Victoria Scott, Janie Watts Spataro, Bonnie Souleles, and Claudia Anderson.

Nicole Runkle survived her second book with me, providing thoroughly professional typing at several stages.

For writing retreats and moral support, I must thank Nancy M. Brown and Gayle Carmichael, two very wonderful friends who shared their homes for extended periods, and my sister Judy Watts, whose Cambridge home served as my East Coast base.

For reading the book and commenting, Brad J. Sherman, Esq., a tax specialist; Robert J. Klein, founding editor of *Money* magazine and President of Novos Planning Associates; Jane Crist, Esq., a securities expert; and Lamar Card.

I also enjoyed encouragement during this period from Elinor Guggenheimer, Mary Alice Dwyer-Dobbins, Martin Harmon, Susan Westerberg Praeger, Barbara Koscala Varat, Eric Zolt, Christine Knapland, Jean Firstenberg, Ron Merl, Edmund Barton, Sharon Mitchell, Linda Poteete-Marshall, and Marian Rees.

Much of the original inspiration for the book was drawn from the memory of my mother, Anna Dempsey Watts. I'm very appreciative and proud of my five-year-old son, Waldo, for the respect he gives my writing.

Finally, Kent Brosveen, my husband, provided both moral and logistical support. From moving computers to cooking supper, Kent has helped almost every step of the way.

Of course any shortcomings in the book are my own; its strengths lie in the wonderful network of supporters.

Half the profits from this book will go to the Ms. Foundation.

THE
Ms. Money Book

INTRODUCTION

Women's financial lives have changed radically over the last two decades, yet improved financial opportunities have not been matched by an increased awareness of personal financial strategies for most women. Progress has been made, but women still have a long way to go to reach full economic empowerment. Despite the proliferation of financial books, columns, radio and TV programs about money, most of us are still puzzled when faced with financial decisions. Part of the reason is that financial guides function like tour guides: you have to know where you want to go before the descriptions are of much help.

Learning to think conceptually about any money decision is the key to taking control of your financial life. This book will not cover every money question you may have; rather, the case studies here—built as composites based on real-life stories—are designed to illustrate principles that can be applied to any consumer's life. My aim is to help you to approach your financial decisions just as businesspeople and MBA students approach their businesses—in fact, the case-study approach is the meat of business and law school educations.

The theory component in this book is meant to focus your attention on the critical aspects of any financial decision. We shall analyze each financial decision in terms of three classic business variables: *cash flow, tax effect,* and *future growth.* If you can look at the effect of an activity on your cash flow, check out its impact on taxes, and see whether it creates financial growth, you'll know enough to make an informed decision.

WHY ANOTHER MONEY BOOK FOR WOMEN?

Since *Ms.* was founded in 1972 women have made rapid progress in many fields; yet American society as a whole is still adjusting to changed social and financial realities. "Good news, bad news" statistics tell the tale.

Top Ten Facts About Women's Financial Lives

1. Women as a group continue to earn less than men, 70 cents to every male dollar, but younger women are narrowing the earnings gap, with white, middle- and upper-class women in their early twenties earning 90 cents to the male-earned dollar.
2. Women have moved into the professions in unprecedented numbers, providing a base upon which a class of women of means can be built. Yet, women still meet resistance in making partner in law firms and attaining other top-level or upper-management slots.
3. Women are the fastest-growing segment in the small business sector, making up 23 percent today. But women entrepreneurs' net profits remain low: under $2,000 annually.
4. Of all married couples, more than half have two breadwinners, contrasted to just over one-third in 1972. Yet the work place fails to reflect the need to accommodate the working family, often punishing rather than rewarding women for their dual roles, with discriminatory benefits packages, for example.

5. Between now and the year 2000, more than 80 percent of the new entrants into the work force will be women, minorities, and immigrants. Despite the increase in the number of women employed, tax provisions give only partial recognition to special working expenses linked to women's traditional areas of family responsibility. For example, parents receive only limited tax credit for child care, and none of the homemaker replacement costs of going to work is deductible.

6. Rising divorce rates have leveled off, but marriage offers little economic security for women today.

7. The proportion of the poor population who are women began to drop in the early 1980s, but the feminization of poverty is still with us. Women over sixteen years of age compose over 61.9 percent of the poor.

8. Children remain women's primary responsibility whether or not the mother is married. More than one out of four children live with only one parent, compared to one out of ten in 1960, and mothers have sole or primary custody of their children in 88 percent of divorces. Because children often are dependent on poor women, 21 percent of all children now live in poverty. At all income levels, employment-related day care is a pressing need.

9. Women are more likely than men to depend entirely on Social Security for retirement.

10. Women are earning more. But, we—like all Americans—are spending more than we are saving, with a savings rate of 4.2 percent of disposable personal income (compared to 8.5 percent in 1971), reflecting only a slight rise from the 3.2 percent all-time low in 1987. Meanwhile, the amount the average consumer owes on credit has risen from a high 15.6 percent of disposable income fifteen years ago to an even higher 20 percent today.

And, women aren't availing themselves of the knowledge that's available. Personal finance books, for example, attract a minority of women readers—men purchase 85 percent of those published in any given year.

The Need for New Priorities About Money

The economic advancement of this generation of American women coincided with the inflation-driven 1970s. The economic climate during that time taught us that spending was attractive: inflation eroded the value of savings, and in the highest tax brackets, for every dollar earned, the government could take up to 70 cents.

But economic times have changed. Inflation has slowed, and the tax structure has changed. Unfortunately, many women have not made the necessary switch from spending to saving. With the current economic climate, it is more important than ever to find new strategies for our cash, taxes, and growth and to accept that there are real-world limits to our spending. Women must change their personal financial habits to meet changing economic circumstances, in part because what we have learned from the experiences of the recent past won't be appropriate to guide us in the future.

OUR CASES

In the following chapters, you will meet women whose lives reflect the major trends of our times. Each has had experiences that offer insights into money management, and each has more to learn about coping with today's financial realities. The case studies are designed to illustrate the changes women need to make in their financial planning. No single case will exactly fit any reader; rather, as a group the cases work together to illustrate the major concerns that the readers of this book are likely to encounter. The cumulative effect of looking at several characters' cash flows, taxes, and growth portraits should underline the relationship among the three factors. Our characters include two moderate-income women, three middle-income households, and three high-cash-flow women.

Olivia Wong, a single woman earning just enough to get by, wonders how she can build a financially secure future on her own. First, she must learn to budget her cash.

Sherry Marshall, a divorced mother of two who lives with

her parents because she can't afford rent, decides to reinvest the money from the sale of her and her former husband's family home.

Dora Delgado, a professor who can afford to buy a home, prefers to steer clear of paperwork and household repairs. Ultimately, she gets involved in real estate, but she also decides to invest in stocks.

Leslie and Andrew Carlson, a young black professional couple, work to create financial equality within their marriage.

Kate English, a high-powered Washington consultant turned full-time mother, faces a hard time emotionally because of her sudden career switch and financially because of associated loss of income.

Melissa Hilton, an attorney whose income has tripled over a decade, has no savings. She puts tax savings to work in buying a home.

Sonny Levin enjoys what looks like a fantasy life-style, but divorce threatens to put her into financial chaos.

Anna Seaver, a successful businesswoman, survives a severe cash-flow crunch and conquers the intricacies of corporate taxes.

Each character's story is analyzed in terms of the principal factors of cash flow, taxes, and future growth. Let us look briefly at how these three fit together.

THE TRADE-OFFS BETWEEN CASH FLOW, TAX IMPACT, AND FUTURE GROWTH

Any financial decision—whether buying a house, purchasing stocks, or reorganizing personal finances upon marriage or after divorce—can be analyzed in terms of *cash flow, tax impact,* and *future growth.*

Let us take a simple example. What woman has not heard the expression "good clothes are an investment"? In fact, *The New York Times* used the expression "investment dressing." Although this idea is often linked to the notion of investing in yourself by dressing well, advertisers blur the line so that we begin to think literally of clothes as a sort of "investment," which they are not.

Here is how you might analyze the "investment" purchase of a designer, woven leather handbag at $500.

First, your *cash flow* will be affected. If you pay cash, you will be out $500 right away. If you buy on credit, you could choose to pay only $50 per month, plus interest, over the next ten months.

What's the *tax impact?* Had you spent the same $500 on a legitimate business deduction, you might have created a tax savings or shelter. But since you bought a pocketbook, not a tax-preferred item, there would be no tax impact, unless the bag is used in a professional setting such as for a stage wardrobe, which might make it deductible.

How about *future growth?* You've just put $500 into a no-growth situation. Unless there's a sudden spurt in the value of used leather pocketbooks, the market value of the purse will go down drastically the minute you fill it with your own paraphernalia. Had you put the same $500 into an interest-bearing account at 8 percent, your money would more than double in ten years to $1,080. In other words, if you buy an expensive leather handbag, see it for what it is: a luxury indulgence, not an investment.

Even as a clothing purchase involves each of the three money basics, so do more complicated financial transactions, such as real estate development, where the formula is used to assess multimillion-dollar investments. Let us analyze a home purchase using "the formula."

First, cash flow changes. If monthly mortgage payments add up to more than rental costs, then demands on cash flow go up. If your rent is $800 a month and your house payments are $1,500, you need $700 more to cover this extra expense and your available cash flow is reduced by $700.

Suppose you decide to turn your purchase into an investment and rent it out? Leaving aside tax considerations for a moment, you now have a higher cash flow every month. If you can rent out the home for more than your mortgage costs, you will be that much ahead. If your home has a $1,500 monthly mortgage payment and you rent it for $1,800, your cash-flow position is improved by $300.

When real estate investors look at a property, they use the

same analysis. The first thing they ask is "What is the cash flow?"

This question is critical because if the property will not generate enough income to *carry itself,* meaning to cover the mortgage, taxes, insurance, and repairs, then it will not be an attractive investment. Instead of supplementing the investor's cash position, the investment drains it, just as an overly expensive home drains yours.

Sometimes investors make a conscious decision to purchase properties that will not generate positive cash flow. An investor may believe that the property will grow in value by more than the extra amount necessary to cover monthly costs. The negative cash flow in this case becomes an enforced "savings plan" for the investor. Assuming the home rises in value, the appreciation will exceed the extra carrying costs, so by sacrificing current cash flow you can build up equity.

Notice the other two factors that an investor weighs if the cash-flow position is not attractive: the *tax situation* and the *prospects for growth.*

When a real estate investor looks at a tax issue, she will concern herself with terms such as *deductions* and *depreciation.* Most people don't know how to calculate the value of a deduction; yet, an informed real estate investor can calculate to the penny tax savings to be made from a particular undertaking.

Future growth is exactly what it sounds like, "increase in value over time," and it is the trickiest issue of all. In real estate, investors ask, "How much will this property appreciate?"

Whether it is a complicated real estate deal or a stock purchase, each financial activity must be analyzed for its future growth component. The appreciation on a single stock and a multimillion-dollar property represent future growth. By contrast, a simple savings account, while it offers cash flow, offers no growth or equity appreciation (other than any extra interest you earn by leaving your interest in the account and compounding).

Remember, as you learned in junior high school math, every positive number has a negative relative. Sometimes growth is negative. A house goes down in value because the plumbing deteriorates. Other lost opportunities for growth include: spending money from savings, charging a trip to Europe on Visa, blowing a week's wages in Atlantic City, or simply seeing your money value erode through inflation. Any diminishing of capital represents negative growth.

HOW THIS BOOK IS ORGANIZED

The book is divided into three parts. Part I consists of three chapters that provide fuller definitions of the concepts necessary to understand cash flow, taxes, and growth. This section is a short course in macroeconomics, tax theory, and finance. The going can get tough in places, but remember that the complicated story of how the economic climate shapes individual prospects for financial growth forms the underpinning for all that follows both for our characters and for you.

Part II centers on our characters. These cases, in turn, are grouped according to the complexity of their financial affairs, reflected in part by the level of their cash flow. Each character's own story is divided into cash, tax, and growth components.

Part III is designed to help you put together a personal strategy for the coming decade. A how-to, working chapter is devoted to each concept, with charts for you to complete on cash flow, tax planning, and growth strategies.

The Appendices contain additional charts and reference materials. Refer to them as you read other chapters.

If you are the sort of person who learns best by building theories from particular examples, turn to Part II (the cases). But if you need theory before you look at examples, begin with Part I.

THE

CONCEPT

CHAPTER 1

STRATEGIES

FOR

GROWTH

A GROWTH PHILOSOPHY

The starting point for financial growth, in the absence of inheritance or windfall, always involves diverting funds from current cash flow or taxes into the future. Whether a gambler spending her last dollar on a lottery ticket, a worker taking a steady payroll deduction, or a young entrepreneur sweeping the factory floor and plotting to own it, those who achieve growth are willing to defer some current gratification in favor of prospective wealth.

One of the preoccupations of our culture is our fascination with undiscovered investment treasures. People allow themselves to be deluded into believing that through clever choices they'll get rich. But the media cover stories of very great financial success precisely because they are the exceptions. Few people will fill their bank accounts by discovering the next Xerox stock, starting Apple Computer, or manufacturing Reebok shoes, to name some visible stars of the past three decades.

Get-rich-quick fantasies, then, serve only to divert us from recognizing reality: steady accumulation is the only sure method to growth. Growth starts with conserving cash flow and generating tax savings.

The first step is to see how you can make trade-offs between cash flow and tax savings that produce the funds for growth. Whether you create funds by forgoing fur coats, using your tax savings to apply to a mortgage, or simply putting aside $25 a month in a savings account or IRA, once you make the decision to favor long-range objectives over short-term expenses, you are on your way to future growth.

PROSPECTS FOR GROWTH: THE ECONOMIC CLIMATE

Ultimately, investing can best be described as betting on the future direction of the economy—whether one expects price levels to rise or fall—in other words, whether to expect inflation or deflation. Boom, stagnation, and bust are all part of the business cycle. Your projection about where economic trends are going (which can sometimes challenge the theories of the "best" professional economists) is the key to where you should place your money.

The most important part of becoming a savvy investor is knowing which way the wind blows and shifting one's investment strategies accordingly. Economic shifts occur with dizzying speed. Look at one example from late 1987: in September, a *Los Angeles Times* front-page story noted soaring real estate prices of 13 percent over six months; fewer than six weeks later, on Monday, October 19, the stock market experienced its record-setting crash.

Even experienced investors and professionals don't have all the answers at such times. But market prices from real estate and bonds are based on the wisdom of the market about the future of inflation/deflation and all the accompanying changes in supply and demand.

Inflation causes prices to rise and the money supply to expand, so money is readily available. Although the relationship between interest rates and inflation is complex, in general, if the Federal Reserve Board does not intervene, interest rates go up as inflation heats up. Lenders expect money to be worth less in the future and therefore desire a higher price from borrowers who will be paying later using "cheaper" dollars.

Likewise, bond prices fall. Bonds pay fixed interest, "locking in" today's rates. If interest rates continue to rise, markets bypass current lower rates for predicted future higher rates, and bonds—with fixed values now lower than the market—fall.

Rising prices cause real estate to become an even more attractive investment. For example, a house worth $100,000 at 8 percent inflation would be worth $146,933 after five years.

The 1970s conditioned people to expect inflation, rising prices, and declining purchasing power for the dollar. By the end of the 1980s this outlook had shifted. The stock market plunge in late 1987 caused people to remember the lesson of the 1930s: a depression is a possibility. In the late 1980s, depression was a reality in regional oil-based markets such as Dallas, Houston, and Denver.

With deflation, prices drop and the money supply contracts. Because of falling interest rates, bond prices go up because they lock in the current (presumably higher) interest. Real estate then becomes less attractive. The same $100,000 house after five years of deflation at 8 percent would be worth only $65,908.

Although such a rate of deflation has not been sustained in the economy as a whole since the 1930s, pockets of severe deflation have appeared. In the depressed Houston and Dallas markets in 1987, average home prices dropped by 15 percent.

Today's investor operates in a global marketing environment. Stock markets are linked electronically. While the United States sleeps, Japan trades. Even real estate is affected—if somewhat more slowly—as foreign investors continue to find U.S. real estate attractive. The open-ended global economy creates volatility, a component of today's investment climate.

Hidden dangers make it all the more important to attend to economic trends, because with some investments you can lose more than your initial capital outlay with severe market drops. For example, much real estate is financed with mortgages; with down payments as low as 5 percent, such a drop may leave the property owner responsible for a mortgage that exceeds the market value of the real estate (although many residential mortgages are constructed so that only the property itself—no matter how devalued—must be forfeited in case of foreclosure).

Ultimately, your investment choices should be set based on your expectations about the inflationary-deflationary cycle.

If you are betting on inflation, invest in real estate, stocks, and collectible items, such as art and antiques. Use credit for buying now and paying later.

If you're betting on deflation, choose cash, bonds, and any investment with long-term fixed rates, such as mortgages.

CONSERVING CASH

Economists estimated that American consumers spent $3.2 trillion in 1988. Some of us spent our portion of this money conservatively, creating savings. For others, expenses outstripped incomes. With shifting economic times and the slowing of inflation, spending patterns that made sense in the early 1970s and 1980s no longer seem reasonable.

In the ten years from 1976 to 1986, average income fell by $1,000 a year in real terms. In the same ten-year period, credit use was two and a half times greater. Too many have used credit to close the gap between income and spending, keeping standards high—often at the expense of future growth. In fact, the average savings of the American family stood at a low 3.6 percent of income in 1986.

We all face the temptation to enjoy life now and spend all the money we make. There are also events that force us to go into debt, such as illness, loss of job, or unexpected expenses. But today, more than ever, the first principle of wealth is building cash.

Our culture too often promotes the notion that spending money we don't have is a substitute for wealth. Advertising urges middle-class people to consume at levels appropriate to those with wealth, not those who are in the middle of building it. Rethink your strategies if you formed your investment and spending habits during an inflationary period, when it made sense to use credit and pay later in rapidly declining dollars. The right path during a slower growth cycle resembles a 1930s conservation mentality more than a 1980s consumption one.

The best way to make money is to conserve it. We must accept that it is all right to be conservative consumers and to say,

"I can't afford it." Or, as wealthy people say when turning down a charity request, "I'm all tapped out." "Too much money is going up in smoke, spent on expensive restaurant meals," as my father-in-law once said.

If you haven't formed wealth-building habits yet, you can start by applying cash-flow management techniques and conserving your cash. The starting point: making trade-offs between current cash flow and future growth through budgeting.

Control Cash Flow Through Budgeting

Perhaps because of their quantitative nature, analyzing cash flow and preparing a budget seem to provoke anxiety. If a consumer wants to achieve new financial objectives, goals have to be set. A budget is a way of reducing those goals to numerical benchmarks. A budget can help you get the means to buy a new car, afford a special vacation, or begin saving for retirement. Most important, budgeting can be the starting point for growth.

According to a study by the Financial Executives Institute, 99 percent of 338 member companies surveyed reported that their companies budget their expenditures. By contrast, researchers report that only 60 percent of consumers budget, and many of these do so only sporadically.

Studies indicate that most people begin budgeting when facing life changes that make organizing essential. The most common events that prompt this kind of financial planning are having a child, moving, recovering from a major medical crisis, or dissolving a marriage. For a consumer who experiences any of these events, budgeting becomes necessary for survival.

Budgeting isn't easy; our own psychology gets in the way. People fool themselves about money and how they are using it. Even for people who do budget, temptations are constant. Stores are set up to maximize profit opportunities derived from shoppers' habits. Food items you do not need are placed at eye level in attractive, colorful displays to encourage purchases; staples are at ground level. The checkout counter is the most desirable product location in the supermarket, for consumers add last-minute purchases there and tend not to check the prices as closely as they would in the aisles. Marketing specialists create special campaigns to convince retailers to place their items in these most desirable spots.

Living in a family does not help either. For most of us, budgeting does not happen in a vacuum. All but 13 percent of U.S. households involve more than one individual, and 71 percent are married couples. For couples, budgeting sometimes presents difficulties because dealing with family finances can exacerbate marital difficulties. When you add children—half of American households include them—new demands on money and time arise.

Even seniors, who in theory should be free from the financial concerns of raising a family, find themselves pressed. Healthcare expenses can eat into savings, and studies have shown that many seniors now worry about their middle-aged children, many of whom experience financial crises.

But a crisis should not be the starting point for a budget. Instead, think positively of the rewards of conserving cash and make the decision to begin budgeting. When cash flow is turned around, the next step is to focus on investing by stages.

STAGES OF GROWTH

Our strategy consists of three stages of growth, each with different goals, and each with a different entry level. The strategy builds on what you have, forming a solid base for future growth. This overview will help guide you as you read later chapters and will prepare you for the step-by-step growth plan in Chapter 9. If you are generally unfamiliar with any particular investment, also see Chapter 9.

Stage 1: Saving for Future Investments

At stage 1 the goal is to save your money by putting it somewhere away from current expenditures. With small amounts to invest, it is not where you put it so much as putting it somewhere. You might choose U.S. Savings Bonds as a savings vehicle. With the money safely set aside out of your cash stream, you will have a nest egg to build on. If you can afford to let your money sit for six months to twelve years, buy bonds (you can withdraw the money in six months, but it takes twelve years for the bond to mature fully, when you can cash it for its full face value). Once an unattractive investment, U.S. Savings Bonds have been revamped, offering more competitive interest and almost absolute safety. Tax deferment, convenience, and a low entry ticket are also attractions.

You can buy bonds from your bank teller. The beauty is that with only $25 you can purchase a bond worth $50, the face value at maturity. Savings bonds now have variable rates of interest; therefore, the date of maturity may vary. At current rates of nearly 7 percent, bonds mature in twelve years. Every time you make a deposit or cash a check, you can peel out $25 or $50 and barely notice that it has gone.

For example, if you save $25 a week, at current rates you will reap $2,600 at maturity in the twelfth year. Just multiply the face amount by the number of bonds for the matured value, for example, 50 (face value) times 52 (one a week), or $2,600. Each year you invest, you can reap another reward a dozen years later. (But inflation can take its toll. At 4 percent inflation, in twelve years the real pre-tax net worth in today's dollars will be $1,624.)

If you start this habit at age twenty-five, by age forty-nine it will be just as if your young self had given your older self an inheritance—in this case amounting to $31,200. (A dozen years of payments at $2,600 if started at age thirty-seven and ending when the final bond matures at age forty-nine. Of course if you reinvested the $2,600 each year, your nest egg would grow larger for later use.) Even if inflation erodes the value, having this money certainly beats having none. Think about it next time you buy two $10 lipsticks and a bottle of nail polish, or four movie tickets.

Whatever the vehicle, the goal of savings is to build up capital. Then, you will have the option to try other kinds of investments.

Stage 2: Securing Your Retirement

The goal of stage 2 is to build up the three main components, or pillars, necessary for a secure retirement. The three-pillared plan consists of Social Security benefits; real estate ownership; and a pension, IRA, or other additional retirement fund.

If you are an employee, you most probably are already funding your Social Security. This enforced savings will eventually serve as the first pillar of your retirement.

The second and most important pillar is real estate. Once you have put aside $5,000 to $15,000, you ought to look at residential real estate. Although $5,000 can't get you through the front door in Los Angeles or New York, there are still deals to be found. If you can find an anxious seller, you may be able to take over a property with a small down payment, using various creative financing devices. For example, depending upon the financing, you might be able to take over an existing loan and get the seller to *carry paper* or finance the rest of the down payment. For the seller this involves no cash outlay, since the seller is simply deferring receiving profits on the property. Or you might find two to three co-investors and purchase a home or condo that one of you will live in and the others use as an investment property. Assuming you have income and decent credit, it is not unrealistic to consider buying real estate at this stage. If you live in an area where real estate is out of your price range, look in areas you know, such as where parents or relatives live and buy a second home or rental property.

Exact comparisons between investments prove difficult. The need to take into account the returns from cash flow and appreciation along with tax savings, corrected over time, means that reliable figures are hard to obtain. Yet by all measures, real estate historically appears to outperform all other investments significantly. According to figures from the Department of Commerce, table 1 shows how after-tax return on investments compared from 1971 to 1984 (with an average inflation of 7.3 percent per year).

TABLE 1. INVESTMENT PERFORMANCE		
	INTERNAL RATE OF RETURN (%)	INFLATION ADJUSTED (%)
Real estate	13.2	5.9
30-day T-bills	4.9	−2.4
Stocks	6.7	−0.6
Bonds	2.3	0.5

Even though some analysts now suggest that real estate will only keep pace with inflation, this is better than eroding each year, as do many investments. From 1980 to 1988, inflation averaged 6.8 percent a year. Simply to stay even, an investment would have had to earn more than that inflation rate. At least for residential and some rental property the additional advantage of tax breaks means after-tax performance is hard to match.

As a key part of retirement planning, a secure living space is critical. But not all of us will be able to afford to purchase our own homes. If you have been permanently priced out of the housing market, it is critical that you take active steps to ensure you can afford to be a renter by retirement time. If you cannot afford or choose not to enter the real estate market, you will need to set up a real estate or home replacement fund for yourself.

The third pillar of financial security is an additional retirement fund. If you can, begin funding an Individual Retirement Account (IRA). Though these funds are not liquid, they offer a tax break because interest earned is tax free until it is withdrawn at retirement, provided you meet basic IRS requirements discussed in Chapter 2 (p. 33). Even if your retirement fund is made up of after-tax dollars, do not bypass this critical element of your plan.

Other options are available, but regardless of which you choose, secure this final pillar. Once you have adequately planned for your retirement you can start thinking about investing, or stage 3.

Stage 3: Investing for Maximum Growth

At this third stage you make riskier investments in order to achieve greater financial growth. Although I do not recommend these investments for most people, only now should you consider playing the stock market, starting a side business, or trying something more esoteric such as collectibles or gold. As you try new ventures, be careful to weigh risk versus the advantages of higher growth. Don't undertake any investment that would jeopardize what you have worked to build.

Stages of Growth Summary

1. Saving for Future Investments
   Begin saving and amass at least $15,000.
2. Securing Your Retirement
   The three-pillared plan includes: Social Security; a home or
   home replacement fund; and an IRA, pension, or other retirement vehicle.
3. Investing for Maximum Growth
   Choices include higher risk/higher yield investments.

Now that you have had a preview of your growth strategy,
let us turn to the next chapter for a primer on taxes.

CHAPTER 2

A

TAX

PRIMER

Although clever tax management is the largest variable in otherwise equal financial situations, many women (and men) who seem financially sophisticated prefer to leave their taxes strictly to their accountants. By making this choice, you deprive yourself of the benefits of understanding tax strategy. Even those who do their own taxes need someone to query about complicated questions, so a competent CPA should be part of everyone's team. However, no matter how good your adviser, only you can take full day-to-day control of your taxes, exploiting the fundamental relationships among your cash flow, tax position, and future growth. Therefore, while you want to use experts, you also need to understand the basic tax rules.

Knowing how the tax structure works will help you save money at tax time. It will also give you the tools you need to engage in strategic thinking about the tax implications of any proposed investment. While the sweeping reforms of the 1986 Tax Reform Act have meant fewer opportunities than before for many middle-income earners to maneuver their tax positions, it is wise to be informed on key technical aspects of our tax structure not only to understand the options you do have for tax savings, but also to be able to follow continuing changes in our tax laws that may affect you. Although the kind of overhaul in the system that we had in 1986 rarely occurs, continuing incremental changes can be expected. For example, the new 1986 law on home mortgage deductions was amended again the next year. As the administration deals with deficit issues, we can anticipate a dialogue on taxes to emerge. Knowing the basics can help you remain informed about how prospective changes will affect your pocketbook.

No wonder the uninitiated feel excluded: conquering the federal income tax code involves learning a new language along with new concepts. Fortunately, regardless of the length of the tax code or the number of legislative mutations, any tax saving will involve only one of five ways to save. They are:

1. obtaining *exclusions* of income without tax consequences;
2. taking *deductions* of expenses subtracted from income;
3. lowering tax *rates;*
4. using *credits* subtracted from the tax liability itself; and
5. utilizing *deferrals* or delays of the tax obligation.

Once you understand these five principles, you will have a framework against which to judge any fine print you encounter. Remember the loophole—or as experts say, *provision*—must fit into one of these categories.

EXCLUSIONS

When we think of saving money on taxes, most of us think of tax deductions. Yet the first—though not the most obvious—place to save money on taxes is to receive income that is legally excluded from taxes altogether. If you can increase cash flow in areas not defined as "income" for tax purposes, you have made an immediate tax saving.

The first step to understanding exclusions rests on defining *income* in a tax setting. In tax terms, there is no exact equivalent to cash flow. Some cash you receive isn't taxable because it's excluded, and some income isn't received in cash. To simplify the relationship between income and cash flow, visualize cash flow as what you actually receive whereas income is what is taxed.

Income appears on the standard long-form tax return, the 1040, with three qualifiers: "gross income," "adjusted gross income," and "taxable income." (See Appendix 1 for a sample 1040.)

Gross Income: This includes all income from wages, salaries, interest, partnerships, and businesses. However, business deductions are removed before business and partnership income is listed on the main form (these deductions are taken on separate forms or schedules).

Adjusted Gross Income (AGI): This is your gross income minus both certain favored (because you do not have to itemize to get them) "above-the-line" deductions, including alimony (or what is now often called "spousal support") paid and deferrals of voluntary retirement programs such as allowable IRAs and Keoghs. The adjusted gross income, which appears on the bottom line of page 1 of the tax return, is used to bring gross income down, thus lowering the floor for certain other deductions, such as those for medical expenses (to be discussed below).

Taxable Income: This is your adjusted gross income minus itemized or standard deductions and personal exemptions. No matter how large your income, you pay taxes only on this last category of *taxable* income unless you are one of the few subject to alternative minimum tax (AMT), a tax primarily effectively imposed on those with high incomes and high deductions.

Beyond gross income a ghostly category of income doesn't appear on your tax return at all, the exclusions. Exclusions may be cash you receive, such as life insurance proceeds, or noncash fringe benefits.

Fringe benefits constitute a majority of exclusions for salaried taxpayers. Although in actuality those who receive them enjoy a higher income than those who do not, benefits such as employer-provided life and health insurance are not paid in cash and therefore are usually excluded. (A premium for life insurance above $50,000 is attributed to income and reported as taxable.) Some other noncash benefits such as personal use of a company car are taxed.

Before the 1986 tax reform, capital gains enjoyed a special exclusion. *Capital gains* are defined as profits made from selling investments rather than earning income. Previously, 60 percent of gains from capital invested longer than six months were excluded from tax. Instead, tax was levied on the remaining 40 percent at the taxpayer's applicable rate. For example, if a person made a $1,000 long-term gain on stocks, $600 was excluded; only the remaining $400 was taxed. In contrast to this "rich get richer" policy, the same $1,000, if earned by a worker on an assembly line, was (and is) fully subject to tax. As of late 1989, there was mounting political pressure for restoring the special capital-gains treatment.

Fringe benefits are not currently taxed, but during the 1986 tax reform, proposals were advanced to include fringes as income, and some inroads were made. Although student scholarships are not taxed, living expenses provided to scholarship students now are. So far, life insurance proceeds, damages from personal-injury lawsuits, and interest earned on tax-exempt government bonds, to mention a few, remain excluded and untaxed. Social Security payments enjoy a partial exclusion for those with higher incomes and a full exclusion for those with lower incomes.

Those who have the particular benefit—employees with fringe benefits or students with scholarships—are better off than those who do not; for example, self-employed persons with no benefits or students whose tuition is paid in after-tax dollars. That is why you are better off when you receive income that is legally excluded from the tax system. Because you get compensation in nontaxed dollars, the value of this income varies according to the amount of your tax bracket.

DEDUCTIONS

If you ever picked up the tab at lunch arguing that "it's deductible," you have some idea of what a deduction is. But if you are like most people, your specifics stop there. You may actually think of the entire amount as a tax saving, but, in fact, your deductions are generally only worth a fraction of their full amount. The value of a deduction is figured according to your tax bracket, which in turn depends on your taxable income.

Depending on the location on the form, a deduction lowers your gross income or adjusted gross income by the face amount of the deduction. In simplified terms, if you are in the 15 percent bracket, a deduction is worth 15 cents on the dollar. This is because a deduction has the net effect of lowering your taxable income, the figure against which the rate would be applied to arrive at your tax liability.

If your gross income stood at $11,000 and you had a deduction of $1,000, your taxable income would amount to $10,000. Then the 15 percent rate would be applied, resulting in a tax of $1,500 and a tax savings of $150. Let us look at how $11,000 is taxed with and without the $1,000 deduction.

TABLE 2.		
	NO DEDUCTION	WITH DEDUCTION
1. Gross income	$11,000	$11,000
2. Deduction	0	1,000
3. Taxable income	11,000	10,000
4. Tax rate	15%	15%
5. Tax (line 3 x line 4)	1,650	1,500
6. Tax savings	$ 0	$ 150

To get this deduction, you have to *itemize,* or list, your deductions rather than filing the "short form." If you itemize, you file your taxes on a "long-form" 1040 and specify deductions on an additional schedule. For personal expenses use a Schedule A, and for business expenses, Schedule C. But note, the expense, if a personal one taken on Schedule A, has to exceed a 2 percent floor (see below) so the deduction will be worthless unless you also have other deductions. (A business deduction taken on Schedule C does not have a floor requirement although other rules affect the availability of some business deductions such as office rent.)

If you skip itemizing, as do two-thirds of all taxpayers, you receive the "standard deduction" or a set amount fixed by law subtracted from gross income. (In that case, using our lunch example, since you cannot take the deduction—let the other person pick up the tab.) If you take this route, file on a short form, 1040A or 1040EZ. In either case, the value of the deduc-tion—itemized or standard—bears the same relation to your tax bracket.

Itemizing allows deductions for a number of expenses that are not available for short-form filers. The types of deductions that can be itemized include medical expenses (but only the amount in excess of 7.5 percent of adjusted gross income); chari-table contributions; state and local income and property taxes (but not sales tax, which was taken off the deduction list by the 1986 law); interest on home mortgages (with some stiffer rules), but not credit card, auto, and other consumer interest, which are being phased out in stages to 1991; and limited casualty losses.

There are also "miscellaneous" deductions, but together they must exceed 2 percent of adjusted gross income before they can kick in. These include unreimbursed employee business ex-penses including transportation, travel, meals (80 percent only), and entertainment; tax return preparer fees; costs of producing investment income; union and professional association dues; of-fice expenses; and costs of searching for new employment.

The standard deduction allocated to nonitemizers is de-signed to equalize somewhat the scales with itemizers. The amount depends on filing status. In 1988, for example, for single persons the new standard deduction is $3,000, up from $2,480. For married couples filing jointly, it is $5,000, up from $3,670, and for single heads of household, it is now $4,400, up from $2,480. The addition of a separate standard deduction for heads of households, that is, persons (except married couples) with dependents—the first time such treatment has been offered—was an important victory for women in the last round of tax reform. Previously, heads of households and single filers had the same standard deduction.

All other things being equal, your total deductions would have to exceed the standard deduction to be worth the effort of itemizing.

Personal Exemptions

Every taxpayer is entitled to the personal exemption. This ex-emption is a flat deduction allotted to each individual in a household. In theory, exemptions are intended to reflect, at least to some extent, the cost of food, lodging, shelter, and other elements of the cost of living. In reality, the exemption is a politically negotiated amount.

With reform, the amount of the exemption was nearly doubled from $1,080 per person in 1986 to $2,000 in 1989. In order to keep large, affluent families from benefiting disproportionately (because deductions would be more valuable to them than to a large, poor family), the personal exemption was put on a sliding scale. At income levels above $149,250 for married couples, $89,560 for single taxpayers, and $123,790 for heads of households, the exemption has been eliminated. (Additional exemptions previously awarded for the blind and the elderly have been folded into the standard deduction.)

Depreciation

Depreciation is an allowance for deterioration arising from age and use. For tax purposes, it is a write-off or deduction of the cost of a tangible asset—such as real estate or machinery—over its estimated useful life.

The amount of depreciation depends on the method of depreciation set by law, which itself depends on the goals of the policymakers at the time. The conservative argument is that if investment is to be encouraged, a bigger depreciation should be offered. If access to large depreciation deductions costs the Treasury too much, as did some pre-1986 tax shelters, then depreciation will be stretched out. To encourage investment in additional assets during the recession of the early 1980s, lawmakers played with the "depreciation schedules" by giving a quicker write-off. However, it is not clear that fast depreciation—or any other tax break—actually leads to productive investment.

If you have never encountered the accounting concept of depreciation, take the easy way and look at depreciation schedules provided with tax-return materials. The key point to remember is that if you can obtain depreciation, you have a paper loss that can create many thousands of dollars of deductions. How these particular deductions can be used is limited by your particular tax status and the new passive loss rules, which are discussed on page 36.

Now, let us turn to what the tax system generally does with deductions once they are itemized.

RATES

You pay a percentage of your taxable income in taxes. That percentage is your effective "rate." The rate is applied against your taxable income, not on your entire, or gross, income. Taxable income is the amount left over after all exclusions and deductions are subtracted. A person's taxable income may be many thousands of dollars smaller than her gross income, but, however large or small the figure, the rate is applied in incremental steps only to this final amount. Keep this point in mind, because as you think about your taxes you always have to remember that your tax rate depends on your taxable income, not your total pay.

The very first section of the Tax Code sets out the rates, which are expressed as a percentage of taxable income. Tax reform cut rates to three percentages: 15 percent, 28 percent, and a super-rate of 33 percent. These rates are down from pre-1986 reform with fourteen rates, ranging from 11 to 50 percent, and even lower still than the 70 percent rate in 1981. (In reality, the rate cut affected primarily those with high incomes. See Appendix 2 for current rate tables.)

How Rates Are Structured

Rate structure, along with deductions and exclusions, embodies the core of tax policy. The greater your taxable income—up to a certain point—the higher percentage you pay in taxes. Everyone pays the same tax on the same amount of taxable income; only the higher amounts of taxable income are taxed at the higher rate. Thus, if your 1988 taxable income is $17,850 and you are single, you are taxed at 15 percent. But if your income is above this amount, then the remainder, up to $43,150, falls in the next tax bracket and is taxed at 28 percent. Any taxable income from $43,150 to $100,480 is taxed at 33 percent, and a flat rate of 28 percent applies above $100,480.

Different rate tables are constructed for different size filing "units." Filing charts are broken into four categories: single, married, head of household, and married filing separately. Except in the case of married persons who choose to undertake the extra paperwork involved and file separately, filing status is not a matter of choice. (If you think your spouse is cheating on taxes and risks losing significant amounts of money, you should file separately. That way, you do not risk penalties or liabilities for the taxes not paid. Otherwise, unless you are in the process of divorce, married people are better off filing jointly than the "married, filing separately" status. *Note:* This latter rate is not the same as the rate for "single." Married people must use one of the two married rates.)

Just as the standard deduction varies to acknowledge that basic household maintenance costs depend on the size and type of the family, the rate tables in theory further recognize the differential costs attributable to running various households. For example, a single person's bracket climbs to 28 percent at a taxable income of $17,850; a married couple's, at $29,750; and a head of household's, at $23,900.

Establishing parity among the various household categories is a tax policy problem that has been debated for the last fifteen years. Policymakers have tried but have not completely succeeded in eliminating penalties deriving from life-style differences, especially marital status. Two-earner families now pay higher taxes as a result of the 1986 tax law's elimination of the two-earner deduction. By contrast, two singles living together pay lower tax on their nearly equal incomes than the same two people would if wed.

The Marginal Tax Rate

At this point, it is helpful to introduce the important concept of the marginal tax rate. The *marginal tax rate* is defined as the amount of tax you would pay on the next dollar earned.

For example, if you currently find yourself in the 15 percent bracket, but you are right at the top of earnings allowed in that bracket, your next dollar would be taxed at the rate of the next higher bracket. Only the new income would be taxed at the higher rate; the base amount is taxed at the old rate. Remember, for everyone, all *taxable* (not gross) income of a particular level is taxed at the same rate. Only income above the cutoff point is taxed at the next higher rate. (Of course, the point must be made that people with higher gross incomes often reduce their taxable incomes by the ability to take many more deductions than those with lower gross incomes.)

Once you know your tax bracket or marginal tax rate, you can use that information to make quick calculations about the value to you of an additional deduction or about the net value to you of additional income. You can also use your marginal rate to see whether a tax-free investment beats a taxable one with a higher total return or yield.

To figure the tax increase or decrease, multiply the applicable marginal tax rate by the amount of the increase or decrease in taxable income, including capital gains.

For example, in the 28 percent marginal bracket, or tax rate, a new, untaxed fringe benefit is worth 39 percent more to you than its face amount—or than an equivalent amount in cash, because you don't have to pay taxes. (The *marginal tax bracket* is the rate you would pay on the next dollar of income. To figure the value, you divide the face amount by .72 in the 28 percent bracket, subtract the result from the original amount, and you have the extra value that you can then convert into a percentage.)

In addition, many readers will also pay state income taxes. In general, this book has not attempted to cover state taxes, as they vary widely. But you should be aware that under current law your state income tax paid is deductible from federal income if you itemize deductions, so any increase in state taxes paid results in a reduction of federal taxes.

In practice, accountants use a "combined rate" or "net rate" to take the federal-state tax relationship into account. To get a complete picture, ask your tax adviser for your effective state rate. For example, in California the top rate is 9.3 percent, but with the federal deduction for state income tax paid, the effective top marginal rate works out to 6.2 percent. (If you do not itemize, an increase in state taxes will not affect your federal rate; therefore, your marginal rate will be higher than for those who do itemize and deduct state taxes.)

But, to keep it simple, develop the practice of at least figuring your federal marginal tax on any transaction. (See Appendix 2 for federal rate tables.)

CREDITS

A tax credit is the amount that is taken directly off the tax you owe. A credit reduces your tax bill dollar for dollar, whereas a deduction is only as valuable as your tax bracket. A deduction for a person in the 15 percent bracket is worth only 15 cents for every dollar of deduction. A tax credit, on the other hand, is worth the full amount of the credit. So if you have a tax credit of $200 and a tax bill of $1,000, your total tax will be reduced to $800.

There are two key credits that matter most to women: the dependent-care tax credit, often called the child-care tax credit, and the earned income tax credit (EITC) for low-income working people with dependent children.

The dependent-care tax credit, for employment-related care, operates on a sliding scale, which depends on the number of children and income. The expense ceilings are $2,400 for one child and $4,800 for two or more, regardless of the actual cost. At the low end of the income scale, a 30 percent credit is allowed for a maximum of $720 for one child and $1,440 for two or more children. The amount is scaled down to a 20 percent maximum credit at adjusted gross incomes of $20,000 and above, which works out to a maximum credit of $480 for one child and $960 for two or more children. (See Appendix 3 for a table of scaled amounts.)

Child care for full-time working parents is extremely difficult to find in urban areas within the congressionally allowed expense amount. Even Congress is installing on-site day care with a $6,000 annual fee, far above its own limit of $2,400 allowable expenses. The national average child-care cost is $3,000 per year. Despite efforts during reform to raise the tax code's unrealistically low ceiling, the allowable expense remains at 1981 levels and is not indexed for inflation.

Also, few families qualify for the maximum tax credit, because a family earning only $10,000 would be unlikely to spend $4,800 in dependent-care expenses. Furthermore, with the new exemptions and standard deductions, persons earning under $11,000 generally do not owe taxes.

Another limitation of this credit is that it is not refundable, which would mean that the low-income household that had no tax bill to which it could apply the credit could not get a refund check for the amount of the credit instead.

By contrast, the earned income tax credit (EITC) is available to working persons with dependents. Even if a person does not owe any taxes, she can file and get this credit refunded. Originally enacted in 1975 and aimed at keeping low-income working parents in the labor force and off welfare, the credit offers up to $800 back in cash to qualified filers.

Like the dependent-care tax credit, the EITC works on a sliding scale. The maximum credit is figured at 14 percent of the first $5,714 of earned income. The credit is phased out at a rate of 10 percent, beginning at $9,000 of adjusted gross income (or, if greater, earned income). The credit ends at $17,000. If you think you qualify, check the tables published by the IRS and distributed as part of the tax-return instructions.

The EITC can be of particular help to divorced women with low incomes who must support dependents. If your earnings fall in this range, be sure to file for this often overlooked credit.

At the opposite economic extreme, before reform, certain investments had legislatively mandated tax credits of 10 percent or more of the full investment in the first year. For example, the investment tax credit, for investing in a variety of activities, offered the following kind of saving: if a company or individual proprietor bought a $50,000 piece of heavy machinery that qualified for the credit, in the first year of ownership the investment tax credit stood at 10 percent, or $5,000; if the business tax liability or taxes owed stood at $12,000, the credit would reduce the tax bill to $7,000; a dollar-for-dollar savings right off taxes.

A few credits, for historic or rehabilitation property, for example, remain but have been reduced. For rehabilitation of properties built before 1936 ("rehabs"), the amount of credit was reduced from 15 to 10 percent of the amount you spend to fix the building. For certified historic structures (CHSs), the credit has been reduced from 25 to 20 percent of expenses. However, a new low-income housing credit has been added, providing approximately 9 percent of construction costs or approximately 4 percent of the cost of acquiring low-income housing each year for ten years.

But access to these credits is not so simple. To these—as well as other shelters—new rules apply, as we shall see below in Chapter 8, pages 170–71.

To review, a credit comes right off your tax bill rather than off your adjusted gross income, as does a deduction. Most credits, like the dependent-care tax credit, can be applied only against taxes paid or owed. An exception: the earned income tax credit, which can be refunded even if you do not owe taxes. *Note:* Do not confuse a withholding refund with your total tax bill. Your tax liability is *all* the taxes you pay in a year, including what is withheld. Even if you are not due a refund, you can still get the benefit of the earned income tax credit and possibly the child-care tax credit by filing for them.

DEFERRALS

The critical ingredient for tax savings is often timing. You don't have to get an MBA or a law degree to understand the advantage of timing. Frequently, timing involves tax deferral. When you legally delay paying the IRS, you are engaging in tax deferral.

The example of deferral most familiar to people is the IRA. Many earners can defer up to $2,000 per year ($2,250 for a couple if only one is employed). A 100 percent IRA deduction is available to those who are not active participants in an employer-sponsored pension plan. The full deduction is also available to those active in a pension plan if adjusted gross income is below $25,000 if single, and $40,000 for married couples filing jointly. The amount of IRA deductions is reduced proportionately and phases out at $30,000 (single) and $50,000 (married). (However, in late 1989, Congress was considering reinstating IRAs for earners at all income levels.)

You defer paying taxes on the income you put in an IRA and on the interest it earns until retirement, thus your earnings increase because you invest pre-tax dollars. For example, say that you are in the 15 percent bracket. If you put $2,000 in an IRA you would pay in pre-tax dollars. If you put in the same amount in after-tax dollars, you would only have $1,700 to invest. Another way to look at it: in the 15 percent bracket you would have to earn $2,353 to net $2,000 to invest. (Divide $3,000 by .85 to obtain the pre-tax equivalent.) Over thirty years, the difference can be substantial, depending on your tax rate and the interest earned.

Or, if you buy a home, it appreciates, and you sell it, under current law you have the right to defer or "roll over" paying taxes on the growth for a period of two years. If you purchase a new or replacement home before the end of that two-year period and the price of the home is equal to or greater than the home you originally owned and sold, you can legally defer federal taxes on the entire gain until you sell your new home and do not buy another.

Why is deferral so important? In addition to the lower rate, paying later when income has been reduced is to the taxpayer's advantage because of the time value of money (see Chapter 3 and Appendix 4). The longer you retain the use of your money to accumulate interest tax-free or to grow as home equity, the better off you are. When you finally pay taxes, you will be paying them with less valuable dollars.

Any activity that is economically productive will eventually give rise to a tax liability; you haven't really rid yourself of the tax obligation, you have just deferred it. You can think of deferred tax as an interest-free tax loan from the government, which is eliminated only at death, when estate taxes replace income taxes.

TAX STRATEGY TODAY

Though it has been years since the unusually broad changes of the 1986 tax reform, many people are still adjusting their tax thinking to reflect the post-reform structure, because the changes took effect in stages. Reform involved many revisions in the law, with new treatments of exclusions, deductions, rates, credits, and deferrals. The most important change from the point of view of creating financial growth is the limitations placed on sheltering earned income. These limitations, called the *passive loss rules,* combined with the abolition of the capital-gains exclusion, mean that investment appreciation is taxed at higher nonsheltered income rates. (The other specifics will be found on page 36, and in the itemizer's checklist in Chapter 8, on preparing your taxes.)

Tax Shelters Explained: A Little History

In an effort to stimulate economic recovery, many tax breaks for investors have been put into effect over the years. Most recently, new tax breaks in 1981 had people flocking to make investments with little or no productive value but with large deductions and credits, which caused even the conservatives who advocated the original strategy to reconsider. Losses on such investments could be used to offset other sources of income, including salaries.

Although tax shelters took many forms, limited partnerships predominated because partnerships—unlike most corporations—could "pass through" tax benefits to the individual taxpayer-partners. Additionally, the limited partnership offered limited exposure and liability to the investors, who were on the hook only for their original investment.

Once formed, the typical partnership undertook activities high in tax benefits but low in growth potential. A popular example was the "sale-leaseback" limited partnership. For example, Company A would sell its equipment, such as computers, trucks, or airplanes, to Limited Partnership B. Then Limited Partnership B would turn around and lease the equipment back to Company A.

You may wonder why Company A would want to lease equipment that it previously owned outright. The reason is this: Company A raised ready cash, or capital, from the sale of the equipment while Partnership B invested in equipment, which before reform created big tax savings. Limited Partnership B could take investment tax credits and deductions, including depreciation and interest expense if the equipment were mortgaged. The lease payments from Company A would pay the mortgage for the equipment, so Partnership B would be left with the tax shelter.

For instance, if the partnership thus created $100,000 the first year in deductions and $10,000 the first year in credits, and there were ten partners, each partner took her $10,000 proportion of tax deductions and $1,000 of credits to "shelter" her other income. She then applied this against her other income to attain significant tax savings. The deductions would be taken off income and the credits directly off taxes, as we have seen.

Typically, doctors, lawyers, and high-salaried individuals were willing to participate in such undertakings even when they clearly offered no future growth because they were, in effect, buying a tax advantage, very often a paper loss that would lower their taxable income and thus decrease their tax obligations.

The existence of shelters such as the sale-leaseback, which generated deductions but had little real economic value—in this sense comparable to corporate takeover activities—was one of the major incentives for the passage of the reform measure. To curtail these unproductive activities, deductions were lowered and most credits were eliminated through new measures known as the passive loss rules. These rules, which form the core of reform, affect every salaried taxpayer who seeks to shelter income.

Passive Loss Rules

The passive loss rules impose a new standard of involvement in activities that create tax-saving loss, and most salaried persons now have far fewer opportunities to shelter their incomes. To deduct a loss, a taxpayer must meet two tests. First, the taxpayer must prove that the activity is one in which she engages for trade or business. For example, if you invest as a partner with your sister in a clothing store that loses money, but you also work full-time as a legal secretary on Wall Street, you probably would not be able to deduct these losses to shelter your $40,000 salary.

The second involves the amount of time the taxpayer spends conducting the business. In the case of the clothing store, if the store were located in Florida and you worked on Wall Street, you would fail the test. The law is not clear yet, with many gray areas. If the store were in New Jersey and you worked there every evening and weekend, the IRS would allow the deduction.

Obviously these tests are a matter of degree. The key point is that the burden of proof is on you to show that you qualify for passive loss deductions. Our sale-leaseback limited partnership would not qualify by legal definition; it is obvious that a limited partner has little direct involvement. Most tax shelters, including those that offer deductions after reform, have been rendered unattractive by the passive loss rules. Most people who want to shelter their income are looking to shelter active income, although passive loss can still shelter other passive gain.

THE REAL ESTATE EXCEPTION

Mortgage interest remains fully deductible on your first and second home, provided that the total mortgages do not exceed $1 million. The debt must be *acquisition* indebtedness, that is, for acquiring, constructing, or substantially improving a principal or second residence.

(A taxpayer who refinances cannot take additional cash and have it count as acquisition indebtedness.)

In addition, the interest on up to $100,000 in a homeowner's equity line can be deducted as long as the combined indebtedness does not exceed the fair market value of the residence. (The 1986 Tax Reform Act was amended by the 1987 Act, eliminating prior requirements linking equity lines to medical costs and college education expenses.)

Rental real estate has been defined as passive per se, or on its face, whether or not you meet the two-pronged test (pre-October 1986 investors had a phase-in, eliminating write-offs by 1991). But, as is often the case with tax law, there is an exception, the "active" standard.

If you actively manage rental real estate, own at least 10 percent of the property, and have an adjusted gross income of less than $100,000, you can deduct up to $25,000 of rental losses from your "active," or salaried, income. For adjusted gross incomes from $100,000 to $150,000, scaled-down losses are allowed; none is allowed above $150,000. (The $100,000 limit applies to single taxpayers and married couples filing jointly; the limit is

$50,000 for married couples who do not live together and file separately.)

In 1987, the IRS published detailed guidelines that you should review if serious real estate investment interests you. The key is keeping the decision making in your hands even if you delegate the details to a rental agent. Interest is also fully deductible for taxpayers in this category, provided that the total deduction, including interest and depreciation, does not exceed $25,000.

Subject to the above limits, you can also take a depreciation deduction. In general, depreciation was stretched out from 19 years to 27.5 years for residential real estate property. This deduction can be worth a bundle. With a $200,000 rental residential property, for example, you would have a depreciation deduction of $7,272 per year for 27.5 years. In the 28 percent bracket, you would rack up another $2,036 in tax savings a year.

An additional rule requires that you be "at risk" to get the deductions, but again Congress had middle-income small real estate investors in mind when writing the law. Even *non-recourse* mortgages, in which only the property itself will be forfeited in the event of default, qualify if the mortgage financed the property and is from a qualified lender.

By contrast, you could not meet the active and at risk standards if you put your money in a real estate limited partnership (structured like our sale-leaseback example but involving real estate instead of machinery or equipment). By definition, the risk would be limited, and the general partner, not you as the limited partner, would be the only "active" participant.

ADDITIONAL EXCEPTIONS

Low-income housing has been called "the only game in town" because it offers a credit that provides one of the few instances to which no active standard applies. You can take the low-income housing credit of 9 percent of the cost of new structures or 4 percent of the purchase price of existing structures regardless of your actual involvement. This exception to the exception means that a middle-income person with no desire to manage real estate could buy a low-income housing limited partnership share and get a substantial tax break. But note that this provision applies only to housing built by 1990; however, Congress routinely adds new special provisions whenever it wishes to encourage a particular sort of investment. To stay on top of such opportunities, check current rules before you invest.

Certified historic structures and older buildings built before 1936 also qualify for additional credits of 20 and 10 percent, respectively, as well as the usual deductions. However, to take the tax breaks against salaried income, these properties require the active standard of involvement applicable to rental real estate, unlike low-income housing.

In addition, the income cutoff for full tax benefits is higher for low-income housing and for certified historic structures and older property ($200,000 adjusted gross income) than for regular rentals ($100,000). There is a phaseout from $200,000 to $250,000, where no benefits can be taken.

Capital Gains

If you make money on an investment, at the time of this writing your profits will be taxed at regular income rates because of the 1986 elimination of the capital-gains exclusion. (The only exceptions, in general, are for home equity rollover deferrals, tax-free real estate exchanges, and inherited appreciation.) The passive loss rule working with the elimination of the capital-gains exclusion renders saving taxes as a salaried investor difficult. The only relief here is lower rates, the trade-off for the change.

There are no interest or depreciation deductions on stock market and other investments that can be used to offset earned income, although interest expenses up to the extent of investment earnings can be taken. Even deductions for capital loss in the stock market are limited to your capital gains plus $3,000 per year (not a change in 1986). If you lost more than that in the 1987 crash, you had to carry it over until the 1988 tax year.

Although such changes in the law make good economic sense from the point of view of fairness and economic soundness of tax policy, and can be justified in terms of overall lower rates, you must wonder where the breaks in our tax system now lie.

The Business Alternative

The answer lies in business. With business—compared to the individual return—the "ordinary and necessary" costs of doing business (with a few changes such as the 80 percent rule for business meals and entertainment) remain fully deductible. Although business tax rates depend on the organizational form —for example, sole proprietorship, partnership, or corporation —even higher corporate rates are not as much a disadvantage as might be supposed because of the many deductions corporations can take.

We shall look at various business options in Chapter 6. As a ray of hope, keep in mind that if a salaried individual starts a legitimate income-producing business on the side and participates in that business regularly, continually, and substantially, and if the business does not show a profit, the taxpayer can use the losses to offset salaried income.

Even here you must be careful. Reform stiffened the performance rules for small businesses. To prove you have a legitimate business and not a hobby, you may have to show a profit three out of every five years, up from two out of five. (There is no hard-and-fast rule, but once the business has passed the two-year mark with no profit, the burden of proof shifts to you to show it is a legitimate for-profit undertaking.) In addition, a special rule aimed particularly at *side businesses,* or businesses run by full-time employees after hours, limits the value of the home-office deduction, which can usually be taken only if it is the principal work place of that business. Generally, you cannot use a home-office deduction—deducting a portion of your rent or mortgage—to create a loss, only to reduce your taxable income, for an otherwise profitable business. (See page 168 for more on the topic of side businesses.)

Conclusion

A middle-income person seeking to create wealth is left with a limited set of options as far as tax savings go. Obviously, real estate investment (other than limited partnerships) makes much sense, but not everyone has the stomach for it, the resources to get involved, or the time to manage the property. Business provides opportunities but also creates risks.

With overall rates lowered, turning to strategies that do not depend on saving tax dollars makes a lot of sense now. However, do not assume that lower rates alone will ensure that your tax burden diminishes.

According to a 1987 Congressional Budget Office study, the results of reform have been to shift the burden of tax from wealthy taxpayers to middle-income and poor taxpayers. The poorest 10 percent of taxpayers paid 20 percent more of their income in taxes in 1987 than they did in 1977, while the richest 10 percent of taxpayers paid 20 percent less. Although poor taxpayers were expected to pay lower taxes as reform took full effect, Social Security and excise taxes would cause a net increase in the federal tax burden at this level.

As you consider your strategy today, note the extent to which you previously relied on exclusions, deductions, credits, and deferrals that no longer exist or are limited in effectiveness by the passive loss rules. Also calculate whether your rate is now higher or lower. Once you've conquered the intricacies of taxes, the next step will be to design your finances to minimize taxes. It is not a matter of filing strategy but of picking financial activities with a favorable tax component.

CHAPTER 3

PRINCIPLES

OF

GROWTH

The overall growth prospects of the economy provide the backdrop against which you prepare your own cash savings, tax savings, and growth strategy. In addition, there are specific principles you should consider in making any investment. These include such items as measurable return on investment, but even more important, personal perspectives such as your own goals.

GOALS

You always need to ask yourself about your goals for any investment. Are you investing for short-term, medium-term, or long-term growth? Retirement? Do you want to build up an estate for your children, your mother, or your spouse?

Most people invest for several goals simultaneously. In order to determine the type of investment you want to make, you need to be able to articulate your goals.

The rationale for an investment will guide the sort of choices made. Age is a big factor. For example, a person in her midthirties can afford to take more risks than a sixty-year-old because she will have time to earn replacement money should the investment turn sour. A person on the brink of retirement would not wish to put hard-earned retirement money into a highly volatile stock market.

As you begin investing, you may not be able to distinguish investments according to goals. But even with very small amounts of money, you can make basic decisions. If you know your first concern is setting aside retirement funds, you may wish to select an Individual Retirement Account (IRA), which can provide tax savings plus growth for qualified taxpayers. On the other hand, if your first investments are a stepping-stone to starting a business, you will not want to tie up your funds in long-term commitments.

TIME VALUE OF MONEY

The time value of money is fundamental to many concepts in the world of finance. Interest rates, the credit system, bill-paying schedules, and many principles of the tax system as well as of the bond and securities markets are all based on the time value of money. It is one of the most important concepts relating to both cash flow and future growth, and it is critical because it is the deciding link in many financial transactions.

Most of us, if we think of the meaning behind the expression "time is money," think of how much our own time is worth. But money, too, goes out to work, and the "salary" it is paid is called *interest*. The inverse of interest, or what money *does not* earn when it is not put to work (representing the cost of lost opportunity by putting money one place and not another), is called the *discount rate*. The discount rate represents your guess or that of the financial markets' about what money will be worth in the future, discounted or devalued back to its current value. (The discount rate is also the interest rate charged by the Federal Reserve Bank—the Fed to its member banks—to control the flow of credit; the two rates will be related because of market forces and the power of the Fed.)

The name of this flip-side calculation is *net present value*

(NPV), meaning how much all the money if received in the future would be worth today, or to put it another way, how much a person would forgo being paid to get money now rather than later.

For example, if you look at table 51 in Appendix 4, you will discover that if the going rate for money today is 10 percent, then a dollar sitting idle will be worth only 38 cents in ten years and less than 15 cents in twenty years; the same dollar will have dwindled to 0.01 cent in fifty years.

Think about the time value of money this way—would you rather have $100 today or $100 in ten years?

Most people would opt for $100 today, and they might even take $90 now rather than wait a year for $100. Taking the $90 now represents a discount rate of 10 percent. If we made the $90 choice, we did so because we intuitively recognize the value of having money in hand, even at a price.

Money in hand is secure, while waiting is risky. Tomorrow you might not get the same amount you were offered today, and chances are great that in ten years something unpredictable could happen to deprive you of your funds altogether.

Banks know the time value of money. Every time you deposit a check and wait for it to clear, the bank is using your money at your expense. Unless you are hard-pressed for funds, bank delays seem simply an annoying inconvenience. But banks earn interest overnight on such funds; Congress estimated in 1986 that banks deprived Americans of approximately 290 million through the practice of delayed check crediting.

This brief introduction serves to alert you that cash has a value when in hand that must be taken into account in any consideration of financial choices. Any time you put your money in someone else's hands, whether as a bank deposit or an investment, your cash has value for which you should be rewarded. If you do not get paid at the going rate for the use of your money, your cash flow and future growth suffer.

THE NUMERICAL MEASURES OF RETURN

Return is the amount you expect to earn. The measurement of return involves some obvious and some not-so-obvious issues such as the *net present value* (NPV) concept.

When most of us think of return, we think of a fixed amount, such as the interest rate on a savings account or the yield or rate of return for a stock or bond.

Entire business school courses are devoted to the concept of measuring return on investment, and there are numerous ways in which return can be expressed. As you look at investments, you are likely to encounter terms such as interest, yield, return on investment (ROI), return on equity (ROE), and internal rate of return (IRR). In general, no matter what the names, the goal of return measures is to reflect the earnings of capital at work. These measures include:

INTEREST

The price paid for the use of money, most often expressed as a percentage per year.

YIELD

The rate of income on an investment. For a stock, the yield is the dividend divided by the purchase price. For a bond, the yield is the annual interest divided by the purchase price.

APPRECIATION

The amount original equity grows in value.

TOTAL RETURN

The capital gain (or loss) plus the sum of dividends or interest on an investment.

RETURN ON INVESTMENT (ROI)

The simplest annual return to figure is to look at the ratio of total annual earnings (whether interest or dividend, positive or negative cash flow) to total capital invested, including debt, usually expressed as a percentage. For example, with real estate, to get the ROI you take the appreciation over a year and divide by the purchase price of the house, which would include the mortgage or debt. A house purchased for $100,000 that appreciated to $115,000 would have a ROI of 15 percent.

RETURN ON EQUITY (ROE)

The net income earned expressed as a percentage return on equity. It is calculated by dividing equity into net income. Assume you put $20,000 down on a $100,000 house. To see ROE, you compare the growth of $15,000 to the $20,000 equity, for a ROE of 75 percent. By contrast, return on investment would compare the growth of $15,000 to the original price of the *entire* investment; if the house cost $100,000, the ROI would be only 15 percent compared to a 75 percent ROE.

For investments such as real estate involving equity growth rather than simply cash flow (see p. 48), this calculation gives a better indication of true return.

Although this example simplifies issues such as real estate fees you might pay, the difference between the two measures should be clear. In the second example, you'd see that for your cash out-of-pocket, you'd be earning a high return that might not be as evident if you looked at the entire investment, including the debt.

PAYBACK

A related but slightly different issue is return of capital. When will the principal be returned to you? Many investors in new ventures look primarily at the issue of when their capital is returned, knowing that once they have recouped capital, what is left is upside potential. The number of years it takes to recapture the original capital is called the "payback." If you put $15,000 into a start-up business and you got your capital back in two and a half years, your payback would be 2.5.

INTERNAL RATE OF RETURN (IRR)

A sophisticated concept, the IRR measures cash return and equity growth in relation to the discount rate. The IRR is technically defined as "that discount rate which causes the net present value to equal zero." However, in all honesty, most people do not understand how to calculate this return, but fall back on specially programmed business calculators.

Even though the concept is elusive, you may encounter it in a sales context. It also is used in many government reports to compare growth vehicles.

What you need to remember is that the simpler measures of return will address only the face of the investment, whereas the IRR tells you the real dollar return when adjusted for the time value of money. Be aware that the concept only works if the person making the calculation uses an appropriate discount rate, which in turn involves an educated guess about the direction of inflation and interest rates.

Opportunity Cost

If you make an investment in real estate, precious metals, or a work of art, these items pay no guaranteed cash flow such as interest but instead promise appreciation in value. Whenever you tie up capital, there is an *opportunity cost,* that is, the difference between what you earn and what you could have earned.

To learn your true return, you need to compare the investment selected to a specified return. If, for example, you could buy a certificate of deposit or a bond that yields 7.5 percent, your opportunity cost is $75 a year (before taxes) for every $1,000 you invest (7.5 percent x $1,000). You need to make certain, therefore, that a nonyielding investment that offers only appreciation will exceed the 7.5 percent readily available.

Overhead and Fees

Whether you are investing in the stock market or real estate, limited partnerships or an apartment house, one essential hidden feature often overlooked in measuring return is the cost of overhead and fees.

If you invest in stocks, you ordinarily have a broker's fee every time you buy and sell your investment. If you invest in real estate, your normal real profit will be reduced by the amount of the fee. You will also have management fees and maintenance fees, depending on whether you rent the property yourself or leave it in the hands of others. If you take out a loan, you will have fees usually expressed as *points* (a point is 1 percent of the face amount of a loan). With limited partnerships, start-up fees and management fees are included. Some money-market funds charge an annual fee of $50 to $100 a year (in addition to a management fee charged to the fund, which you never see).

Cash-Flow or Growth Investments

Of great importance to growth potential is whether your equity, that is, capital invested, will appreciate or grow, rather than simply earn interest. Investment advisers divide investments according to whether they produce "cash flow," or earnings, rather than "growth." In general, the higher the ongoing cash flows from an investment, the lower the growth. Often cash-flow investments are safer than growth vehicles.

A savings account represents a simple sort of cash-flow investment. The account pays interest, but the amount originally invested, in this case the deposit, does not grow in value.

The disadvantage to this type of investment is that your upside potential is limited. Even though you can count on the cash coming in, your principal will never grow (although in the case of a savings account, if you leave the earnings on deposit, they will compound).

When inflation is high, money sitting in a nonequity vehicle, including bonds, Treasury bills (T-bills), and certificates of deposit (CDs), actually declines in value. For example, at 6 percent inflation, a dollar is worth only 73 cents at the end of five years. (The NPV analysis expresses this relationship.)

By contrast, investments that offer equity appreciation, such as real estate, generally parallel the direction of the growth of the economy. A stock is an ownership interest in a company, an interest that will grow if the economy and the company are on the upswing. That growth is represented by the rising price of the stock on the market.

On the other hand, if a recession or depression occurs, equity investments will usually decline. Thus, these investments are riskier because they always involve the potential for loss, although they also offer higher positive advantages as well.

The type of investment chosen—cash flow or growth—would depend on your needs. If you were planning to live off your investment earnings, you would want "cash-flow" vehicles such as mortgages, for example. But your growth potential would be zero. On the other hand, at the beginning of a career, a high-earning young professional would be better off diverting additional cash to future growth.

Liquidity

Whenever you are making an investment, but especially those for growth, you must always concern yourself with the issue of how quickly you can turn an asset into cash. Investors usually refer to this timing by the shorthand term *liquidity,* or marketability at whatever the present value.

The standard example is that real estate is less liquid than the stock market, although the term is relative. If you had a highly appreciated property and needed money quickly, you might be able to get a loan, whereas if your stocks had declined sharply and you needed to sell, you would lose money. In the sense of not losing value, the stock was less liquid although it was readily salable.

You don't ever want your investments positioned so that you find yourself "land poor," with plenty of assets and no cash. Before you select any investment, think about how long it will take to turn it back into cash. To some extent, your judgment call will depend on when you will need the money. If you are in your thirties and starting a retirement fund, liquidity will not be a high priority. If, on the other hand, your near-term goal is a down payment on a real estate purchase, you will want liquid funds.

If in doubt, stay liquid.

RISK

Even with the best thought-out plans, outside factors can intervene. From changes in the economy to natural disasters, unpredictable circumstances that can produce loss rather than positive return have to be taken into account.

You may only be a victim of bad timing, making less profit than otherwise possible. For example, suppose that your
company transferred you from Boston to Los Angeles, so that
you sold your home and reinvested in a new home in Los
Angeles.

If you had left Boston for Los Angeles in 1980, you would
have left behind a depressed real estate market for a market that
had just experienced a boom. To purchase a home in Los Angeles
at that time, you would have needed all your equity from the sale
of your Boston home and more. But if you had sold your Boston
home in 1980, you would have missed reaping profits from a
record-setting housing boom only a few years later—Boston area
houses achieved as much as a 20 to 30 percent growth rate in
some years in the mid-1980s. Meanwhile, your Los Angeles home
would not have grown at all; in fact, its value would have stayed
the same or even declined. You would have thus swapped a
lower-priced home for a higher-priced home, missing out on one
real estate boom and experiencing the decline of another real
estate market.

For any investment you must consider the chance of losing
the original capital invested. Perhaps you watched the Dow
Jones climb from 1300 in the year 1984 up to its dizzying height
of 2700 in August 1987. And at some point along the way you
decided to get into the action. If you were not fortunate enough
to get out of the market before the October 1987 crash, your
equity would have been slashed overnight.

The ever-present possibility of loss is expressed by the concept of risk, called the "downside" in Wall Street vernacular.

One part of the standard wisdom is that the greater the
reward the greater the risk. But this equation does not always
hold. For example, investing in residential real estate in most
major cities represented very high returns in the late 1970s, with
little risk. (This point did not hold true for Texas cities hit by the
oil price collapse.)

In general, when returns offered by a specific investment far
exceed the going market, take a careful second (and third) look.
Not only might you lose your anticipated profits, but in some
situations, you can lose more than your initial capital. To take
two examples, with stock options, you may be required to meet
a margin call and put up more money. If the business turns sour,

you could lose all your assets, not just what you have invested originally.

Financial risk is relative. Your perception of risk depends on both your assets and your personality. People with generous reserves can afford to invest in activities that those with limited assets should not consider. A good rule of thumb: do not invest more than you can afford to lose in growth vehicles; choose cash-flow investments instead.

Even though very few investment strategists talk about preservation of capital, keeping one's capital intact should play the major role in any investment decision. Think in terms of gambling. You ante up at the gambling table with $1,000, and you win $100. If you are a wise gambler you will set the $1,000 aside and play with the $100. Unless you have enough money that you feel you truly don't care about loss, you are better off with a less risky investment.

It is not easy to measure risk because almost any measure makes certain built-in assumptions. Even insured savings accounts, U.S. Treasury bills, and high-grade corporate bonds—traditionally regarded as the safest of investments—embody a degree of risk. A sharp rise in inflation will lower the value of both the investment and its earnings. But where only lower earnings—not loss of capital—is the downside, you are on secure ground.

Or, take the standard investment guides, Moody's or Standard & Poor's Stock Guide, which rate some 5,000 common stocks from A+ to D on the basis of stability, earnings, and dividends. All these ratings provide guidelines, but in a sharp market downturn, even an A+ stock isn't likely to preserve your capital.

Spreading Risk

One way to ameliorate risk is to diversify investments. If money is divided into different kinds of investments, losers and winners may balance one another out.

While the "don't put all your eggs in one basket" school of thought sounds logical, many women do not have enough investment funds to diversify. However, if you have sufficient funds (some advisers say at least $200,000 before you move beyond medium risk), select some investments from each category that appeals to you. Or, consider a mutual fund, where at least your stock or bond investments are diversified.

In general, investment experts agree on a ranking of investment types by risk (if you are unfamiliar with these items, see Chapter 9).

Very Low Risk, Very Low Return: Treasury bills, short-term certificates of deposit, and money-market accounts.

Low Risk, Low Return: Short-term bonds.

Medium Risk, Medium Return: Low-leverage real estate, high-yield stocks, medium-term bonds.

High Risk, High Return: High-leverage real estate, cyclical and growth stocks, long-term bonds.

Very High Risk, Very High Return: Over-the-counter (OTC) stocks, new issues, junk bonds, options.

SUBJECTIVE FACTORS

There are hidden features of any investment that involve the investor or the investment itself. No investment should be undertaken that does not fit you, the investor.

What "hassle factor" can you tolerate? Does the investment fit your needs, your personality? Does it fit your portfolio in the sense of diversity? Have you looked at the role your age may play?

Risk-Taking Personalities

A study comparing high-risk, or "active," investors with low-risk, or "passive," investors found distinct personality differences. The high-risk investors were much more likely to have been entrepreneurs than the low-risk investors. High-risk investors have strong egos and a desire to control their investments rather than delegate the control to an adviser. Risk takers are not team players; they are more concerned with self-approval than the approval of others. As a result, high-risk investors were willing to jeopardize current life-styles to achieve their financial goals.

There's a Wall Street saying that women are "risk-averse" (although there are no statistical data to support this view). However, being risk-averse is not necessarily negative. Anyone, including women as a group, who has less to risk should take a conservative investment posture.

The Hassle Factor

Your time and energy are critical ingredients. If you are a busy executive or a pressed homemaker, you cannot afford an investment that eats away time you do not have. It is a given that you will spend far less time going to your local bank to open a savings account than buying a run-down house in a deteriorating neighborhood, with plans to remodel and sell it for a profit. The difference here is what I call the "hassle factor."

My favorite example: A successful New York executive walked down Fifth Avenue on the way to a meeting for a deal that could have resulted in profits for her participation of many thousands of dollars. Rather than thinking about her forthcoming presentation, her mind was on a few hundred dollars she had lost the previous day in the stock market.

If you are likely to find yourself distracted by the investment, you will be better off taking lower earnings, leaving you free to enjoy both your job and your investment.

Personal Preferences

You also have to decide whether a particular investment fits your knowledge and personal preferences. For example, if you grew up in the South, you probably regard land as supreme. On the other hand, if you have spent your entire life in an urban area, where most people live in apartments, you may feel more comfortable in the stock market.

Social concerns matter to many investors. Socially conscious investors support their principles through such means as avoiding investments in companies with stakes in South Africa, nuclear involvement, or unfair employee policies. A few brokers today are aware of socially responsible investors' concerns, and some specialize in servicing this market. There are also socially responsible mutual funds. Just ask.

All of these subjective issues must be taken into account. They are often of greater importance than the "harder" issues, such as numerical measures of return. But only you can determine whether an investment fits you personally. Ask yourself if you have the time, energy, understanding, and risk-taking inclination required for a given investment.

Now, it is time to see how these principles affect our characters' lives.

PART II

MEET

OUR

CONSUMERS

CHAPTER 4

HOW

SMALL INCOMES

CAN GROW

Here and in the next two chapters, our real-life consumers' stories will be grouped by income level because the strategies available generally correlate with income. Budgeting techniques are accessible to everyone, no matter how modest the earnings. Although some tax strategies help even modest earners, tax savings start to become a viable possibility as earnings move into the midrange. To create easy growth, a critical mass of income and tax savings must be reached; therefore, higher-income people enjoy the maximum opportunity to benefit from the trade-offs among the three. But if your earnings are modest, do not despair. As we shall soon see, you can make effective incremental changes that will improve your position.

As we look at our characters' cash flow, taxes, and growth, three financial forms are associated with these three concepts. The *budget sheet* represents cash flow; the *1040,* taxes; and the *balance sheet,* growth. In this chapter on moderate-income women, the focus is mostly on budgeting. In Chapter 5, with middle-income individuals and couples, the emphasis is on tax savings. In Chapter 6, the last of our character chapters, with high-cash-flow women, the focus becomes growth.

OLIVIA WONG

Olivia Wong's case affirms that the principle of trade-offs among cash flow, tax benefits, and future growth applies, even when the range of trade-offs is limited. Regardless of how modest a person's earnings, room to save exists. Even if high-growth investments or owning a home are out of the question, the pre-tax investment in an individual retirement account (IRA) can maximize what is saved.

Olivia's Cash Flow

Twenty-nine-year-old Olivia Wong holds a steady job, earning $1,200 a month before taxes as a customer service representative at a local credit union. A salary of $14,400 a year means that Olivia's cash flow is tight.

Although she keeps track of her expenses informally by remembering many of them, she has never taken the time to see exactly where her admittedly modest income goes. She has always felt that it did not make sense for her to budget because she did not earn much money. But after reviewing her finances, we concluded that the only way she would be able to set aside savings from her tight cash flow would be to work out her expenditures and income on paper. With this information in hand, she can modify her expenditures.

As you think about Olivia's effort to analyze cash flow, keep in mind that a budget is a plan for the future—what is to be spent—whereas a cash-flow statement is a summary of what is being spent now. The cash-flow statement includes two components, an expenditure summary and an income summary.

Because Olivia's bookkeeping system consists of files of disorganized receipts, invoices, and bills, her first step is to organize her information into categories and begin to group her expenses so that she can see where her money is going.

Olivia employs categories published by the Department of Commerce in its Personal Consumption Expenditure data reporting as a starting point (see p. 143, Chapter 7).

Olivia then starts with what she knows. Her rent is $300 a month (she shares an apartment with a roommate). For transportation, she drives an old Chevy Nova that she has paid for completely. (She is thinking of buying a newer car.) Her repairs are minimal, so under auto maintenance she puts down $20 a month; she will check whether this sum represents all her car repair expenses over the past year. She also adds her car insurance payment of $50 a month, and she estimates that her gas and oil run between $30 and $50 a month. From telephone bills to clothing expenses, Olivia has sketchy ideas of average costs.

Olivia next moves to her easily available records to fill in the details. She obtains many of the basics from her checkbook and credit records. She looks over the past month or two and adds these expenditures under her established broad categories.

After she has finished all written records, Olivia estimates cash and casual expenditures. The best way to gather such data is to prepare an expense diary, which she decides to do. Though this exercise is tedious, it is a one-time undertaking that will provide necessary information.

She begins by writing down expenditures on a daily and weekly basis in a small pocket diary. Maintaining her usual spending behavior, she includes everything, even items that, on second thought, she might not buy the next time.

After keeping the diary, she is surprised at some of her expenses (see table 3). Her restaurant and fast-food outlays really add up. For example, she had written on her estimated

TABLE 3. OLIVIA WONG
SAMPLE CASH DIARY

ITEMS BOUGHT	COST
Date: Thursday 2/16	
Lunch at fast-food restaurant	$ 3.00
Candy bar and diet Coke	1.25
Magazine	3.00
Stamps	1.00
Date: Friday 2/17	
Lunch at fast-food restaurant	3.50
Candy bar, diet Coke, gum	1.55
Groceries	39.86
Date: Saturday 2/18	
Dinner (w/tax and tip)	8.33
Drinks	5.00
Movie	6.00
Pay phone	.75

expenditures that she spent $80 a month for food, thinking of grocery store expenses. But based on three days of her diary, she finds her restaurant meals cost an average of $7.54 a day, or an estimated $225 a month, far more than her earlier $80 estimate for all food expenses.

Once Olivia finishes her cash diary, she integrates this material with the information from her checkbook and bills.

Because she has reviewed her checkbook for one month's time only, Olivia has to check expenditures such as car repairs, which occur on a less regular basis, by looking back in her rec-

TABLE 4.   OLIVIA WONG—MONTHLY EXPENDITURES

	AMOUNT
1. Housing	
Rent	$ 300
Utilities	20
2. Food	
Groceries	80
Restaurants	225
3. Clothing	50
4. Transportation	
Installment payments	0
Insurance	50
Fuel	40
Maintenance	20
5. Phone	24
6. Household purchases and supplies	10
7. Entertainment	40
8. Personal care and improvements	30
9. Medical and dental expenses	75
Subtotal (before tax expenditures)	964
10. Taxes	
Federal income tax	121
State income tax	50
Social Security	90
State unemployment	25
Subtotal, Taxes	286
TOTAL MONTHLY EXPENDITURES	$1,250

ords. If she cannot find enough information to make reliable monthly amounts, she should estimate.

Note that Olivia lists her federal and state income taxes, Social Security, disability, and unemployment as expenditures so that she has a clear idea of these costs. Especially with federal taxes, the amounts could change depending on her tax savings strategies, so it is important to think of them as expenditures rather than as givens.

The results of her effort are shown in table 4, page 60.

Next, Olivia writes down her total income. Because she is paid twice a month, she multiplies her credit union paycheck by 24 and divides by 12 for an accurate monthly income figure.

TABLE 5.   OLIVIA WONG—MONTHLY INCOME

	AMOUNT
1. Income from employment	
Salary	$1,200
2. Investment income	
Taxable interest	20
Total Monthly Income	$1,220

Finally, all the information is consolidated into one statement of monthly income and expenditures—called a cash-flow statement, simplified below.

TABLE 6.   OLIVIA WONG—MONTHLY CASH-FLOW STATEMENT

	INCOME	EXPENDITURE
Total	$1,220	$1,250

Comparing her estimated expenditures of $1,250 to her income of $1,220 a month, Olivia sees a small difference of $30. Olivia thinks that her diary expenses for restaurants had been a bit high and that with more careful tracking of cash expenditures, she will come out about even.

Her next step is to budget. Because her current expenditures are not excessive except in restaurants, "budgeting" does not mean revamping her spending habits but selecting areas to trim back. In addition to planning expenditures low enough to close the monthly gap of $30 between income and expenditures, Olivia needs to budget to create growth for herself.

Olivia thinks that if she reduces fast-food expenditures by packing lunches, she can save $85 a month or just over $1,000 a year. Olivia decides to trim $115 a month from her restaurant tab ($30 to close the gap and $85 in new savings), for a new projected expenditure of $110 a month on restaurants. Given her small income and fairly modest habits, her "budget" simply becomes her expenditures adjusted to reflect the new lower planned restaurant outlays.

It is difficult for busy women like Olivia who don't have time to cook to restrict restaurant meals. Shopping and cooking activities seem all but impossible to factor into their schedules.

But Olivia can save money by being selective. She orders out and eliminates the tip and looks for neighborhood restaurants that serve quality food at lower prices. She orders from the low end of the menu and eliminates extras such as drinks, desserts, and side dishes that add up and can double her bill.

Likewise, Olivia's clothing expenses are not excessive at $50 a month, but she can wait for sales, shop at discount stores, and try to buy classic styles that stay in fashion.

Given her limited resources, Olivia should consider borrowing from a friend or relative for one-time use items such as evening gowns or specialized vacation clothes, including seasonal clothes she does not need when at home.

Although, like most women, the pressure on Olivia to be fashionable is intense, Olivia realizes she must try to limit her shopping. To curb any temptation to overspend, Olivia decides to pay cash for clothing.

With these practical strategies in hand, Olivia is now ready to face tax and growth strategy.

Olivia's Taxes

Olivia believes nothing she can do will improve her tax situation. As a single woman earning $14,400 a year, Olivia feels her tax bracket is just high enough to hurt, but too low to make it worth her while to get involved in complicated tax strategies. In fact, despite the 1988 reform phase-in, her 1987 and 1988 tax bills are virtually identical, seeming to prove her point.

Reform for Olivia spelled out a $5 per year tax savings. When we compare 1987 to 1988, the first full year of reform, we see just how the reform changes affect smaller income earners. In 1987 a lower rate of 11 percent, a smaller standard deduction, and smaller exemption brought her total tax bill to $1,460. In 1988, a year in which rates supposedly lowered, Olivia's rate actually *rose* from the previous minimum rate of 11 percent to the new bottom rate of 15 percent. Her higher rate is offset by the increased standard deduction for single filers and increased personal exemption, and her tax bill totals $1,455, just $5 less.

At tax time Olivia's paperwork burden has been light. The "short form" 1040EZ is reserved for those who do not itemize and whose interest income totals less than $400 per year. Since her interest income on her $3,500 savings comes to $250 a year, Olivia files on the EZ. To complete her return, Olivia takes her wage and withholding information from her W-2 form from her employer and adds her taxable interest income. Since the 1040EZ provides the amount of the standard deductions and exemptions right on the face of the form, she merely has to fill in her income, do a couple of calculations, and her tax return is complete. (See table 7, p. 64.)

Although simplicity at income tax time is desirable, with a little more work Olivia can improve her position without over-burdening herself. Because of her low income, not much room for maneuvering exists. She does not earn enough money to create deductions by buying real estate. Also, although her expenditures on items such as medical care is high considering her salary, these expenses do not exceed the 7.5 percent of her income required to warrant filing on the "long-form" 1040.

Olivia is the perfect candidate for the tax savings and growth benefits of an IRA, the vehicle for making a textbook trade-off between tax savings and growth.

Olivia's Growth

Olivia has managed to save $3,500, on which she earns her $250 a year interest, but with an IRA she will build toward her long-

TABLE 7.   OLIVIA WONG—FEDERAL INCOME TAX SUMMARY

	1987 1040EZ	1988 1040EZ	1988* 1040A
1. Wages	$14,400	$14,400	$14,400
2. Interest	250	250	250
3. IRA deduction	0	0	1,000
4. AGI	14,650	14,650	13,650
5. Standard deduction	2,540	3,000	3,000
6. Personal exemption	1,900	1,950	1,950
7. Taxable income	10,210	9,700	8,700
8. Tax withheld	1,460	1,460	1,460
9. Tax owed	1,460	1,455	1,305
10. Refund	$ 0	$ 5	$ 155

*Figured with an IRA of $1,000. To take the IRA deduction, the 1040A or regular 1040 must be used.

term future while making a modest saving on her taxes. An IRA will allow Olivia to reverse for herself the trend of women having to rely solely on Social Security for retirement.

As she is not a pension plan participant and her adjusted gross income of $14,650 is far below the qualifying amount of $25,000, Olivia could legally create a $2,000-a-year tax deferment for herself by opening an IRA. But Olivia's budget doesn't allow her comfortably to put aside the full $2,000. She has already decided to set aside $1,000 a year, or $83 a month, by cutting back on restaurant meals. Now, with tax savings in mind, she determines to use her brown-bag lunch savings to assure her future security with the IRA.

To get started, Olivia opens her IRA with a firm that offers a monthly payment option. This way, she can save some money each month and put it tax-deferred directly into her IRA. Also, although the IRA offers the beauty of "forced savings"—there are tax disincentives to withdrawal before age fifty-nine and a half—Olivia's savings remain available for emergencies.

However, you should not be intimidated into bypassing the IRA because of these disincentives. They amount to 10 percent of the amount of the IRA, plus the taxes you would owe now on the money earned. If you really need your money, you can withdraw it. In fact, some advisers suggest putting funds away tax-free if you are not certain whether you will need them. You can withdraw the funds at what is called a "crossover" point, and your penalty will equal your tax savings to date, depending on the amount the IRA earns.

With Olivia's small opening amount, the exact choice of type of IRA account is less important than simply getting started. Later, when she has more money accumulated, Olivia can switch her account to obtain a higher rate. Or, she may consider a "self-managed" IRA so that she can invest some of her funds in higher growth activities, such as a mutual fund (with this small amount, a more risky stock market IRA investment would not be recommended).

Even with only $1,000 a year, in her 15 percent tax bracket, Olivia's money if invested at 10 percent interest will have grown to $15,939 in ten years compared to $13,681 without the IRA, a difference of $2,258.

Another way to make the comparison is to look at the tax saving with her IRA. A $1,000 IRA would reduce her taxable income by $1,000, from $9,700 to $8,700 (assuming she paid the full $1,000 before April 15). Her taxes drop by $150 a year, assuming the same income and tax status, as reflected on Olivia's tax summary chart with the 1040A.

For a quick estimate of annual savings, the same result can be seen if the new $1,000 deduction for the IRA is multiplied by Olivia's 15 percent tax bracket, for a tax saving of $150.

(This latter calculation works exactly only when you know the marginal tax bracket or the amount of taxes that would be paid on the next dollar owed, as discussed in Chapter 2. With the simplified tax brackets, for practical purposes most taxpayers can assume that their marginal bracket will be identical to the highest rate they pay: 15, 28, or 33 percent.)

To take the IRA deduction, Olivia must switch from the 1040EZ filing format to the 1040A. The 1040A is not much more complicated than the 1040EZ. (For sample forms, see Appendix 1.) By making this extra bit of effort at tax time, along with investing in an IRA, Olivia has increased her future growth at a 15 percent discount to herself. Although the IRA will not make her rich, she will be far better off than if she continued her habit of eating fast food rather than putting away $83 a month.

Conclusion

Olivia's best choice lies both in making modest additional savings in her current budget and in finding ways to increase her income. Obviously, until she makes more money, it will be hard for Olivia to create solid long-term security. Olivia's best investment is in the form of human capital—that is, herself. She might take additional classes at the local college or embark on a training program that will open up higher income career options.

In the meantime, she should add as much as she possibly can to her IRA, up to the $2,000-a-year limit. Every dollar she sets aside from her income will mean a more secure future.

SHERRY MARSHALL

Sherry Marshall, a recently divorced mother of two, approached me for financial advice at a women's committee meeting. Her focus, understandably, has been on getting her emotional life in order following a traumatic divorce and her husband's remarriage. Now, Sherry must turn to dealing with her postdivorce finances.

Sherry's Cash Flow

When she came to my office one evening after work, we started to examine her financial situation where everyone must start—with her cash flow.

First, we filled in income and expenses forms.

As a temporary secretary, Sherry is paid hourly, and her incoming cash varies. Generally, her employment income runs about $1,400 a month, typical in a field traditionally composed of women. In addition, her former husband, George, pays $685 a month in spousal and child support (she has custody of their two children), which he is obliged to pay for three years.

For investment income, Sherry receives $1.65 a month in taxable interest, $20 a month in nontaxable interest, and $5 a month in dividends, bringing her total investment income to $26.65 a month or $320 a year.

TABLE 8. SHERRY MARSHALL—MONTHLY INCOME	
1. Income from employment	
Salary	$1,400.00
2. Investment income	
Taxable interest	1.65
Nontaxable interest	20.00
Dividends	5.00
Total Income from Investments	26.65
Total Income Without Spousal/Child Support	1,426.65
3. Spousal and child support	685.00
TOTAL MONTHLY INCOME FROM ALL SOURCES	$2,111.65

Counting earnings investments and child support, her monthly income of $2,111, or $25,332 yearly, looks comfortable. However, Sherry has decided to live solely on her earnings rather than get used to a higher standard of living, which the three-year transitional help from her husband would encourage.

Sherry is afraid that George's support will not last. George remarried quickly and has a new child on the way. As a social worker, George does not earn much himself. Statistically speaking, Sherry's instincts are valid—according to Census Bureau figures, only 60 percent of men pay spousal support after the first two years, and only 39 percent of women receive the full child support awarded.

If she subtracts George's payments, Sherry does not have enough earnings to pay rent and cover all her other expenses. Fortunately, the family has been able to move in with her parents temporarily, resulting in savings on both rent and child care. However, not all women are so fortunate, and eventually Sherry will need to reestablish her own household.

When we examined Sherry's expenses, a few really stood

out. Installment payments on her recently purchased new car, which Sherry insisted is a necessity, run $150 a month. Since her divorce, Sherry has redone her personal image. She lost weight, cellophaned her hair, exchanged her glasses for contact lenses, and joined an exercise class. But spending $450 a month (over 30 percent of her own earnings) for personal care, clothes, and a new car seems excessive for a woman who feels she cannot afford to rent an apartment.

If Sherry wants to save, she needs to develop practical solutions similar to Olivia's. First, she should try to save money on clothes. The same advice applies: shop at savings and discount houses, wait for sales, and buy with cash.

She could save $45 a month by exploring free exercise alternatives such as running, cycling, and walking, and she could curtail expensive hair treatments or try drugstore products.

Finally, Sherry will have to become realistic about major purchases, such as her car. It does not make sense to sell her new car now, for she would lose more through depreciation than she would gain by selling it. But next time, she should look for a good used car with low mileage. (See table 9, p. 69.)

We next turned to the questions that had brought Sherry in for advice, the issue of how to invest the capital from the sale of the couple's home and what to do about her credit card debt.

In 1977, Sherry and George Marshall purchased a home for $29,500. By the time the couple sold the home in 1981, its value had risen to $177,000. Using most of the proceeds from their first house and reinvesting them in a down payment, they were able to qualify for a mortgage on another home that they purchased for $245,000 in 1982.

The real estate market flattened out in the intervening years. When the couple split up in 1986, their second home sold for $251,700, only slightly more than they had paid for it. By the time all the selling costs were subtracted, Sherry's share of the profits from both houses amounted to $77,100.

When we met, she had made a plan to settle all her outstanding debts, including some to family, out of this sum. In fact, she had already moved $4,200 of her capital from her interest-bearing credit union account to her non-interest-bearing checking account for the purpose of paying her debts.

I urged Sherry to hold off paying both credit card and fam-

TABLE 9. SHERRY MARSHALL—MONTHLY EXPENDITURES

	AMOUNT
1. Housing	$ 0
2. Food	390
3. Clothing	150
4. Transportation	
Installment payments	150
Insurance	60
Fuel	40
5. Phone	35
6. Household purchases and supplies	15
7. Club membership	45
8. Personal care and improvements	150
9. Medical and dental, health and disability	150
10. Debt reduction (excluding home and autos)	150
11. Contribution	35
12. Storage	30
Total Monthly Expenditures	$1,400

ily debts from her capital. Instead, by applying the $685 monthly spousal support to debt, she would be able to pay her balances in full in about six months. In the meantime, her capital would stay intact, earning interest, and she wouldn't be tempted to upgrade spending to match her new cash flow. Especially for a person in her vulnerable position, having several credit cards with high limits available for recharging might be hard to resist.

(Despite this advice tailored to Sherry's situation, as a general rule, you should pay off your debts before commencing a savings program. The interest paid on credit cards is higher than what you would make through savings. Exceptions to this rule include people whose investments earn more than the amount they pay for credit and those who would be tempted to reuse their credit. Of course, if you do not have the discipline not to overcharge, consider retiring your cards to a safe place, using them once or twice a year to keep them active, and paying cash.)

If Sherry does not buy a home, she will face a tremendous tax problem because the IRS expects Sherry to pay taxes on the gain from the sale of her homes if she doesn't buy another home within the two-year legal limit for deferral on a home repurchase. We shall examine Sherry's tax alternatives below, but the point is that unless Sherry conserves her cash she will not have any alternatives to consider.

With conservation in mind, our discussion then turned to the interest being earned on the capital. While the credit union rate competed with stock house money-market funds, two points worried me. First, Sherry could earn more if she could predict when she would be ready to buy a house; if she were going to wait six months to a year, she could commit the funds to higher-interest certificates of deposit.

Second, in light of her current frame of mind, putting her capital in a less accessible location made sense. Temptations inevitably arise for anyone with an unaccustomed liquidity. To someone who earns $16,000, $70,000 feels like a lot of money. With two-and-a-half-years' earnings accessible to Sherry, I feared the next $4,000 would be even easier to remove from her account than the first $4,000 had been.

Though she certainly would not become rich, if she could conserve her cash Sherry would have a strong, positive position from which she could rebuild her life.

Sherry's Taxes

While Sherry had several questions, her chief tax concern centered on trying to purchase a replacement home within the two-year period allowed so she could defer, or roll over, the gain. If she did not purchase a home of equal or greater value, much of her equity would be required to pay her tax bill on the profit from both homes.

The Marshalls' real estate situation represents a classic example of the benefits and costs of tax deferral. Up to $125,000 of gain from selling a home can be rolled over indefinitely. But once the tax comes due, it may exceed available cash.

In the Marshalls' case, they had owned two homes as marital property. House no. 1 was purchased for $29,500 and sold for $177,000, producing a gain of $147,500. House no. 2 was purchased for $245,000 and sold for $251,700, producing a gain of

$6,700. The total gain on the two houses amounted to $154,200, which they would split since they had taken title together. If a new house was not purchased at an equal or greater price than the $251,700 home, both Sherry and her former husband would owe a large tax bill.

TABLE 10.   THE MARSHALLS' GAIN AND ROLLOVER

House No. 1	Net Sales Price (selling price less costs)	$177,000
	Less Purchase Price	29,500
	Gain	147,500
House No. 2	Net Sales Price	251,700
	Less Purchase Price	245,000
	Gain	6,700
Total Gain		154,200
Sherry's 50 Percent of Total Gain		$ 77,100

Because the two had divorced, each of them could defer their portion of the total gain and apply it to the purchase of a new home, the price of which could be divided equally between them. Therefore, if they each bought homes of $125,850 ($251,700 divided by two), each could defer his or her half of the gain.

See what happens to Sherry's taxes if she has to pay taxes on the $77,100 on top of her regular income. Before tax reform, only 40 percent of Sherry's gain ($30,840) would have been taxable, resulting in a tax bill of $15,420 at her then prevailing 50 percent tax rate. (Since her home was sold in 1986, Sherry's income tax bill for the gain of $77,100 would be taxed at her 1986 rates, which would have been higher than now as a result of adding the taxable portion of the gain to her taxable income of $8,000. The taxable gain of $30,840 would put her in the 35 percent marginal tax bracket.)

TABLE 11.   SHERRY MARSHALL'S CAPITAL GAIN TAX (PRE-REFORM)

Capital-gain exclusion	($77,100 x 60%)	=$46,260
Taxable gain (40% taxable)	($77,100 − $46,260)	=$30,840
Tax liability	($30,840 x 35%)	=$10,794

By contrast, had she sold her house in 1988, after tax reform, Sherry's tax picture would have been different. In that case, if she had not purchased a replacement home, her full $77,100 profit would have been taxed at regular, but for Sherry, lower rates; still for Sherry this would have resulted in a higher total tax, since the lower rate is levied on the entire gain. Her tax rate would rise with the additional income from the gain (see table 12). As head of household with two dependents, the first $23,900 of taxable income would be taxed at 15 percent (see Appendix 2 for marginal rates for other filing statuses). Her earned income and alimony less deductions come to a taxable income of $18,332 (contrasted to her total income of $25,332 reflected on p. 67). The remainder of the 15 percent bracket would be the first $5,568 of gain ($23,900 top bracket amount less regular taxable income of $18,332) for a tax of $835.

The next $37,750 of gain would be taxed at 28 percent for a tax of $10,570. The final $33,782 of gain (total gain of $77,100 less $5,568 gain taxed at 15 percent and $37,750 taxed at 28 percent) would be taxed at 33 percent for a tax of $11,148. The total tax on the gain would amount to $22,553 in 1988.

This complicated example illustrates two vital points. First, you can see how income is taxed in brackets. Remember, the first part of all income is initially taxed in the lowest bracket; only as the income becomes higher is it taxed in higher brackets.

Second, for a person such as Sherry, the one-time gain taxed at full rates creates a disproportionate tax liability in one year,

TABLE 12.   SHERRY MARSHALL'S INCREMENT (STEPPED) TAX ON PROFIT FROM SALE OF HOUSE (1988 RATES)

PORTION OF GAIN	HEAD OF HOUSEHOLD TAX RATE*	TAX
$ 5,568	15%	$ 835
37,750	28%	10,570
33,782	33%	11,148
Total Tax		$22,553

*See Appendix 2, Schedule Z.

which cannot now be averaged with earlier or later lower earnings years.

If she cannot purchase a home, Sherry will have had to amend her tax return by filing a 1040X (the X signifies an amended return) for 1986, the year in which the house was sold. The amended return would include the taxes that would now be owed. (Sherry can take the 1986 pre-reform capital-gains treatment, but anyone selling her home in 1987 or after would not get this break and would have to pay tax on the full capital gains. The same procedure of amending the return for the year in which the sale occurs applies.)

Sherry Marshall's example illustrates the power of tax deferral, as well as the tax savings that occur with a favored capital-gains treatment, particularly in the post-reform era. Even with lower rates, the longer that taxes can be deferred, especially large amounts like a home gain, the better off the taxpayer will be. However, the pitfall is that with a large rollover and little cash, the taxpayer may owe more than she has left.

Sherry's Future Growth

Even during their marriage, the Marshalls never earned a combined income of more than $30,000 a year. But they participated in the great California real estate boom of the 1970s. Through no real work on their own and very little planning, the couple's equity growth on their two homes had amounted to $154,000—about 26-fold over nine years—for an average annual return of 290 percent. (See table 13, p. 74.)

This profit presents a stunning picture of the growth power of real estate. The key was in the couple's timing: their entry into the housing market coincided with the beginning of the upward swing.

Their success also demonstrates the effect of leveraging. With only $5,900, the Marshalls were able to command a property in the marketplace worth almost $30,000. As their property grew, up to the point of sale, the same $5,900 held down property worth thirty times as much.

A 10 or 20 percent of purchase price down payment will

TABLE 13.   SHERRY AND GEORGE MARSHALL—SALE
OF PRINCIPAL RESIDENCE

Computation of Gain

1. Selling price of residence less expense of sale	$251,700
2. Basis of residence sold*	97,500
3. Gain on sale	$154,200

*Calculated by subtracting the cost of the new residence ($245,000) from the gain post-poned from the first residence ($147,500).

---

command an entire property. Depending on interest rates and the economy, the homeowner then earns not only on the original equity, or down payment, but also on the amount that is mortgaged. For example, assume a home is purchased at an 8 percent mortgage interest rate. If real estate appreciates in value at only 8 percent, the property purchased at 8 percent interest would stay even with the cost of the 8 percent mortgage. But if the property is purchased with 8 percent mortgage and the real estate growth rate stands at 12 percent, then the owner is gaining the difference of 4 percent per year over what she is paying the bank for the money borrowed. On the downside, if real estate appreciates at only 8 percent and the property is purchased with 12 percent interest, then the purchaser would be losing 4 percent per year—the difference between the amount paid for the money borrowed and the growth rate.

In the late 1970s, interest rates on homes purchased stood at under 8 percent and the growth rate was as high as 20 percent per year. Soon the banks could not afford to lend money at these rates, leading to steep increases in home interest rates in the early 1980s—at one point up to 17 and 18 percent for mortgages —and the growth of variable rate mortgages.

With her real estate cash profits of $77,100, Sherry's balance sheet showed a net worth of $80,180. Look over her assets and liabilities.

You will see that some of the items are "soft." Although cash is clearly worth the face amount, her household furnishings, which she figured might cost $15,000 for replacement, but would bring only a fraction of the amount—approximately $3,000 as reflected in table 14 (see p. 76)—on the market as used furniture. Her new car could probably resell for $10,000, and her IRA $2,600. Her total assets, then, come to $92,980.

Her liabilities include her auto loan of $9,000, $2,000 on charge accounts, and other bills at $1,800. Total liabilities stand at $12,800. (This figure does not include the taxes she would owe if she were unable to purchase a replacement home.) To calculate her net worth, Sherry subtracted her total liabilities from her total assets. Considering her relatively modest earnings of just under $17,000, Sherry's balance sheet reflects a relatively good position (especially, as we shall soon see, compared to some of our high-cash-flow individuals).

One dilemma that Sherry faces centers on her cash position were she to reinvest most of her $77,100 in real estate, which she must do because her monthly income is insufficient to service a larger mortgage. With this much tied up in a new home, Sherry's liquidity will be low. But as a young woman with a number of earning years in which to amass additional savings and parents who can help in case of emergencies, a home purchase makes sense. Although the real estate market would probably not experience growth as great in the future as it had in the past, the risk of investing her capital in a home is low. Owning property would provide a home for her family and cushion them from rent rises.

Buying a home fits her goal of long-term growth rather than current income, but the drawback is its effect on cash flow. With a down payment of $70,000 and $5,000 in closing costs, her monthly outgo will rise to approximately $1,000 for interest and principal on her projected mortgage loan, $105,000 at 11 percent, a very large monthly payment considering her earned income of $1,400. Since she now pays no rent living with her parents, the entire cost will be a new cash expenditure. Sherry will almost certainly require help from her parents to make the purchase even if her alimony and child support continue.

As for tax consequences, Sherry will save paying on her gain because she can roll over her portion of the taxes that would be due as a consequence of the profit on the two previous homes. This tax obligation can be postponed indefinitely should she decide to stay in her new home or again replace that home with another home purchase. As for current deductions, with her low income, her three exemptions, and her full child-care tax credit,

TABLE 14.   SHERRY MARSHALL—BALANCE SHEET
(SEPTEMBER 30, 1988)

What Is Owned (Assets)

Cash and cash equivalents	
Cash in checking accounts	$ 4,200
Cash in savings accounts, credit union	72,900
Personal property*	
Household furnishings	3,000
Car	10,000
Real estate	0
Investments	
Stocks, 6 shares, Standard Oil	280
IRA retirement savings	2,600
Total Assets	**$92,980**

What Is Owed (Liabilities)

Current bills	
Charge account balances	$ 2,000
Other bills including storage, doctors,	1,800
taxes, property ($6,168)	
Amount owed on loans	
Auto loan	9,000
Total Liabilities	**$12,800**

Net Worth Computation

Total assets	$92,980
Total liabilities	12,800
Net worth (assets minus liabilities)	$80,180

*Estimated current market value.

Sherry owes no federal income taxes. Thus, the tax savings that would be generated by her purchase are meaningless to her until she can raise her income.

This last point is worth emphasizing. Not everyone can use tax savings that may be created as a result of a particular investment. If the taxpayer cannot use the tax savings, then it is not a saving at all—a point sometimes lost in a sales context.

As Sherry came to the end of 1988, the two-year tax deadline for purchasing a home drew near. She located a $175,000 condominium near her parents, made an offer, and concluded the purchase, thus taking advantage of leveraging growth and tax savings on rollover. Sherry closed the year feeling in better command of her financial life.

CHAPTER 5

MAXIMIZING

MIDDLE

INCOMES

Being a middle-income consumer today is not easy. On one hand, people whose incomes are adequate but not generous have been educated to believe that finances can be improved and that material comfort is attainable. On the other hand, these same consumers face a variety of everyday pressures on their incomes, from an increasing tax burden—despite reform—to higher costs of living. Finding a balance between current needs and growth goals takes skill and patience, as illustrated by the three cases in this chapter.

Dora Delgado, a New York biology professor who pays a good bit of her income in taxes, fears making a commitment to real estate, even though it would provide her with tax relief and growth potential.

Leslie and Andrew Carlson, a young professional couple who own a home, need to create further tax savings and growth opportunities.

Kate and George English face hard times, illustrating that not all financial lives serve as rational models of behavior. But all these characters have in common sufficient income to complete stage 1 (adequate savings) and stage 2 (securing their retirement)—provided they follow the necessary steps.

DORA DELGADO

A thirty-five-year-old tenured biology professor, Delgado feels secure in her job. She can well afford to take some risks, but having grown up in an economically disadvantaged setting, Delgado's motivating concern is to avoid poverty. Therefore, she's not a risk taker. In fact, Delgado has erred on the side of caution.

On the positive side, with her conservative approach, Delgado has managed to conquer stage 1 of growth—savings. And because her university-sponsored retirement plan is in order, she has built part of stage 2—her retirement fund—as well. She has enough cash set aside that she could add to her security by investing in real estate. But her fears of the uncertainties associated with real estate—for example, the possibilities of repairs—have limited her perspective and her actions.

Dora's Cash Flow

Dora has been a conscientious budgeter since college, and her cash flow is managed well. Her income and outgo are balanced, including over $200 a month routinely set aside for savings.

Dora's problem is not her cash flow, but her taxes and her growth. (See table 15, p. 80.)

Delgado's Taxes

Professor Dora Delgado sees that although she and a colleague, Professor Hill, earn almost identical salaries, their financial pictures are very different. Professor Hill's taxes are next to nothing, while Dora shells out over $8,000 a year to the federal government. The difference is that Professor Hill owns real estate and Delgado owns none.

Tax savings through real estate deductions provide Hill the break that Delgado needs. Hill has figured out that she can

TABLE 15.   DELGADO'S INCOME AND EXPENDITURES

1. Income from employment	
Salary	$3,529
2. Investment income	
Taxable interest	29
Nontaxable interest	209
Total Monthly Income	3,767

Monthly Expenditures

1. Housing	
Rent	$1,000
Utilities	40
2. Food	
Groceries	100
Restaurant meals	250
3. Clothing	150
4. Transportation	
Taxi	250
Subway	80
5. Phone	50
6. Household purchases and supplies	20
7. Health club membership	120
8. Personal care and improvements	100
9. Medical and dental expenses	75
10. Travel	250
11. Savings	215
12. Taxes	
Federal income tax	687
Social Security	265
State income tax	115
Total Monthly Expenditures	$3,767

legally divert money from the federal government to her own pocket by investing in highly leveraged real estate. Instead of paying taxes, she is mortgaged to the hilt. But with exactly the same cash going out each month from each professor—Hill's to service the mortgages and Delgado's to service her tax bill and rent—Hill participates in real estate growth and tax savings. Delgado's best solution is to buy a home in order to gain interest and property tax deductions. By the time she had made the decision to buy, the Manhattan real estate market had risen out of her reach. Delgado's solution, then, was to look for a cooperative in a less expensive area and commute to work.

As outlined in table 16, the purchase price of the cooperative apartment she bought was $125,000, with $25,000 cash down. Her cash savings after tax amount to $156 monthly (line 13).

TABLE 16.   ANALYSIS OF HOME OWNERSHIP COSTS

Basic Facts

1. Purchase price of home	$125,000
2. Cash down payment required	25,000
3. Loan	100,000
4. Monthly payments: principal and interest (10.5% interest 30 years fixed)	914
5. Monthly deposit for property taxes	156
6. Maintenance for cooperative	100
7. Monthly deposit for insurance, approximate	50
8. Total monthly payment (lines 4, 5, 6, and 7)	1,220

Expense Items for Income Tax Purposes

9. First month's interest*	886
10. Monthly property tax deposit	156
11. Total deductions (line 9 + line 10)	1,042
12. Tax bracket†	15
13. Tax savings per month (line 12 x line 11)	156

Total After-Tax Cost

14. Total monthly payment (line 8)	1,220
15. Less estimated tax savings (line 13)	156
16. Effective monthly cost in cash, after taxes (line 14 minus line 15)	1,064
17. Subtract equity* being gained monthly (line 4 minus line 9)	28

Actual monthly cost	$ 1,036

*Interest amount decreases by a small amount each month and equity increases by the same proportion.

†In table 17, Dora's actual savings on the 1040 reflected in line 8 are higher because of other deductions taken and because some of her income is taxed at 28 percent, making the effective tax rate approximately 20 percent.

Looking at the comparison of her tax return with and without the real estate deductions, it is evident that by filing the 1040, Dora's annual taxes drop considerably from $8,250 to $4,990, almost 40 percent. Her $14,460 in Schedule A itemized deductions include a number of deductions previously unavailable to her as a short-form filler. For example, like many university professors, Dora has unreimbursed employee business expenses such as conference travel and manuscript preparation costs. These expenses can be deducted only when they exceed the 2 percent adjusted gross income floor for miscellaneous itemized expenses. When filing on the short form, Dora lost these deductions, but now she claims $1,150 in unreimbursed employee business expenses as part of her miscellaneous deductions. Combined with her real estate deductions, the total monthly savings are almost $275, even greater than the $156 from the property alone, and her actual monthly housing costs are only $36 more (rent of $1,000 compared to actual monthly cost of $1,036; see table 16). She has the advantage and security of the increasing equity in her home investment.

(If you, like Dora, are an employee with reimbursed or unreimbursed business expenses, take note of the method of filing. Unreimbursed expenses should be put on Form 2106, "Employee Business Expenses," which are in turn listed as part of the miscellaneous itemized deductions on Schedule A. These deductions must exceed 2 percent of annual adjusted gross income to be

TABLE 17.   DORA DELGADO—TWO RETURNS COMPARED 1988

	1040ᴇᴢ	1040
1. Wages*	$42,350	$42,350
2. Interest*	350	350
3. Adjusted gross income	42,700	42,700
4. Standard/itemized deductions	3,000	14,640†
5. Personal exemption	1,950	1,950
6. Taxable income	37,750	26,110
7. Tax withheld	8,249.50	4,990
8. Tax owed	$ 8,249.50	$ 4,990

*Because of rounding, figures are slightly different from table 15.
†With mortgage interest as well as other itemizations on Schedule A.

taken. To take the mortgage interest deduction, Dora must also complete Form 8598, a new form that summarizes mortgage interest taken.)

Middle-income and higher earners are much more likely than lower-income persons to be able to take advantage of tax savings opportunities and switch to filing the long form. But, anyone paying a substantial tax bill should investigate whether she—like Dora—can save on taxes by filling out a long-form 1040. Table 39 on page 158, in Chapter 8, will show you how to project these calculations in advance of tax season.

Delgado's Future Growth

In buying her home, Dora has overcome her cautious approach to finances. With a toehold in the real estate market, she has completed investment stage 2, securing her retirement. Her stage 3—investing for maximum growth—revolves around exploring the stock market.

Dora has recently noticed her university retirement fund has two kinds of investments, one for "security" and one for growth. The growth-oriented fund, invested in the stock market, appreciates at a far greater rate than her safer investment, which is in Treasury bonds. Since she has been increasingly curious about the market, the good news from her growth fund encourages Dora to try her hand in the stock market with $10,000 she recently inherited from an aunt.

With no inheritance taxes due, because her aunt's estate paid these taxes before disbursement, Dora's nest egg can build a small portfolio. Because of Dora's conservative bent, she divides her liquid assets into two portions, similar to the fifty-fifty split that has been made with her retirement fund, one for security and one for growth.

With the first $5,000, she opens a money-market account at a major brokerage house. The account appeals to her because it allows her to earn money-market interest rates, which run up two to three points higher than a savings account in a bank, while enjoying a safer investment than the stock market. The fund also offers a checking account, allowing her to draw her funds out instantaneously if need be, and a Visa card, actually a debit Visa. (A debit card takes money directly from a deposit account, but it looks exactly like ordinary plastic credit card. With a debit card, the user has the advantages of credit without the disadvantage of running up high bills. Since consumer credit interest is not entirely deductible in the post–tax reform era, and will not be deductible at all after 1991, having such a card makes sense. With this debit Visa, Dora's money *earns* interest rather than causing her to pay interest; however, she can still use the Visa to rent a car or purchase theater tickets by phone.

Dora decides to put together a sample group of stocks with the second $5,000. She has read the business section of the newspaper for several months and feels that with some guidance, she can make a selection that will suit her goals: to equal or exceed the return that she makes on her money-market account while conserving her capital.

Dora is not naïve; she knows that the stock market is very risky. And for this small an investment, it will be difficult to organize a balanced portfolio with a significant number of stocks in each category of risk. Nonetheless, she feels that with her specialized knowledge in biology and the sciences combined with her continuing reading, she can do better than the proverbial monkey throwing darts at a stock page. To get started, Dora puts together what she thinks is a balanced portfolio of stocks that interest her. Her next step is to take her "shopping list" to a broker.

Since Dora doesn't know any brokers personally, she turns to networking. By asking around among her faculty colleagues, she learns of two brokers, both women, who meet her requirements. She wants to amass a socially conscious investment portfolio, and she prefers a broker who will not waste her money by *churning,* or repeatedly buying and selling, her stocks in order to create higher commissions. Dora wants to avoid South Africa, nuclear power, and the tobacco industry while supporting firms that hire and promote women and minorities, which turns out to be harder than she imagines it will be.

She considers using a discount broker rather than a regular one, as she can save $50 to $100 per trade. But with her small amount of money, getting a cheaper rate will not make enough difference to outweigh her main goal: locating a broker who fits her two chief criteria. She settles on the house where she has

opened her money-market account. She feels that this relationship will give her greater flexibility should she decide to invest
further funds from her money-market account in the stock market, and the recommended broker there meets Dora's standards.
Also, she likes the idea of keeping all her money with one house,
thus becoming a valued customer.

After reviewing the standard risk factors with Dora, her
new broker asks her to evaluate the amount of risk she can
tolerate, ranging from high to low. The broker then reviews
Dora's own preliminary selection of stocks and assists her in
making final choices to fit her desired medium-risk, medium-
return socially conscious portfolio.

Dora's portfolio includes a low-risk computer stock, a riskier
entertainment stock, a solid biotechnical company, and an established sportswear stock, adding up to a medium-risk mix. In
addition, she adds two mutual funds. Since she has already established a money-market account, which is basically built
around the same ingredients as a very low-risk, very low-return
investment would be, she does not feel that she needs this low-
risk component to balance her portfolio.

Dora is excited to see that although she is a newcomer to the
market, her stocks all have gained in value. Her portfolio growth
has not quite equaled the interest her money-market account
earns, but she is prepared to let her money stay put—the only
way to profit. But Dora has not forgotten the crash of 1987; she
makes sure that she keeps in the market only money that she
can afford to see eroded overnight. Although she has no high-risk
investments, she knows that even her medium-risk stocks can
turn sour if the market takes another plunge.

As Dora filed her 1988 tax returns, she noticed again the tax
difference between her real estate and her stock market investments. While she can deduct her interest and property tax on
her home, she has to pay taxes on the small dividends from her
portfolio. Not only does the stock investment provide taxable
income and no deductions, but if Dora loses a substantial amount
of money in the stock market, only $3,000 will be deductible in
a single year. By contrast, if she loses money when she sells her
home, the full amount will be deductible.

The stock market is a game, and Dora is involved not just
for making money but for the pleasure of following the market

itself. She knows that, like a gambler in any other setting, she is playing the odds. Unlike many investors, she realizes the nature of her involvement. Many people in the stock market forget the gambling aspect and find themselves surprised by a down-turning market.

Dora is a woman making real progress on her financial growth. Her assets remain modest, but her approach is sane. With careful, continual involvement, she will eventually build a solid financial footing. In addition, because she has taken control of her own financial future, she feels more able to progress in other areas of her life.

LESLIE AND ANDREW CARLSON

Leslie and Andrew Carlson are a young professional couple with two children, one a newborn. Like the majority of couples, they are a two-earner family. Also, like more than half of mothers with young children, Leslie is in the paid labor force. Andrew is a participant in a business partnership; Leslie runs a computer business from her home. Leslie's business has been taking a loss lately for two reasons: her net profits are never very high (typical nationally of female-owned businesses) and she cut back on new contracts after the birth of their second child.

Leslie's decision to seek advice arose from her realization that, despite being in business for herself and using her computer expertise in keeping track of family expenditures, she did not fully understand the bigger financial picture. Now having temporarily reduced her business commitment following the birth of a second child, Leslie has become aware that the financial balance of power in her marriage needs adjusting.

Leslie and Andrew's Cash Flow

The first step that the Carlsons need to take is to analyze their cash flow. Since Leslie keeps regular books on the computer for family expenditures, she only needs to group expenses by function to convert them to a budget format. In this way, she is able to look at broad expenditure categories to analyze how the family spends its after-tax funds. From there, creating a budget simply amounts to setting up desired spending plans, or the "budget," in the next column of her computer spread sheet. The hard part of this exercise is to figure out goals so that spending can be reallocated to match new priorities.

SETTING GOALS AND CREATING A BUDGET

Leslie's immediate goals are to create an education fund for the children and to put aside money in savings. Andrew agrees but wants to add an investment component to their cash-flow picture. To achieve any of these possibilities, money will have to be set aside from current expenditures, or tax savings will have to be made.

To translate their general goals to specific dollar commitments, Leslie creates an expenditure budget.

The Expenditure Budget. The Carlsons establish an expenditure budget, by category, so that they can control and evaluate their spending. This budget will also serve, when it is reviewed at the end of the budget period, as an aid in making new plans, thus closing the loop by providing feedback for future undertakings.

The expenditure budget differs from a cash-flow analysis in several ways. The budget takes into account not only what a person thinks she will spend, but what she is actually spending; by contrast, cash-flow analysis simply reflects what was spent.

Leslie decides to set up a four-column analysis on her computer. Column 1 lists last year's figures for actual expenditures by category; column 2, the budgeted amount; column 3, actual expenditures this year; and column 4, the *variance analysis* (the difference between the amount budgeted and spent). Leslie programs her computer to make this final calculation automatically. This budgeting system is ideal for the Carlsons since they are already involved with computers and own the requisite spreadsheet program.

LESLIE AND ANDREW CARLSON'S BUDGET

| | LAST YEAR | | THIS YEAR | |
| EXPENSE | ACTUAL | BUDGET | ACTUAL | VARIANCE |

Reallocating Resources. In order to start savings, a college education fund, and an investment fund, Leslie begins to analyze where current expenditures can be cut. The couple decided to reduce restaurant meals and entertainment expenditures. The money reflected in the "budgeted amount" column for these items has been adjusted so that the education fund of $110 per month or $1,320 a year can be created. Next Leslie and Andrew review furniture and clothing expenditures. Both Leslie and Andrew can reduce their clothes budget, as projected in the "budgeted amount." New furniture purchases will be curtailed in favor of garage sale acquisitions, and the money saved will go toward an investment fund. Finally, Andrew decides to dispense with the gardener, do most of the work himself instead, and hire a neighborhood teenager to mow the lawn for $10, thus saving another $140 per month. The final results of the cash-flow and budget effort are shown in table 18, pages 89–91.

YEAR-END REVIEW

When the budget year is complete, Leslie will add up the monthly totals by category, then compare these totals with both budgeted amounts and last year's expenditures. In addition, because Leslie's income varies, the couple will want to look at the overall money spent and be sure annual income exceeds annual expenditures.

The review will provide a chance to see how they have done and to set goals for succeeding years. However, while cost cutting and careful controls will help, they will not solve the Carlsons' basic problem. It is clear if you look over Leslie and Andrew's budget that the couple must find a way to divert funds from their current heavy tax burden to make dramatic improvements in their growth funding. Like many self-employed middle-income people, their tax bite is high and their budget is tight.

The Carlsons' Taxes

Leslie and Andrew Carlson own a home, but even with their mortgage deduction, their taxes—including self-employment

TABLE 18. LESLIE AND ANDREW CARLSON'S
MONTHLY BUDGET

	LAST YEAR	THIS YEAR		
EXPENSE	ACTUAL	BUDGET	ACTUAL	VARIANCE
1. Housing				
Mortgage	$1,000	$1,000		
Real estate taxes	150	150		
Condominium dues	140	140		
Homeowner's insurance	120	120		
Water and sewer	25	25		
Heat	20	20		
Electricity	35	35		
Gas	13	13		
Subtotal, housing	1,503	1,503		
2. Telephone	125	125		
3. Food and beverage				
Home	350	350		
Restaurant	150	100		
Subtotal, food	500	450		
4. Clothing and shoes				
Wife	120	80		
Husband	100	75		
Children	60	60		
Subtotal, clothing	280	215		
5. Household operations				
Laundry/dry cleaning	80	80		
Repair	50	50		
Gardener	150	10		
Subtotal, household	280	140		
6. Child care	260	260		
7. Life insurance	85	85		
8. Medical				
Doctor	25	25		
Dentist	25	25		
Prescriptions	20	20		
Subtotal, medical	70	70		
9. Automobiles				
Payments	145	145		

TABLE 18—*Continued*

EXPENSE	LAST YEAR ACTUAL	THIS YEAR		
		BUDGET	ACTUAL	VARIANCE
Insurance	90	90		
Maintenance	20	20		
Subtotal, automobile	255	255		
10. Household equipment				
Furniture	100	100		
Tools	10	10		
Subtotal, household equipment	110	110		
11. Personal business				
Lawyer	50	50		
Accountant	25	25		
Banking fees	5	5		
Subtotal, personal business	80	80		
12. Nondurables				
Travel	100	100		
Entertainment	160	100		
Organization dues	100	100		
Magazines	20	20		
Toiletries	55	55		
Subtotal, nondurables	435	375		
13. Miscellaneous				
Husband	50	50		
Wife	75	75		
Children	20	20		
Subtotal, miscellaneous	145	145		
14. Investments				
Savings	0	65		
Education fund	0	110		
Investment fund	0	80		
Subtotal, investments	0	255		
Subtotal, expenditures	4,128	4,068		

TABLE 18—*Continued*

EXPENSE	LAST YEAR ACTUAL	THIS YEAR BUDGET	ACTUAL	VARIANCE
15. Taxes				
Federal income tax	342	342		
Self-employment tax	487	487		
State income tax	100	100		
State unemployment	50	50		
Subtotal, taxes	979	979		
TOTAL MONTHLY*	$5,107	$5,249		

*Total expenditures do not exactly match income because of Leslie's business income, expenses, and loss.

taxes—in 1988 came to 19 percent of their adjusted gross income and 36 percent of taxable income.

Previously employed by a large corporation, two years ago Andrew formed a business partnership. Although his partnership pays him slightly more than his previous salary, in estimating his earnings Andrew had not taken the self-employment tax into account. The self-employment tax—13.02 percent up to a total indexed income of $45,000 in 1988 and $48,000 in 1989—is the payment that a self-employed person must make to Social Security in lieu of the combined employer and employee contribution of 7.51 percent each. The rate rises to 15.30 percent for 1990, but self-employment earnings under $400 annually are not subject to this tax. Since a flat rate applies and the tax is not bracketed according to income, this tax is not progressive. For a self-employed person like Andrew whose income falls near the top of the ceiling on which the tax is levied, this tax drives up the effective tax rate considerably.

By contrast, although they have two children with child-care expenses of $260 a month, the child-care tax credit provides no relief because Leslie's business is losing money. In order to qualify for the credit, both spouses must show earned income, and in the case of a business owner, the income must exceed business expenses to qualify.

On the positive side, with their children, Leslie and Andrew become big winners in the exemption category. Their personal exemption jumped to $1,950 per person in 1988, for a total of $7,800 (up from pre-reform of $1,080 per person or a total of $4,320 in 1986).

TABLE 19.   ANDREW AND LESLIE CARLSON—1988 INCOME TAX RETURN (1040) SUMMARY PROJECTION

1. Partnership (Andrew, Schedule E)	$ 58,000
2. Business income (Leslie, Schedule C)	< 5,000 >
3. Adjusted gross income	53,000
4. Itemized deductions (Schedule A)	17,800
5. Personal exemptions (4)	7,800
6. Taxable income	27,400
7. Tax owed*	4,110
8. Self-employment tax†	5,859
9. Total tax owed	$ 9,969

*Married couple, filing jointly, taxable income up to $29,750 fixed at minimum rate of 15 percent.
†13.02 percent of self-employment income up to $45,000 ceiling.

Let us take a closer look at another component of the Carlsons' return, Leslie's business deductions.

BUSINESS LOSS

Like any business filer using Schedule C, Leslie has the opportunity to take many more tax deductions than are available to a garden-variety employed 1040 filer.

Before the new law went into effect, if a person operated a small unincorporated business, she might have had to show a profit two out of every five years for the IRS to allow the loss, which is deducted against other income. Now a profit must be shown in three out of every five years (or else the burden of proof is on the taxpayer to show that the business is in fact a for-profit business and not simply a tax shelter or a hobby).

In Leslie and Andrew's case, this new rule could hit hard. Leslie has cut back on her commitments with the birth of their second child. Her emphasis now lies on longer-term projects with fewer immediate cash returns, thus the profit outlook in the short term is dim.

If Leslie is to continue her business and utilize the deductions, she will have to review the new rules on home offices as well as the new profit guidelines.

The new narrow home office rule reads: "Deductions for the business use of a home will not create a business loss or increase a net loss from a business." That is, if the business is showing zero profit or already showing a loss, one cannot add the business use of the home office to create a larger loss. In Leslie and Andrew's case, the rule works to their detriment. Part of the loss that Leslie shows in the couple's estimated 1988 taxes is attributable to the deduction for the business use of their home, a loss *not available* to lower the 1988 tax bill. The couple's final tax return—to be filed later with an extension—must reflect this change.

With an income of $7,500, Leslie is now allowed to deduct only $500 for her home office because of the new formula. Of course, she can still deduct her other expenses, such as dues, publications, typing, and Xeroxing. If you, like Leslie, have a home office deduction, get the special IRS brochure on this extremely complicated rule (IRS Publication No. 587)—and be alerted that your deduction, like Leslie's, may have been diminished.

Despite these changes in the deductibility of business losses, the real value of having such a business, especially in a two-earner salary situation, can be readily seen. In Leslie and Andrew's case, in at least two out of every five years, Leslie can afford to show a loss provided it is not from her home office deductions. As long as Leslie continues her efforts in the computer field, she will have a deduction that will benefit the family as well as the potential for future income when her efforts return a profit.

In fact, any salaried person who engages in a legitimate side business, not a hobby, can continue to create losses that offset a high salary. The passive loss rule does not apply to these losses. To be sure, the IRS scrutinizes such activities, but a legitimate active effort can provide shelter—and possibly profit.

But, for now, Andrew and Leslie will have to show less business loss and refigure their 1988 taxes.

SALARY REDUCTION 401(K) AND KEOGH OPTIONS

Given the fact that the couple had no retirement program under way, they considered having Andrew devote a portion of his income to a 401(k) salary reduction plan, one type of salary reduction option, also known as a CODA (cash or deferred arrangements). This plan works as follows: if the employer, in this case a company of which Andrew is a part-owner, decides to establish a "plan" as required by the Internal Revenue Code, then a base amount of up to $7,000, indexed for inflation, of the employee's income can be put into the plan right off the top of income.

The amount contributed does not enter the stream of income that is reported to the IRS in the year earned but instead tax is deferred until the funds are distributed from the plan to Andrew and Leslie. In the 15 percent bracket (excluding self-employment tax), if they could afford it, Andrew and Leslie would be wise to take the full $7,000 contribution available. Of that figure, $1,050 ($7,000 times 15 percent effective bracket) would represent cash tax deferral to the couple—legally delaying the payment of money that would otherwise be used to pay this year's taxes.

There's one more catch. Under the antidiscrimination provisions designed to protect rank-and-file workers, employer's contributions depend on the amount deferred by lower-paid employees of Andrew's business. The company has only one no-nowner employee. To meet the IRS test for deferred income, Andrew's 401(k) cannot exceed 125 percent of what the employee "voluntarily" contributes. For Andrew to put away $7,000, Andrew's employee or the firm on her behalf would have to pay $5,600 for a comparable 401(k) deferment, hardly an attractive proposition financially for Andrew.

(Although the 401[k] is not widely offered by companies, this last provision creates an attractive opportunity for employees. In order to get their own deduction, some employers match employee contributions. Check to see if your employer offers a 401[k] and a matching contribution.)

Since Andrew is self-employed, another option would be contribution to a Keogh plan, another voluntary contribution program for self-employed persons. There are two types of Keogh plans: a defined contribution, where a set amount is put aside annually, and a defined benefit, where an annual after-retirement benefit is selected. For younger people, the defined contribution makes more sense; as a person approaches her midforties, aiming for a particular retirement income and paying enough to reach that by retirement is the preferred course of action. For the defined-contribution plan, up to 20 percent of net earnings from self-employment with a maximum contribution of $30,000 per year can be set aside. With $58,000 in 1988 earnings, Andrew could theoretically put in up to $11,600. However, here again the antidiscrimination provisions kick in. Andrew would have to match his 20 percent Keogh with a comparable amount (20 percent) for each employee of the business. Practically speaking, reform limited the usefulness of these plans for a small business owner with employees. (For more details on these plans, see Chapter 9.)

MARRIAGE AND MONEY

For Leslie and Andrew, getting control of their finances involved more than simply setting aside money. Although Leslie was the family budgeter, she had left taxes, which she "hated," and long-term planning to Andrew. When the Carlsons had bought their first home, Leslie had taken time to learn about home interest and property tax deductions. As a businessperson, Leslie also understands the tax environment for her own business situation. But she had not moved beyond understanding these deductions to think in strategic terms about taxes.

The budgeting experience has allowed Leslie to view financial knowledge differently. As she works to equalize control over the family finances, she understands the power of hands-on involvement. But, as she becomes more knowledgeable, Andrew resents having "his" territory invaded. But Leslie persists. Having observed the effects of a lopsided economic partnership in her own childhood, she now realizes that her own marriage resembles her parents' to a startling degree.

Andrew's "cultural programming" says that men should keep the reins on the family money. But he is becoming convinced that the change could be positive. Instead of being the sole person responsible for the couple's economic future, he is beginning to see Leslie—despite her minimal earnings contribution—as his economic partner.

To symbolize their new cooperative spirit, the couple organizes the family's bank accounts into "yours," "mine," and "ours" categories (formerly, Andrew had exercised primary control over the account). Leslie and Andrew open a joint account to pay all household bills. In addition, each opens an individual account for clothes and personal items.

With her newfound knowledge, Leslie takes seriously the idea that marriage is an economic partnership. When the couple acquires assets in the future, she will make sure that the title accurately reflects their ownership intentions. Leslie has also made sure that the couple has prepared a will reflecting their plans for their children's guardian to ensure that the couple's resources would be properly managed.

Any married reader should also follow Leslie's example and protect her own economic position. (See additional information in Appendix 5.)

The Carlsons' Three-Cornered Growth Foundation

With their marital partnership on a more solid footing, Leslie and Andrew could count their future growth blessings. Through careful budgeting and planning, they had acquired all the important cornerstones of a solid future—a home, Social Security, and plans for adding a 401(k). This puts them in our "stage 3" investment group, that is, investing for maximum growth.

Tax incentives had spurred them to a home purchase and retirement plan. Now, Leslie and Andrew are positioned to diversify, and their next task consists of identifying new investment directions. But as Andrew's income continues to rise and Leslie returns to work, they will be tempted to increase their standard of living rather than devote their resources to investing. If Leslie and Andrew can keep on course, they can engage in investments to create maximum growth.

KATE ENGLISH

Kate English, a Washington-based civil servant, is accustomed to a good income and high purchasing power. With her $41,000 annual salary, she should be able to live decently, although not luxuriously. But she married George, a free-lance photographer, who brings in just over $11,000. His business expenses run high—too high. And now, the couple has the added expense of a baby.

Not surprisingly, Kate and George experience a credit crunch, and in a long-distance call, Kate asks how to deal with their creditors. After talking through her problems and getting some tips, she sounds relieved.

A few days later, Kate calls with the news that George has purchased a new dark-room setup, and she has gone along with his decision. When reminded of her credit crisis, her response is "George feels he can't afford to pass this opportunity up—he won't have to buy new equipment for several years."

A couple of weeks pass, and Kate phones again. This time she is near tears because the hospital that had delivered her son, Jason, has been calling to collect the remaining money the couple owes. Reminded that the hospital cannot "repossess" Jason, she is encouraged to work out a payment plan.

Soon another call comes. "Suzi's is closing their doors and I have been able to buy clothes to last for years at a fraction of their cost. I'm thrilled—I have cornered almost half their stock of imported silk negligees as well."

Although shopping as "therapy" isn't uncommon, Kate and George have graduated from shopping as therapy to needing therapy to stop shopping. Fortunately, she had the courage to call a therapist for an appointment to examine the psychological issues motivating their irrational patterns.

Consumer Targets and Consumer Resistance

Not all of Kate and George's overspending can be laid at their doorstep. While it is partly a result of personal problems, much of their behavior reflects a response to a marketplace that is designed to encourage excessive spending. Retailers and advertisers maximize profits by techniques designed to take advantage of consumer shopping habits. For instance, consumers make up to 80 percent of purchasing decisions when in the store.

A few points could benefit from some further exploration.

Although it is not always easy, one can combat the intense "spend-spend-spend" messages in our culture and the media. Cut costs by using the tried but true advice we have all heard.

To start, plan to shop only when you need something specific. Check your refrigerator before going to the supermarket. Make a list and do not stray from it. Never go to the supermarket when you are hungry. Shop for bargains. Use coupons when you have them. Resist the messages that are designed to get you to spend and spend some more. Also, don't shop as therapy (if you do, buy bubble bath, not a new handbag). Indulge yourself in other ways.

A key difference between business or government purchasing and personal shopping is planning and accountability. A business expenditure is ordinarily planned. But even if the purchasing decision is made at the last minute, most organizations require a purchase order. Generally, that purchase order has to be signed by someone other than the initiator, thus creating accountability.

As a civil servant, Kate uses paperwork for department purchases. As a first step to bringing her spending under control, Kate agrees to make a purchase order for whatever she plans to buy (see table 38, p. 153, for form). The couple has adopted the rule that nothing costing over $50 will be acquired without first completing some "paperwork."

Unfortunately, Kate and George's financial difficulties involve more than overspending. George's free-lance business has been sketchily managed, and his haphazard bookkeeping leads to a tax audit.

The Englishs' Tax Audit

To cover the gap between what they had spent and the couple's tax bill, Kate and George had tacked extra expenses onto George's legitimate business deductions, thus lowering their tax bill considerably. The IRS soon notified them of an audit.

Kate and George will never know exactly what triggered the review. With a home-based business showing consistent losses, they were already in a high-risk category for audit. Added to their excessive deductions, Kate had forgotten to report a state income tax refund as taxable income (federal income tax refunds are not subject to federal income tax).

Kate should have stopped here and involved a CPA as well as using resource books such as *How to Do Business with the IRS* by Randy Blaustein. But, as the family paperwork expert, preparing for the audit fell on Kate's shoulders.

As she reviewed their records in preparation for their initial IRS meeting, Kate saw that George's documented expense receipts fell short of amounts listed on the return. In addition to having exaggerated expenses, he overestimated the portion of their home used for office space. (As we saw with the Carlsons, under the 1986 tax law, such deductions were curtailed when the business loses money; but in the earlier year being audited, this rule had not yet gone into effect.) Unfortunately, even though Kate serves as the family financial manager and prepares the couple's returns, she had relied too heavily on George's estimates and failed to notice the discrepancies.

George had generated only $11,922 in income for the year being audited but reported deductions of $33,293 for a total business loss of $21,371. Also, as with Leslie Carlson, George's business loss served to offset the taxes paid on Kate's salaried income. This loss, when subtracted from her $41,000 income, put the couple's adjusted gross income at $19,629. (*Note:* The passive loss rule had not gone into effect, but if it had, it would not apply because George actively pursues his business.)

As reflected in George's Schedule C, he claimed car and truck expenses, dues and publications, laundry and cleaning (presumably of his office), and $15,000 in travel and entertainment. Had this been a start-up year, George's expenses might have made financial sense. But the IRS finds unconvincing expenditures so large for a couple with $41,000 worth of income. His $21,000 loss—more than half their income—appears out of proportion, and it is. (See table 20, p. 100.)

As Kate reviews the information requested by the IRS for the audit, she finds the detail required staggering.

Let us look at the items on the IRS list:

Item 1: Bank Account Deposits and Client Income. As she begins to work her way through the check registers, it is clear

TABLE 20.   GEORGE ENGLISH—SCHEDULE C PROFIT
OR (LOSS) FROM BUSINESS OR PROFESSION

1. Gross income	$11,922
2. Advertising	256
3. Supplies	1,331
4. Bad debts	278
5. Bank service charges	493
6. Car and truck expenses	2,970
7. Depreciation and Section 179	60
8. Dues and publications	1,104
9. Insurance	659
10. Laundry and cleaning	1,132
11. Legal and professional services	1,157
12. Office expense	359
13. Rent on business property	4,800
14. Repairs	256
15. Supplies	1,331
16. Travel and entertainment	15,107
17. Utilities and telephone	2,000
18. Total deductions	33,293
19. Net profit/loss	<$21,371>

that she and her husband made interbank transfers frequently. These transfers created an impression of additional income.

Item 2: Receipts for Schedule C Items. George has stored the receipts and has no idea where they are among his many boxes.

Item 3: Automobile Expenses. For automobile expenses, the IRS offers a per mile allowance for business travel, documented with a log. Since most of George's photography takes place around the Washington metropolitan area, proving almost $2,970 worth of business-related automobile travel at 22.5 cents a mile—over 13,000 miles of travel—would prove difficult.

Item 4: Travel and Entertainment. The travel and entertainment expense gap overshadows the auto problem. George could not come near documenting a valid business purpose for the $15,000 of long-distance travel and entertainment expenses the Schedule C reflected.

(The IRS may audit for up to three years or in cases of fraud or tax evasion in a failure to file, indefinitely. Taxpayers should keep returns and backup data for a minimum of three years after the date they filed their returns.)

Kate had also made a few technical errors on the couple's return. She had mistakenly taken day care as a Schedule A expense instead of putting it on the 1040 where it belonged. The IRS agent also pointed out that George's job-seeking expenses should be on Schedule C rather than Schedule A. Both these problems, although minor, served as additional indicators to the IRS that the return was not carefully prepared.

Through "creative bookkeeping," Kate and George had reduced the family tax bill from $4,404 to $829. Though they had been thrilled to receive a $3,500 refund, now they are paying a high price for this tax saving. Kate's worst fear is of being accused of fraud. Halfway through the audit, Kate realizes she needs expert advice and seeks professional help. But she takes care in her choice, checking with friends and interviewing several attorneys specializing in tax matters before making her choice.

The expert relieves Kate's worst fears, telling her that she is being audited by an Internal Revenue agent, not a "special agent" who conducts criminal investigations. Much relieved to learn that the IRS does not suspect outright fraud, but is simply reviewing an apparently sloppy consumer filing, Kate realizes she should have involved a lawyer or a CPA from the beginning.

Before the audit is over, Kate's health has suffered from the accumulated stress. She finally realizes that one's health and sanity are always more important than tax savings. Kate's lesson—and yours: if you feel that you cannot support an "aggressive" position on a tax return—whether a legitimate deduction or not-so-legitimate one—certainly do not take it. An audit can be time-consuming, expensive, and harrowing.

No Growth

Before she married George, Kate had made several growth investments. But her profits had been used to cover the gap between annual cash income and outgo. Rather than increasing wealth, the couple faced the downside of growth—financial retrenchment.

FILING FOR BANKRUPTCY PROTECTION

When the double blows of the tax audit and Kate's illness hit, the couple began to review more drastic steps to curtail their increasingly belligerent creditors. Kate turns to considering the protection the bankruptcy code offers both businesses and consumers. Although being behind in one's bills is certainly no signal for bankruptcy filing, Kate and George's position has advanced to the point that paying their debts seems increasingly unlikely. However, to make the legal admission of financial defeat that bankruptcy signifies requires courage, and Kate spends agonizing hours researching her alternatives.

Kate learns that bankruptcy will not only get the creditors off her back, but will also serve temporarily to halt the IRS. Although she has few assets remaining to protect, the bankruptcy will prevent both the creditors and the IRS from "garnisheeing," or seizing, her salary, which would be an embarrassment as well as create further financial pressure.

As a thorough researcher, Kate investigates the various forms of bankruptcy before acting. She finds that Chapter 11—named after its Code section—which features prominently in the business pages, is primarily reserved for larger business reorganizations.

Chapter 7 is the asset liquidation form of bankruptcy for both individuals and businesses. Even though the couple do not have many assets to protect, and therefore have little to lose through liquidation, they do have an expensive automobile. The car is worth $10,000 above its outstanding loan, while the federal bankruptcy law allows a consumer to keep only up to $1,200 in equity in a car (although a somewhat higher equity can be protected under federal law if there are no other assets).

Chapter 13 looks the most promising. In the 1984 Bankruptcy Act revisions, Chapter 13 debt reorganization, which works something like a scaled-down version of Chapter 11, was expanded to include small businesses as well as individual filers. With a Chapter 13, Kate and George can pay whatever portion of their income is deemed by the court to be "disposable" for three years, after which their remaining debts will be dismissed.

Chapter 13 is also the only chapter in the federal bankruptcy code that provides specifically for both taxes and student loans. Although most student loans cannot be dismissed under bankruptcy proceedings, student loans that are older than five years can be forgiven under Chapter 13. Kate has an unpaid student loan that would qualify.

After conferring with their adviser, Kate learns that Chapter 13 will allow her to block further IRS action and to work out a payment plan in the case of her more recent tax transgressions. But the best news is that tax liabilities more than three years old not fraudulently incurred could be dismissed. Since the IRS has not accused Kate of fraud (even though she herself knew that she stretched her expenses considerably), Kate and George were perfect candidates for the sort of relief provided by Chapter 13. (Even some kinds of fraudulent debts are dismissed or reduced under Chapter 13.)

With some $40,000 in debts and an income of $41,000, the Englishes are marginal candidates in relation to their debt-earnings ratio. They could pay off these debts with perseverance and avoid bankruptcy, which will stay on their credit report for ten years.

On the other hand, the laws are designed to provide a "fresh start." Kate feels the family will be too hard-pressed if they attempt to satisfy all their debts. Though the psychic cost of having a bankruptcy on their record will be high, for Kate and George, the cost of continuing to fend off increasingly aggressive collectors is higher. With great relief, they find an attorney specializing in insolvency and file for Chapter 13 protection.

Looking Forward

Setting new goals now becomes Kate and George's number-one priority. They are determined to bring their budget within their current means, to pay their future tax obligations in full, and to set up savings.

Kate faces the realization that she must encourage George to shift gears and seek a salaried position. While he values the freedom offered by his free-lance work, the couple has paid a high price for hanging on to George's business—and the associated tax deductions—during a period of declining revenue.

Although there are no hard-and-fast guidelines to evaluate

cash flow and credit difficulties that accompany entrepreneurial
risk taking, it is clear that George's business expenses, at three
times his income, were far too high. Even taking into account his
exaggeration in reporting to the IRS, George clearly needed to
limit his expenses, as would any entrepreneur starting out.

A fledgling entrepreneur must believe in his or her business.
This optimistic frame of mind is often the source of trouble for
an undercapitalized undertaking. A key to avoiding the Englishes' cash flow and credit difficulties is to budget and plan for
business expenditures just as for personal ones. Financial projections are a must so you can predict rough patches.

Any business preparing financial projections needs a minimum of two "schedules" or projection sheets: a profit-and-loss
statement and a cash-flow summary. A profit-and-loss statement
addresses the overall amounts of revenues, or money to be generated against which expenses must be charged; cash flow addresses the timing of receipts and payables. When the
businessperson compares the two, she can see the gap that has
to be covered either through capital or borrowing.

Let us look at an example worked out for a small business.

A company sells $10,000 worth of photographic services in
January. The cost of the sale—that is, $4,000 for labor and $2,000
for materials—is $6,000. Operating expenses, including rent,
utilities, telephones, staff, stationery, and so on, are $2,000.

TABLE 21. PROFIT AND LOSS	
Gross sales	$ 10,000
Cost of sale	−6,000
	4,000
Operating expense	−2,000
Net pre-tax income	$ 2,000

With a net pre-tax income of 25 percent ($2,000 net income
divided by total costs of $8,000), this profit-and-loss picture looks
attractive. But it does not take into account cash flow, or the
timing of the money's coming in and going out.

If the company delivers its product to the customer on January 28, when will it get paid? Most businesses pay on a thirty-,
sixty-, or ninety-day schedule. The earliest the company can
expect payment is the end of February. Say the buyer pays 50

percent of the bill in thirty days, 25 percent in sixty, and 25 percent in ninety. The company receives $5,000 on March 1, $2,500 on April 1, and $2,500 on May 1.

In the meantime, what about the $6,000 in costs? If the costs included $4,000 for labor and $2,000 for materials and services were produced in January, the company would have to pay the labor then too, although it, like the buyer, could delay payment to the vendor. The company could pay nothing in January and February, but it would have to pay for materials in March, because vendor credit is very important to continuing in business. In addition, operating expenses of $2,000 per month would continue. Here's how the schedule might look.

TABLE 22.   CASH FLOW

	JANUARY	FEBRUARY	MARCH	APRIL	MAY
Cash in:					
Buyer	$ 0	$ 0	$5,000	$2,500	$2,500
Cash out:					
Operating expense	2,000	2,000	2,000	2,000	2,000
Labor	4,000	0	0	0	0
Materials	0	0	2,000	0	0
Net cash flow	$(6,000)	$(2,000)	$1,000	$ 500	$ 500

Even though the company made a profit, January and February would be rough months from a cash-flow point of view. It is exactly at this point the entrepreneur will turn to credit to support cash flow until the projected profit materializes.

Had the owner borrowed the $8,000 needed for these two months and sales went sour, the prospects for this businessperson look dim. Unfortunately, right at this point people are most vulnerable. They have invested time and energy. It is hard to know when to draw the line and call it quits. Often people will stretch their credit trying to extend the life of the business. Essentially, that is what happened to George and Kate.

Conclusion

Kate and George's troubles must be viewed in context. Cash-flow and credit difficulties often accompany financial risk taking. Statistics show that at any time, about 10 percent of consumers experience financial difficulty. The rate for business owners is much higher. But risk taking is often the key to making money; so, as women move into business activities, more are bound to encounter experiences such as Kate and George's. These problems come with the territory. Two rules of thumb can help. First, know when you have a good hand and know you don't. Second, survive and move on.

CHAPTER 6

HIGH-CASH-FLOW

WOMEN

The lives of our high-cash-flow characters provide an opportunity to view tax and growth strategies in bold relief. With cash flows that allow freedom of choice and flexibility, these people should enjoy a rosy financial picture.

Yet, none of our three high-cash-flow characters is financially secure. Melissa Hilton is a successful young attorney who owns her own home, pays too much in taxes, and has almost no savings. Sonny Levin faces the challenge of cutting back on her expenses while learning that understanding her tax returns holds the key to negotiating her marital settlement. Anna Seaver's business flourishes, but her cash flow does not keep pace.

Their stories will also provide examples for us as we continue to explore the mysteries of home purchases, equity growth, tax shelters, marriage and money, and business. But, even more important than these informational and technical skills, these characters illustrate the theme that having more income does not guarantee financial ease. It is not what you have but how you spend it that makes all the difference.

MELISSA HILTON'S STORY

Suppose you are a salaried attorney earning a good annual income. You are single, free of financial problems and personal involvement that might impede taking quick action. You do not overspend, have a relatively modest debt load, and your cash flow breaks even.

You do have one big burden: a large tax load. Combined with your high expenditures, your financial picture adds up to an expensive present life-style but a no-growth future. You have the ability to make a near textbook-perfect tax savings maneuver, swapping high taxes and low rent for lower taxes and a higher house payment. In a nutshell, that is Melissa Hilton's story.

A Decade of Taxes

Melissa became a partner in a business associated with her law firm in 1981; therefore, from 1981 to 1985 her major income was divided between two sources: salary and partnership income. Other than that, her schematic tax form, if charted over time, resembled that of many single, well-paid working women.

When she began her law career in Los Angeles in 1980, Melissa commanded a salary of $43,750. Melissa had liberal personal deductions on Schedule A, but in 1980 she failed to track carefully her high unreimbursed employee business expenses.

With only these two main deductions, as a salaried employee who did not own a home, Melissa paid $8,270 in 1980 in federal income taxes on an adjusted gross income of $44,902 and a taxable income of $33,456. Theoretically, this income put her close to the 45 percent bracket, but with her deductions and exemptions, her effective bracket in 1980 stood at 19 percent.

By 1981, looking for ways to save tax money, Melissa started keeping everything from business lunch to parking garage receipts and annotating them on the spot. Her careful work paid off—she now reported $7,471 in unreimbursed employee business expenses up from $2,233 in 1980. Unfortunately, her raise wiped out all of her hard work. With a salary jump of $8,606 (from $43,750 to $52,356), Melissa's tax bill fell only a few dollars—from $8,415 to $8,025. New deductions put her effective bracket at 26 percent in 1981, and with taxes of $8,000 a year, too much of her livelihood went to the government. Melissa resolved to decrease her tax bite by acquiring a home.

THE VALUE OF A MORTGAGE DEDUCTION

Melissa Hilton stands out as a woman who knows what she wants, goes after it, and gets it. She moved from a $400 a month apartment with a roommate to a $300,000 home in West Los Angeles, all in the blink of an eye.

Melissa Hilton's informed use of her tax savings to make her mortgage affordable, combined with her negotiating skill in locating a real estate partner, is a model of good management. The strategies she used apply equally whether you are Melissa Hilton dealing with the high-priced real estate market of West Los Angeles or a woman in a town where the average house costs $60,000.

Although Melissa wanted to buy a home, she knew according to then prevailing, somewhat stricter lender's rule of thumb, that the price of the house purchased should equal no more than two and a half times her annual income. (Lenders have become somewhat more lenient as housing prices have risen.) Using this guideline, Melissa only qualified for a house in the $112,500 price range. In West Los Angeles, where she worked, houses at this price disappeared from the market during the late 1970s real estate boom.

Melissa had accumulated no savings to speak of, so she had no cash for a down payment. Her solution was to make the purchase by splitting the house with an investment partner who provided the down payment and shared the tax shelter benefits of home ownership with her. Although she could have involved a relative or a friend, Melissa took advantage of a job change to negotiate for this fringe benefit package. Her new employer provided the down payment on the condition that she forgo a salary increase for two years.

Melissa's deal provided that when she sold the home, she would have to return her partner's down payment from her share of any profits. But she felt this trade-off was well worth the risk. She would be able to benefit from tax savings and participate in equity growth. She had leveraged her money 100 percent, since she acquired a mortgage without putting any of her own money into the down payment. She also cut her tax bill substantially.

After looking in less expensive parts of town, and deciding against a commute, Melissa finally purchased a house in 1982 for $293,000, with a total monthly payment of $2,707.

Using the data shown in table 23 (p. 111) in the Analysis of Home Ownership Costs, Melissa was able to make a nearly exact estimate of her tax savings, which she did before making her purchase. With total monthly cash tax savings of $634, Melissa's house was more affordable. Taking into account her tax savings, the effective monthly cash cost of the house was reduced from just over $2,700 to just over $2,000. (Of course in reality, Melissa shared the tax benefits with her partner, an option that would be more limited post-reform.)

Primarily through the addition of her portion of the deductions from her home, her annual tax bill was reduced from over $8,000 in 1981 to just over $1,600 in 1982, thereby lowering her effective tax bracket from 26 percent in 1981 to 14 percent in 1982.

After the deal was completed, Melissa realized she had forgotten one important detail. While she had created new deductions for herself, she had failed to adjust her withholding form with her employer to reflect the tax savings. Suddenly she experienced so severe a cash-flow crunch that even canceling her only indulgence—fresh flowers delivered to her office every Monday morning—would not solve it. A quick calculation released several hundred dollars a month in overwithholding, and Melissa settled in to enjoy her new home. Having made the ideal exchange—cash flow from herself to the government in exchange for the same amounts paid into a home mortgage—Melissa put herself in a position for potential growth at Treasury expense.

Even after adjusting her tax bill, Melissa still could not save enough with her new deductions to make up the difference between her old rent and her new home. Taking into account the tax savings, Melissa's monthly house payment came to 53 percent of her 1982 gross monthly income of $4,400. So she found a roommate to share the large house. In turn, the roommate's rent had to be declared as rental income, creating additional taxable income for tax purposes.

TABLE 23. MELISSA HILTON
ANALYSIS OF HOME OWNERSHIP COSTS, FIRST HOME

Basic Facts

1. Purchase price of home	$293,000
2. Cash down payment required	73,000
3. Loan (10.5% interest 30 years fixed)	220,000
4. Monthly payments, principal and interest	2,263
5. Monthly deposit for property taxes	244
6. Monthly deposit for insurance, approximately	200
7. Total monthly payment (lines 4, 5, and 6)	2,707

Expense Items for Income Tax Purposes

8. First month's interest*	2,195
9. Monthly property tax deposit	244
10. Total deductions (line 8 + line 9)	2,439
11. Tax bracket†	26%
12. Tax savings per month (line 11 x line 10)	634

Total After-Tax Cost

13. Total monthly payment (line 7)	2,707
14. Less estimated tax savings (line 12): 1,806.53	634
15. Effective monthly cost (line 13 minus line 14)	2,073
16. Subtract equity* that is being gained monthly (line 4 minus line 8)	68

Actual Monthly Cost	$ 2,005

*Interest amount decreases by small amount each month and equity increases by the same proportion.
†1982.

ESCALATING: NEW INCOME, NEW DEDUCTIONS

Two years later, Melissa's negotiating skills had paid off in more than her personal real estate. By 1984 she had accepted a new and more powerful position in the business-law world, and her prospects for advancement indicated that her income would rise dramatically over the coming years.

After owning her home for just two years, Melissa realized that she would be more secure if she could get out of her partnership with her former employer. But the real estate market had declined.

Melissa, ever the negotiator, talked her partner into taking the house over. She signed the house over with no profit. Her alternative would have been stiff real estate fees—and losing money on the sale. For example, if the house sold in the flat market for the same as its purchase price of $293,000, the real estate fee at 6 percent would have amounted to $17,580. With other sales costs, the total cost would have been approximately $20,000. Melissa would have had an equity loss of $10,000 (her half share of the total loss of $20,000), not counting her previously enjoyed tax benefits. Instead she simply signed her share over to her partner and went shopping for a new home.

With no profit, she had no capital-gains tax. Had there been a profit, Melissa would have been able to defer capital-gains tax if she purchased a replacement home in less than two years.

With her track record as a homeowner carrying a high monthly mortgage, Melissa was able to convince a lender to let her qualify for a house well above the $177,500 she could purchase if he used the standard "rule" that a house should be less than two and a half times her income.

The house she picked out in the Hollywood Hills close to her new office cost $227,500. Since interest rates had dropped to just under 9 percent in 1984, her monthly payment of $1,843 on this home was far lower than the $2,707 on her previously higher-priced house. Since she had no partner and all deductions were now hers exclusively, the new home produced greater deductions. In addition, Melissa had $3,408 a year or $284 a month in real estate tax deductions.

Besides her real estate tax savings in 1984, Melissa also reported losses of over $5,000, which reduced Melissa's gross income from $70,952 to $67,067. Although the losses were primarily derived from her business partnership participation, they did not all represent actual cash outlays. Before the 1986 tax law, some portion of losses from many partnerships reflected the tax-shelter benefits derived from tax credits and depreciation then available. These figures demonstrate the pre-reform power of using nonsalary losses to offset salaried income.

As a high-salaried person originally with no dependents, Melissa was hard hit by the 1986 reform. Though reform was designed to make taxes more equitable, her earnings put her right in the group that saw the most change (but also presumably could afford to pay more taxes). Her high tax bill of $31,467 on a 1987 taxable income of $103,942 put her marginal rate at 38.5 percent. By comparison, in 1986, her tax liability on a gross income of $57,308 stood at $15,292, a rate of 26 percent.

Because Melissa has become accustomed to structuring her finances to minimize her taxes, looking to 1989 and beyond, she has started searching for alternatives to provide trade-offs among cash flow, tax savings, and future growth.

Hilton's Future Growth

Melissa Hilton was sitting on top of the earnings world as 1989 began. She had just received a raise, putting her income at $150,000 base pay, plus an expected bonus of $35,000, for a total of $185,000. Melissa has more than quadrupled her earnings in a decade, but her growth has stalled. While her cash flow had increased fourfold in under eight years, her net worth had only grown to $67,000. As she approached age thirty-five, this high earner had not switched spending gears. The good news was that she was not deeply in debt.

Over lunch, Melissa confessed that she felt almost as financially pressed earning $185,000 a year as she had at $45,000. This state of affairs was a result of different forces: Melissa's unlucky timing in entering the real estate market, just as it hit a flat point, and her continually rising standard of living.

Melissa's timing in making her real estate investments could not have been worse. When she purchased her home in 1982, interest rates were up, therefore, hefty monthly payments—which Melissa made assuming she would build up equity through market appreciation—deprived her of the ability to engage in savings. When she had her home appraised in preparation for putting it on the market two years later, she learned that her equity in the house had declined. Even real estate is not a sure thing if a sale must occur in a down market. (See table 24, p. 114.)

Looking at her balance sheet, Melissa's assets of $317,500 are offset by liabilities amounting to $250,450, including her mortgage. She is left with a net worth of $67,050. (See table 25, p. 115.)

Although her bottom line is nothing to sneeze at, Melissa

TABLE 24.   MELISSA HILTON'S REAL ESTATE

	HOUSE NO. 1	HOUSE NO. 2
Purchase price	$293,000	$227,500
Sale price	293,000	250,000*
Year of purchase	1982	1984
Year of sale	1984	N/A

*Estimated market value

could do better with her earnings. Melissa makes over ten times as much as Sherry Marshall, but her net worth is only $67,050 compared to $42,000 for Sherry. If Melissa wants a secure future, she has to improve this record.

Look at her take-home pay. In 1988, Melissa's take-home pay stood a $121,500, in excess of $10,500 a month. With a mortgage under $2,000, Melissa had $8,000 a month disposable income. Even taking into account a car loan running about $360, Melissa still had more than $7,000 available.

Why hadn't Melissa saved more? Her choices about spending reflect the trap into which high earners often fall. Every expenditure looks so small in comparison to income that soon the Melissas find themselves spending more than they realize. If Melissa is curious about where her money is going, she can keep track of her expenses the way Olivia Wong did when she was establishing her cash flow. This tedious task often points out areas of spending a consumer may forget.

To create growth, Melissa will have to engage in some kind of investment program. She is exploring alternatives that involve the least hassle. The most painless way for her to start saving is to opt for her firm's 401(k) retirement plan and have the funds deducted before she receives her paycheck. Not only will this plan force Melissa to save, it also gives her a tax break. With a projected marginal tax bracket of 33 percent in 1989, she would save $2,310 in actual taxes on the maximum allowable $7,000 contribution.

But $7,000 represents under 5 percent of her annual income. Melissa has now started looking at additional real estate. However, a second home with no rental income would require cash flow to support it, although she could deduct the mortgage pay-

TABLE 25. MELISSA HILTON—BALANCE SHEET (DECEMBER 31, 1988)

What Is Owned (Assets)

Cash and cash equivalents	
Cash in checking accounts	$ 5,500
Cash in savings accounts	2,000
Money owed you (bonus)	25,000
Personal property*	
Household furnishings	20,000
Special items (car, art, etc.)	15,000
Real estate*	
House	250,000
Total Assets	**$317,500**

What Is Owed (Liabilities)

Current bills	
Charge account balances	$ 500
Credit cards	2,900
Utilities	150
Mortgage	1,843
Other bills	1,757
Amount owed on loans	
Mortgage	227,500
Auto loan	13,000
Life insurance loans	2,800
Total Liabilities	**$250,450**

Net Worth

Total assets	$317,500
Total liabilities	250,450
Net worth (assets minus liabilities)	$ 67,050

*Estimated current market value.

ment from her taxes. Other real estate investments offer severely diminished tax benefits for her earnings bracket.

The strict rules under tax reform, designed to wipe out abusive tax shelters, require a high level of personal involvement in the investment for it to qualify to offset salaried income. An exception to this rule applies to taxpayers with less than $100,000 adjusted gross income, but with Melissa's high adjusted gross income of over $150,000, she could not qualify for the exception. Instead she would be subject to the strict new passive loss rules, discussed in Chapter 2, that limit her deductions to offset passive income. Thus the interest and depreciation would be fully deductible if Melissa had profits from other passive investments but are not deductible against her salary.

As Melissa's income grows, her ability to create income sheltered from taxes becomes critical. Even more important, she has to learn to save a portion of her very high disposable income. If she does not start to trim her life-style now, she will find herself a decade hence without any real security, despite her impressive earnings.

SONNY LEVIN

A bright, articulate woman met me one afternoon at the University of Southern California faculty club. For several days she had been leaving message after message as we continued to play telephone tag. The cause of her urgency: her husband, Barney, who is an executive in an advertising agency, was pressing her for a list of her monthly expenses as the first step toward reaching a spousal support and property settlement.

Her high-priced divorce attorney had provided expense forms to fill in, and Sonny could not bring herself to do them alone. Not only did she find figures and forms intimidating, but she also could not bear to come to grips with the reality of ending her marriage. As we talked, it became clear that Sonny did not have all the information she needed to proceed. As unbelievable as it seems in the late 1980s, Sonny didn't know what her husband earned nor could she list the family's bank accounts. The bookkeeper paid all the bills from his office, so Sonny had no way of knowing how much her husband spent. Instead she operated with a generous household allowance. Even her credit profile was in Barney's name; though she used several charge accounts, all but one of the credit cards in the family had Sonny's husband as the cardholder of record.

While Melissa Hilton enjoys freedom and control, Sonny

Levin experiences *being* controlled. Her story highlights possible difficulties facing a woman today who pursues traditional marriage as her "career choice." With marriage offering less security, women like Sonny find themselves left with a high-cash-flow life-style they can no longer afford. Or, like Sherry Marshall, they find themselves without adequate income to support their families.

Sonny Levin now faces being a single mother and moving from the home in which she has raised her daughter. Sonny's marketable skills will not earn an income to support the lifestyle she has enjoyed; therefore, she must arrange her post-divorce finances to minimize taxes and maximize her cash flow and future growth.

Sonny's issues resemble Sherry Marshall's. Both will pay a large proportion of their accumulated savings in taxes if they don't defer their gain from selling their homes, and each must now earn a living. Like Sherry, Sonny has to cut back or find a way to earn more money. But Sonny will feel deprived on an annual income—at least while alimony lasts—that to Sherry would be luxurious. Also, whereas Sherry's parents live in the same neighborhood and their home served as a refuge during transition, Sonny has no immediate family.

An additional concern for Sonny is the obvious disparity between her life-style and her husband's. Barney arrives in a limousine for his custody visits, underscoring Sonny's reduced circumstances in her daughter's eyes—and her own.

Sonny's Cash Flow

The "budget" sheet Sonny's attorney asked her to complete indicated a luxury life-style on a monthly cash-flow basis. Expenditure items included a few not found on many middle-class budgets: pool maintenance, a gardener, four kinds of lessons, grocery store charge accounts, and household help by category, live-in or live-out.

As we completed the forms by estimating as best we could, it became clear that this high-cash-flow woman is facing a nearly inevitable adjustment to living on less. Her budget stands at $12,000 a month. Her monthly living expenses exceed what many women earn in a year. What will happen when the child support and alimony cease? (See table 26, p. 119.)

Sonny will need to unravel the couple's complicated tax forms to assess her prospects, and she also needs to understand them to interpret Barney's previously unknown income.

The Levins' Taxes

In short order, Sonny finds herself considering the proper mix of alimony, or spousal support (which is taxable to her and deductible for her husband), and child support (which is neither taxed nor deductible). *Note:* Spousal support is the term preferred by feminists, but alimony still appears on the 1040, so in this tax discussion we shall use alimony to match the form. She must also deal with the potential taxes on capital gains from rolling over three previous residences. For a person intimidated by budget forms, tackling the 1040 can seem nearly impossible. However, Sonny learned that understanding her tax returns provides the key to the level of her alimony award. Court guidelines for alimony and child support are often built on a net income figure derived from the tax return, so Sonny determines she will persevere.

SPOUSAL AND CHILD SUPPORT

The income guidelines for Los Angeles County, the county in which the Levins live, provide a sliding scale division of income. At Barney's earning level, 40 percent of his "net" monthly income is allocated to the custodial spouse, that is the spouse keeping one child. This figure rises to a maximum of 50 percent with three or more children—you may wonder about the fairness of this division. Why do four persons (usually a mother and children) share the same allocation as one (usually the father)? The tax return comes into play because the "net" income derives from that form, although the net income is not equal to either adjusted gross income or taxable income.

Keep in mind that the recipient spouse—Sonny—will owe income tax on the alimony portion while the person who pays the spousal support gets a tax deduction. For instance, if Sonny

TABLE 26.   SONNY LEVIN'S MONTHLY EXPENDITURES

1. Housing	
Mortgage	$ 3,025
Property taxes	400
Insurance	150
Utilities	100
House maintenance	
Gardener	300
Pool maintenance	150
Subtotal, housing	4,125
2. Food	
Grocery store account	800
Restaurant meals	1,650
Subtotal, food	2,450
3. Clothing	1,000
4. Transportation	
Insurance	150
Fuel	150
Maintenance	50
Other transportation—taxis for lessons	50
Subtotal, transportation expenditures	400
5. Phone	100
6. House cleaning	
Daily household help	650
Live-in	500
Subtotal, household help	1,150
7. Personal care and improvements (massage, hair, facials)	400
8. Medical and dental, health and disability insurance	150
9. Psychologist	400
10. Education (private secondary school)	500
11. Entertainment	200
12. Vacations and travel	500
13. Charitable contributions	100
14. Lessons	
Piano	80
Art	45
Trumpet	60
Dance	100
Subtotal, lessons	285

TABLE 26—*Continued*	
15. Boat dock fee	150
16. Club membership	250
TOTAL AFTER-TAX MONTHLY EXPENDITURES	$12,160

receives $40,000 a year, Barney lands a $40,000 deduction worth $13,200 cash savings in his 33 percent bracket. Sonny will owe approximately $6,000 in federal income taxes on that amount.

Proponents of this tax policy argue that it creates a tax incentive for the high-earning payor (usually a husband) to support the lower-earning recipient (usually a wife). Balancing this view is the notion that spousal support formulas award less money proportionally to the wife, and the policy of taxing spousal support serves further to reduce divorcing dependent spouses' incomes. (Parenthetically, the alimony deduction is also given special treatment on the tax form. Alimony is removed from income before adjusted gross income is reached, thus providing a lower adjusted gross income floor for medical and miscellaneous deductions.)

The Los Angeles court guidelines allow mandatory social security (FICA), SDI (state disability insurance), and federal and state taxes to be deducted to arrive at net income figures, but voluntary retirement deductions, such as Barney's Keogh, are not subtracted. Although the Keogh is used to lower net income for tax purposes, it is not deducted for spousal support because such contributions are voluntary. Also, Schedule A itemized deductions and personal exemptions are not included for the purposes of figuring net income. In Sonny's case, with high deductions, this formula means the "net" income she will share will be higher than the adjusted gross income on the tax return. (The courts have discretion about whether job-related expenses and employee benefits will be allowed as deductions to ascertain net income.)

To arrive at an estimated measure of income that the court would allow her, Sonny had to subtract the couple's tax liability of $32,537 from their adjusted gross income of $195,000 to arrive at a figure of $162,463. The $30,000 Keogh contributions are added back to arrive at $192,463, the figure the court would use.

TABLE 27.   BARNEY AND SONNY LEVIN
1988 INCOME TAX RETURN (1040)

1. Interest income	$ 5,000
2. Partnership income (Schedule E)	220,000
3. Total income (line 1 + line 2)	225,000
4. Keogh adjustment	30,000
5. Adjusted gross income (line 3 minus line 4)	195,000
6. Itemized deductions (Schedule A)	102,350
7. Personal exemptions (3 at $1,950)	5,850
8. Taxable income (line 5 minus lines 6 and 7)	86,800
9. Tax owed (see rate chart, Appendix 1)	21,115
10. Self-employment tax (maximum)	5,859
11. Total tax liability (line 9 + line 10)	$ 26,974

Using the maximum of 40 percent of "net" income ($192,463 as defined by the court, higher than the taxable income figure on table 27 of $86,800 but slightly lower than the gross income of $195,000) for alimony and child support, Sonny and her daughter would be entitled to a total of $76,985 a year, far higher than what Barney had proposed. But it amounts to half her current annual budget of $144,000.

The length of time of the award is as critical as the amount received. Following the passage of the no-fault divorce law, the courts changed alimony from a "permanent" award to one based on a rule of thumb relating alimony to the duration of the marriage. But this practice has put women like Sonny and Sherry into an untenable economic position, because few single women with children can match their former spouse's earnings.

Statistics show a sharp decline in the postdivorce standard of living for wives and a raised standard of living for husbands. Recognizing this trend, California has enacted a provision treating marriages of over ten years as "long term" and allowing the court to retain jurisdiction so that spousal support can be continued if necessary. Barney wishes to confine his spousal support to as few years as he can negotiate while Sonny feels that keeping the door to the court open will provide her a safety net. This option becomes another bargaining chip.

Finally, because Sonny will have to pay taxes on her alimony, and child support is not taxable, Sonny will negotiate to minimize the alimony portion of her award, categorizing it as child support instead. However, this strategy could backfire should Sonny herself need support beyond the years she receives child support.

THE LEVINS' ROLLOVER

Even with the division of property in this community-property state, tax considerations play a role. (Marital property in the eight community-property states is considered to be owned equally by both spouses. In the separate-property states, owner-ship—except of the family home—will be determined by title. Most states recognize special rights of both spouses in the family home regardless of how title is held, but it is wise to indicate one's intentions through careful taking of title. See Appendix 5 for more details on who owns what under state laws.)

Barney has offered Sonny his half-share of the family home in exchange for her giving up claims to his advertising business. However, Sonny will not be able to keep this home because the payments and upkeep are too high. If she sells it, she will face a tax problem.

The Levins' real estate growth started with their first home, which was priced at $92,500. As each successive home was sold and a new one purchased, they had climbed the equity ladder, reinvesting their capital in increasingly expensive properties. With an original investment of $18,500 (20 percent down), their total profit stood at just over $200,000.

Measuring cash-on-cash return only, they had watched their investment increase more than tenfold in a dozen years. Trans-lated into percentage terms, they had made 1100 percent on the investment or 91 percent per year, a tremendous amount of profit.

Like the Marshalls, the Levins made this money in a ris-ing real estate market, but both examples illustrate that to make money in such a situation, one has to have chips on the table.

Sonny and Barney's total profit for four houses amounts to $507,500. When adjusted for improvements and total commis-sions, the amount on which taxes would be owed is $203,974; therefore if Sonny takes the home, sells it, and cannot replace it, she will owe income taxes on $203,974 in the year of sale.

Sonny's federal taxes on the sale would be 28 percent of $203,974, or $57,112.

TABLE 28. LEVINS' CAPITAL GAIN	
Sales price, current home	$600,000
Adjusted price, original home	92,500
Gross profit	507,500
Less	
Capital improvements	221,656
Sales fees (all homes)	81,870
Net gain	**$203,974**

Purchasing a replacement home will defer this tax indefinitely, and the law allows some relief for divorcing couples. The rollover can be split if two homes are purchased. If Sonny buys a home with a purchase price of $300,000 or more, and Barney does the same, no capital-gains taxes will currently be owed. If Sonny and Barney can agree, Sonny can defer the house taxes. But as a part of her settlement negotiations, Sonny must assume that there is a possibility that she will not be able to purchase a replacement. In that case, she must remember that her after-tax cash will be reduced by her estimated taxes of over $57,000.

By contrast, Barney's business ownership will not be sold, therefore it will not be currently taxed. Assuming the two items—the house and business rights—were equal in value at the point of separation, Sonny would be short-changed by the amount of taxes owed unless she could purchase a replacement home. Even then, taxes will eventually be owed on the gain stretching back to their first home (unless Sonny waits until she is fifty-five and takes advantage of the one-time $125,000 tax-free allowance).

DIVIDING THE KEOGH

Using the principles of deferral to reduce current taxes and defer income until retirement, Barney had amassed a large Keogh retirement fund. Under California community-property law,

these monies are community property, therefore, Sonny is entitled to half. (If the couple had resided in a separate-property
state, the voluntary pension funds, if derived from his earnings,
would have been his alone.)

To determine the amount of that Keogh, Sonny turned
again to their tax returns. The couple's old 1040s revealed a gold
mine. Barney had estimated his retirement fund at $75,000, but
the tax returns reflected total contributions to Keogh at
$150,000 plus interest or other income earned. Sonny's 50 per-
cent share of these years came to $75,000 plus interest. (Had she
known who the Keogh trustee or administrator was, she also
could have ordered a report.)

To summarize, many of Sonny's financial concerns revolve
around complicated questions concerning alimony, child support, and property settlement, all of which are threaded with tax
issues. When Sonny started her consultation, she could barely
read a tax return. Now, although she certainly would not qualify
herself as a tax expert and she continues to solicit professional
advice, she has improved her financial position through learning
to overcome her fear of the 1040. By doing this homework, Sonny
can now go to the bargaining table and meet with her own advisers with an arsenal of information—much of it gathered from
her returns.

Sonny's Growth

The tax law does not require that the actual cash be reinvested
in succeeding homes but simply that the price of the home equal
or exceed that of the previous home for full rollover, so figuring
Sonny's cash position after the home sale requires additional
analysis. (Special values apply when the purchase price of the
new home is lower than the sale price of the old.) When they
bought their third home, Sonny and Barney had not put all their
cash into the home but took a mortgage of $300,000 on the
$325,000 property.

Since the couple had agreed that Sonny would take the
house, her postdivorce cash position, assuming she did not repurchase, would rest on the house sales price minus mortgage and
sales costs. Assuming a sale of $600,000, a mortgage of $300,000,

and real estate fees of $36,000, the cash realized on the sale will be $264,000 without taxes. If she has to pay taxes, she will have a cash nest egg of $197,000.

With more than a quarter of a million dollars in cash with which to purchase a replacement home and for savings, Sonny's position seems to be on a solid footing. However, unless she and her daughter are willing to reduce their admittedly very high standard of living dramatically and not touch their $264,000 cash from the house, their capital will be depleted in under two years at their current projected $144,000-a-year life-style. Even generous child support and alimony payments will cease eventually. If Sonny uses her cash to bridge the gap and maintain her life-style, she will soon deplete her savings.

Sonny must put herself on a budget that looks beyond the years of guaranteed support. Assuming that she has a net income of $75,000 a year, from spousal and child support, Sonny will have to pay taxes estimated at $6,000 a year. (She will pay taxes on only that portion which is spousal support and not on the child support.) If she receives the money for the next five years, she should plan to live on no more than $50,000, including paying her new mortgage, to conserve $19,000 of her $69,000 after-tax income. Over a five-year period, not counting interest she could earn on the principal, these savings would amount to $95,000, thus providing a cushion when alimony ceases.

For Sonny's future growth, the subjective factors are most important of all. She must take control of her emotions and put her considerable skills to work on consolidating the assets that she has. In order to do this, she has to establish clear-cut goals for herself. For instance, her two goals might include investing in a home and in herself.

The home will provide financial security as well as tax roll-over. Over time, her home equity will grow, but even more important for Sonny, as rents rise she will be able to enjoy a much better life-style than if she becomes a renter. By improving her own prospects, through further education or management training, she will be providing the best possible insurance for her future security.

While in the middle of a divorce, Sonny finds thinking in these terms difficult. As one recently divorced woman said: "You're the richest you'll ever be the first year after divorce," a reflection of the perception that women in control of newly liquid cash often have. Sonny's challenge will be to remember that her cash on hand will not last. She must adjust her attitudes and her expenditures accordingly.

ANNA SEAVER

Anna Seaver, a high-powered architect, decided that if she could make money for her bosses, she could make money for herself. Her switch from employee to entrepreneur brought new opportunities, much satisfaction, and several unanticipated problems.

For several months Seaver's company has been involved in the preliminary design stage—creating and packaging an idea. Eventually, buyers will commit the money to a complete design. While she is waiting for a sale, Anna is seeking a bank line of credit based on her success in the first years of her company, but so far she has been turned down.

Our mission: To figure out why the loan hasn't materialized and to help her get through this tough time.

Seaver's Business Cash Flow

One thing is clear: my client lives daily with cash-flow peril. She had started her business with good credentials but too little of her own capital. Since she had spent her life in "quality" undertakings, her idea of how to begin a business included renting an office in a high-priced district. Along with the office, she had brought several of her high-paid staff with her. When her company hit its slump, meeting the rent and the payroll was increasingly difficult as each week rolled by.

Finally, consulting with other people in the business, including her own attorney, it became clear that the bank had turned Seaver down because of her financial statements.

Normally, lenders and investors want to see two "schedules" or projection sheets, a "profit-and-loss statement" (P&L), and a "cash-flow summary." Profit and loss addresses the overall amounts of money generated; cash flow addresses the timing of the receipts. The personal budget sheet is somewhat similar to a cash-flow summary, and the balance sheet is somewhat similar to the P&L statement.

Seaver didn't have cash-flow statements but did have P&L statements, a year-end accounting. Although Seaver had completed a very large project that year for just over $2.1 million, the income was not reflected in the figures. In the last year, the picture on paper looked like this:

TABLE 29.   PROFIT-AND-LOSS STATEMENT

Gross income	$528,244
Expenses	222,534
Pre-tax profit/loss	$305,710

No wonder Seaver could not get the bank loan for which she had applied. Her pre-tax profit was respectable, but her gross income made the company volume of over $2 million appear as only half a million dollars. The company's need for a large bank loan to fund the cash-flow gap did not make sense from this picture.

Soon it became clear the business manager and bookkeeper had made an error that consumers often make. Rather than reporting gross income—or all the revenues that the business received—the bookkeeper had reported net income after expenses and taxes were taken out. (Consumers sometimes make this mistake when applying for a home mortgage. Here, the lender's rule of thumb for qualifying is calculated on gross income, not net income after taxes. The uninformed person who puts down net income on a mortgage application may end up with no mortgage. The net income figure would give the mistaken impression that she did not meet the income requirements.) Seaver brought in outside accountants to straighten out her books. Her revised profit and loss (see table 30, p. 128) presented by their statement matched her more impressive tax return.

Seaver shows a profit in previous operating years, but her cash flow is still tight. She needs a cash-flow statement to present to bank managers and presidents. With her accountants and business consultant, she worked out a schedule of income and expenditures to show the prospective lenders how she utilized

TABLE 30.   REVISED PROFIT-AND-LOSS STATEMENT

Income	$2,253,480
Expenses	1,947,770
Gross (before tax) profit/loss	305,710
Tax liability	7,328
(see table 31, p. 000)	
After-tax profit (income minus expenses)	$ 298,382

her funds to even out her business cash flow. (Look back at pages 103–105, the end of the English case, to see how cash flow and profit fit together in a less complicated business.)

On the way to shop for bank loans, we discussed Seaver's options. The choices she faces might not be easy. Aside from closing her business, she can lay off staff or take out an additional business loan. Either option has its costs. If she dismisses her staff, she may not have enough skilled people on hand when she receives the green light for her next project. To keep her staff, Seaver will have to decide how to collateralize her business loan. If the bank will not lend her money based on the strength of her business performance, she will be required to pledge her home, in which she has considerable equity, as security.

Swapping future growth and security (for example, her home) for cash-flow needs (in this case, her business) illustrates a classic trade-off of current cash flow against future growth. Placing her home on the line for her business may leave her without equity in the long run, and in the short run, a second mortgage will add new payments to her monthly cash-flow needs.

Before looking at Seaver's solutions, let us review the position tax benefits growing from her corporation.

Seaver's Taxes

BUSINESS STRUCTURE PRIMER

Anna Seaver benefits from owning her own business. She enjoys many deductions not available to a salaried person, even though as a sole owner of a corporation she pays taxes on the portion of her income she draws from the corporation.

Seaver followed her lawyer's advice and selected the corporate format when her business began. Even though the lawyer's advice was perhaps proper, she had not fully appreciated the tax implications involved.

If you, like Seaver, are unfamiliar with the advantages and disadvantages of incorporation, it is vital to conquer these basics before starting a business.

Briefly, a business can take one of three forms: a sole proprietorship, a partnership, or a corporation. The choice you make depends on a variety of factors, such as legal liability, tax consequences, and degree of control you want to maintain. The structure can have a significant bearing on your ability to raise capital and on your own financial position.

There are no hard-and-fast guidelines about when or whether to incorporate. For example, at what revenue level is one ready to incorporate? The answer is, any level. Some companies incorporate from the beginning, when revenues are zero. Other very large companies, particularly in the real estate development field, never incorporate, even with millions of dollars in revenues.

One key variable is the issue of tax consequences. As we shall see in Seaver's case, a corporation that is owned by a single individual is subject to tax twice: once at the corporate level and once at the individual level if a salary is taken.

Since creating and maintaining a corporation costs money, you certainly would want to explore the specific consequences given your factual situation before making such a decision.

Here are some general pointers about the differences among the forms of business organizations.

Proprietorships. There is only one owner of a proprietorship, and this individual is legally liable for the business. Taxes are filed on Schedule C as part of the individual 1040. Profits and losses become part of the individual's income and deductions, and the applicable rate is the individual rate of the owner.

Partnerships. Partners share the right to manage the business and share the profits. Each partner—except in a limited partnership in which liability is limited to the amount invested—has an unlimited obligation to answer personally for business liabilities. Partnership income and loss is distributed annually and taxes are paid at individual rates by the partners on their own 1040 returns on Schedule E.

Corporations. Corporations are state-chartered artificial entities that have a status of their own, independent of the owners or investors. *Publicly held* corporations offer shares to a large number of investors. *Closely held* or *closed* corporations are privately owned by a few people. Both these types of corporations are taxed at the corporate level with rates that differ from those applied to individual taxpayers. *Nonprofit*—or Section 501(c) in the tax code—corporations operate for educational, religious, or charitable purposes and enjoy tax-exempt status. *S corporations* (before 1982 known as "Sub-chapter S" corporations) pass along profits and losses to their investors, with no tax at the corporate level. Today S corporations offer the best position for a smaller business with one or a few owners.

The advantages of incorporating include limited liability on the part of investors, possible tax savings, and an enhanced ability to attract investors. The disadvantages include cost of organization, additional paperwork, and possible tax costs. Lenders certainly prefer to see that the businessperson has gone to the effort to organize in this way, even though the lender often requires personal guarantees before business loans will be granted to either a partnership or a corporation.

Two-thirds of women that start businesses open sole proprietorships. By comparison, 59 percent of the men start corporations. Other statistics show that women have a harder time raising start-up capital. It is not clear whether the dearth of women-owned corporations is a function of capital access or whether women are not aware of the advantages of incorporation.

Seaver had overcome this start-up hurdle and had chosen to incorporate, thereby creating a complex tax profile and impressive tax savings. This strategy worked pre-1986. Today regular non–S corporations are a much worse deal for a small business owner.

Compare Seaver's corporate and individual returns (tables 31 and 33). Of particular interest, Seaver's case illustrates what happens when a single individual owns a corporation and how changing tax laws can affect business strategy. Despite the many benefits of the corporate tax entity, because Seaver is the only owner of her corporation, any income she personally withdraws from the corporation will face the possibility of being taxed twice, once at the corporate level and once at the individual level. The classic corporate tax game here is to avoid a double taxation.

THE CORPORATE RETURN

The main corporate return, the 1120, is deceptively simple. While corporate taxation is a tremendously complex topic, the U.S. Corporation Income Tax Return Summary occupies only a page. However, there are many schedules that must be included to arrive at this summary form. Let's focus on the summary page to provide an overview. (See table 31, p. 132.)

In the Seaver corporation's return, the gross receipts are $2,253,480. The "cost of goods sold"—the project design—ran $1,756,521, for a gross profit of $496,959. In addition, her corporation earned $31,285 in interest for a grand total of $528,244 of income.

In the deductions section, the total expenses of the corporation are listed as $222,534. The taxable income before the special business deductions is $305,710. (*Note:* The taxable income figure matches that on page 000, but other figures will not match because of differences in accounting for computing taxes.)

Now we come to some of the peculiar features of a business tax life.

Although individuals can no longer income-average (which allows income to be smoothed out if there are high and low years), corporations and businesses operated by individuals filing on Schedule C can continue to carry forward losses and thus achieve income averaging by deducting losses from a previous year on the current year's return. For example, Seaver's company had carry-forward losses of $247,382, all fully deductible. Generally, a corporation may carry a net operating loss back to each of three years preceding the year of loss and may carry a loss forward to each of the fifteen years following the year of the loss. Seaver's net operating loss deduction lowered

TABLE 31.   SEAVER CORPORATION—1987 U.S. CORPORATION INCOME TAX RETURN

Income

Gross receipts or sales	$ 2,253,480
Cost of goods sold	< 1,756,521 >
Gross profit	496,959
Interest (earned on cash advances)	31,285
Total Income	528,244

Deductions

Compensation of officers	32,400
Salaries and wages	16,022
Repairs	2,205
Rents	26,132
Interest	10,161
Contributions	2,642
Depreciation	4,215
Advertising	6,797
Employee benefits	5,471
Other deductions	116,432
Total Deductions	222,534
Taxable income	305,710
Net operating loss deduction (see page 000)	< 247,382 >
Net taxable income	58,328
Total tax due liability (Schedule J, table 32)	$ 7,328

the taxable income on which tax would be calculated from $305,710 to $58,328.

The explanation lies in the secret of Schedule J, Tax Computation carried on a separate schedule (see table 32). The total preaudit tax on the Seaver corporation's profit in 1988 stood at $58,328. However, the corporation can take a general business credit, totaling $51,000, for the Seaver corporation. With this credit, the corporate tax is lowered to $7,328 on a pre-tax income of $305,710 or an effective rate of 2.4 percent.

While it must be noted that 1986 tax reform did away with many of the credits available to corporations, credits earned before the beginning of 1986 remain available until they earn out. Since many of these credits stretch for several years, businesses will continue to enjoy them.

TABLE 32. ANNA SEAVER—SCHEDULE J TAX COMPUTATION

1. Income tax	$58,328
2. General business credit	51,000
Total Tax	**$ 7,328**

If you had wondered what all the fuss about corporate taxation was about, Seaver's credit picture provides a startling example.

Corporate rates have also been reduced. Until 1986, the highest rate on corporate taxes stood at 46 percent; now it is down to 34 percent, with a 5 percent override on income from $100,000 to $335,000. Income over $335,000 is taxed at a flat 34 percent. (See Appendices 1 and 2 for sample forms and rate tables.)

Contrast these rates to individual ones. The "married filing jointly" rate for individuals will jump from 15 percent at a cutoff point of $17,850, while a corporation doesn't reach this comparable cutoff until $50,000. (But a second tax will eventually have to be paid at shareholder level when shares are sold.) Although the gap between lower corporate rates and higher individual rates has narrowed, corporate tax rates still enjoy an advantage over individual rates for taxable incomes up to $75,000.

These advantages should make it clear why Seaver's advisers had encouraged her to form a corporation in a pre-1986 tax context. Very few advisers would incorporate this business for tax reasons today, another indicator of the importance of understanding tax basics and keeping abreast of changes in the law.

SEAVER'S INDIVIDUAL RETURN

Seaver's decision to create a separate corporate entity allowed her to use a sophisticated form of deferral. With her corporation, she could plow profits back into the company, drawing out as taxable salary only $32,400.

For a person intent on long-term growth, this strategy made sense. Seaver reinvests her profits (or losses) in the corporation, drawing income only as needed. Rather than subjecting her earnings to higher taxes, she watches her equity grow. As her company's profits increase, she and her officers should draw larger salaries (paying tax at only the individual level) so that corporate taxable income will be kept down to $50,000 per year, thereby minimizing corporate taxation.

In fact, she may never have to pay taxes on much of her company's growth, one of the attractions of corporate acquisitions and mergers. For example, were she eventually to sell her corporation or were it to be acquired by another corporation, this acquisition could itself become a nontaxable event. Let us say that a large national design firm decided to acquire Seaver Corporation. Seaver could receive stock shares in the acquiring corporation in exchange for her shares in her corporation. By and large this exchange would be a tax-free event. But, if Seaver sold her stock in her corporation outright, she would be taxed on all her capital gains. If she had her corporation sell its assets, which is increasingly the only way big buyers will sell companies, she will pay double tax.

Let us look briefly at the point where Seaver's corporate and individual tax returns mesh. If you compare, you will see the links between the corporation's 1120 return and Seaver's individual 1040. For example, Seaver's salary of $32,400 is reflected on both the corporate and individual returns.

Although the income has been subject to tax once at the corporate level and once in Seaver's return, the $32,400 becomes a corporate deduction for the corporation. The $32,400 shows up on Seaver's individual return as income and is taxed there. The rate, of course, will depend on Seaver's other personal deductions.

TABLE 33.   ANNA SEAVER—1988 INCOME TAX RETURN
(1040)

1. Wages	$32,400
2. Interest	400
3. Dividends	1,560
4. Capital gain	1,625
6. Total income	35,985
6. Itemized deductions	12,655
7. Personal exemption (1)	1,950
8. Taxable income	21,380
9. Tax liability	$ 3,665

Her salary illustrates the complex considerations involved in making a decision to interface a personal income tax return with a corporate one. The picture can be even more complicated when the same person owns all or a significant portion of the corporation, as in Seaver's case. The interface always involves considerations of double taxation, and calculations must be done in order to tell what is the most advantageous tax position to take.

AMENDED RETURNS

Filing an amended return is not an unusual occurrence for a corporation, because information may come in late. Seaver's corporation had to file amended tax returns because the outside accountant uncovered several mistakes in the company's original returns, prepared by her former accountant.

In fact, any taxpayer can file an amended return for refund within three years from the time the return was filed or within two years from the date the tax was paid, whichever is later. For example, if you sell a home, defer the taxes, and later decide you cannot purchase a replacement home, you must file an amended return for the year in which the home was sold. *Note:* If you filed originally on a 1040, 1040A, or 1040EZ, the amended return is on a form 1040X. If you, like Seaver, filed on a corporate return Form 1120, the amended form is 1120X.

Seaver's Growth Prospects

Although the number of women in business rises annually, women entrepreneurs still are struggling for business success. In the context of personal financial growth, a business owner such as Anna Seaver may find herself caught in a squeeze between business objectives and personal security. Owning a business all too frequently seems like a bottomless pit to the pressed entrepreneur who must often obtain her capital from her own resources.

Anna Seaver's dilemma reflects women's common business experience. Studies by the Small Business Administration (SBA) show that women starting a business rely on their own individual savings for 44 percent of their capital. The average woman business owner starts with half the capital of a man, capital of under $10,500 compared to the average man with $20,700. Although Seaver started her company with more funds than the average woman, her need for a business loan nevertheless derived in part from undercapitalization.

After a business has been established, the gap between men and women widens. Established businesses owned by men, according to the same SBA study, have equity capital of $45,000, but those owned by women have under $20,000. Women had to rely on their personal savings for a large percentage of their operating equity for established businesses—the national average is 55 percent—while for men the figure is 34 percent. Even though women put so much of their own resources into their undertakings, profits are low, averaging under $2,000 a year.

Compared to this average, Anna Seaver's reward from her company is high. After only eighteen months in business, Seaver's company grossed $2.25 million with a pre-tax profit of $305,000. However, just as the statistics suggest, it is to her own savings that Seaver must look to guarantee loans for operating funds.

The company has also started to create assets consisting of partial ownership of projects developed in joint venture with other companies. These properties will continue to generate a stream of income for the corporation in addition to the revenues from ongoing production activities. Creating properties, compared with simply offering services, provides additional tax benefits, since properties are depreciable.

Although Seaver enjoys potentially high rewards with her company, she also faces high risk. In a volatile business, if Seaver's assets are at risk, her personal net worth could be demolished in a flash.

Seaver knows that she should be very cautious about putting her personal resources on the line, but her company's assets are not sufficient to guarantee the financing she needs. If Seaver wants to keep her company afloat, her choices boil down to finding investors or placing her home at risk.

Seaver has managed to build a substantial net worth of over $290,000. Most of her personal equity lies in her house. With a low mortgage of only $70,000, the cash value of her $285,000 home is $215,000. Although this is a handsome sum, if her company does not get a paying project for a year, the company overhead alone will exceed her home equity.

In addition to possibly losing her assets, Seaver also faces other opportunity costs or the economic price of choosing this course of action over another. These include earnings forgone, diminished pension contributions, a reduced standard of living during this lean period, and a lower savings rate resulting from a minimum start-up salary.

SEAVER'S BUSINESS PLAN

To make the decision whether or not to risk her home, Seaver puts her company's prospects in a business plan. Originally undertaken to organize materials to present to commercial lenders and investors, the planning process allows Seaver to view her company in a more cohesive and thoughtful way. We shall review her planning process here in a very abbreviated form.

To create a plan, Seaver thinks through her business in terms of the product and its market. She commits these thoughts to paper, along with the factual details of her corporate history. The previously prepared financial projections for the company are added. The whole plan is tied together as a presentation package, complete with photographs of her most outstanding designs. (To learn more about the planning process, see Appendix 6, "Resources for Entrepreneurs.")

In addition to being a tool for obtaining financing, the plan serves as a guidepost for company development. The process of working out the business plan gives Seaver a chance to see what her company has accomplished and makes her future goals more concrete. When complete, the plan sets up realistic expectations about cash flow, which allow Seaver to face facts. When Seaver finishes her planning process, she realizes that she should not jeopardize her future personal security for business objectives, however worthy. She makes the wise decision to trim back on overhead, allowing her company to continue without placing a further burden on her personal assets.

Her decision reflects Seaver's maturity and her ability to comprehend the most important growth principle of all, knowing when enough is enough. Preservation of capital is the starting point for growth, a maxim too easily forgotten. With capital intact, even if equity does not grow rapidly, the chance for future growth survives. Once capital has been eroded—whether in a business venture or by overspending—it is very hard to replace. Particularly in a case such as Seaver's, where her excellent home equity represents the combined growth deriving from a long tenure as an employee and solid growth in the real estate market, it would be almost impossible for her to earn new funds to replace this equity.

Seaver is smart enough to recognize her limits and to adjust her business activities accordingly.

Now, with the benefit of our three groups of consumers' experiences, it is time to turn to creating your own strategies for success. The next three chapters will be devoted to looking at your cash flow, taxes, and growth. By the time you have finished these three chapters, you should be confident of your own chances for success.

PART III

STRATEGIES

FOR SUCCESS

IN THE

COMING DECADE

CHAPTER 7

YOUR

CASH

FLOW

Making a budget designed to help you cut back on current consumption in favor of future growth is the single most important step you can take. All growth starts with bringing spending under control. If you have been spending money as fast as you have earned it, you are not alone. But just as the 1980s were a time of consumption, the 1990s will be a time of conservation. The best way to limit spending is with a budget.

Tracking your cash flow is an opportunity to gain control. Not everyone needs to budget. But just as businesses and governments must set written guidelines—called "budgets"—to establish spending limits, people serious about changing their financial lives will have to make some attempt, however informal, to account for what has been spent and to plan future spending.

If you are a person who has avoided setting up a budget because you have seen it as a restriction rather than an opportunity to set goals, this chapter should provide a chance to think along more positive lines. Of course, as we have seen, not everyone must budget—some people already control their cash flow very carefully, and their energies would be better focused on tax or growth strategies. Nevertheless, whether you budget now, wish to start, or cannot bear the thought, understanding the principles of budgeting will lay a basis for conserving cash.

If you cannot tolerate the thought of reducing your financial life to a column of figures, pick one or two spending areas where you can cut down and conserve cash for growth. After all, the point of a budget—whether you are rigorous or casual in your approach—is to live within your means and create savings. Set a realistic savings plan for yourself. Stick to it and let your other expenses follow suit.

If your spending is out of control and you cannot make ends meet, you should take time to conquer budgeting basics. This chapter provides the steps to follow in that case.

To get started, familiarize yourself with three steps:

1. analyzing cash flow;
2. setting goals; and
3. allocating and tracking resources.

ANALYZING CASH FLOW

A budget represents planned future activities based on data from the past. Accounting for what has been spent forms the basis for analyzing the outgo side of your cash flow, while your income provides the rest of the equation.

A cash-flow analysis is distinguished from a budget in that it represents no particular goal or plan. It merely sets forth your present behavior. After thorough cash-flow analysis, you can begin to budget, or decide how to allocate your resources.

Categorizing and Gathering Expenses

To have a clear picture of what you make and spend, get it all down on paper.

First, expenses must be summarized. The easiest place to begin is to list them by category. Exactly how you group items is less important than using a system that makes sense to you.

Some advisers suggest dividing expenses into "fixed" versus "variable." *Fixed* expenses might include mortgage or rent, auto, insurance, and other items that remain the same month after month. *Variable,* or discretionary, payments include food, light, water, telephone, clothing, and recreation.

Of course, in theory almost any expense can be raised or lowered once you have made up your mind to change it. As a rule, it is best not to prejudge any expense as "fixed."

For categories, as a starting point, you might employ the Department of Commerce breakdowns for the U.S. Personal Consumption Expenditure data. National household budgeting statistics are included here so you can review your expenditures to see how they measure up against those of other consumers. But remember, costs vary widely, and yours may differ from those reported there. For example, housing costs nationally are skewed downward by averaging in those who own their own homes outright and pay no monthly mortgage or rent.

COSTS	PERCENTAGE OF INCOME
Housing	15.9
Food and beverages	17.8
Clothes and shoes	6.0
Household operation	6.4
Furniture and household equipment	4.9
Autos and parts	6.6
Gas and oil	2.8
Transportation services	3.5
Medical	11.4
Personal business services (accountants, lawyers, banking fees)	6.9
Other nondurables (tobacco, newspapers, toiletries)	7.1
All other	10.7

After you have set up general categories, you should break them down according to what you find you have actually spent. For example, if, under housing, you have mortgage, property taxes, and repairs, then you need to keep track of each under the general category of housing.

As you work along, you may identify items that you are not

sure how to label. For example, where should automobile insurance be placed? It could fit under auto, or you might want to create a new category for all insurance expenses. Organize your categories in a way that feels right for you. A summary budget form similar to that used for our characters is on pages 145–46.

Next, move on to gathering the information that is available from your financial records. If your bookkeeping is disorganized, you will need to organize your records. After you have exhausted your written records, you will need to estimate cash and casual expenditures.

The best way to gather data about cash expenditures—and the way the government itself gathers these data—is to prepare an expense diary. You will only have to do this once. Charting your daily expenses will fill the gaps in information for items not paid by check or credit card.

Once you have finished your cash diary, you will want to integrate the material gathered this way with the information you have found from reviewing your checkbook and bills. Quarterly or annual expenses must now be added. You will need to review credit card bills and department store receipts to locate additional seasonal expenditures. Look at all your financial records to get a complete picture.

At this stage you should review your tax return for expenditures you might have forgotten, such as interest paid, business expenses, and others taken as deductions on Schedule A, "Itemized Deductions," and Schedule C, "Profit or Loss from Business."

In addition, when you review your tax returns, you can add into your annual expenditure summary the total taxes you have paid. If you participate in withholding, then you can get the total amount withheld and add to that amount any additional taxes paid with your return. The total will represent your federal tax bill. Of course, if you were entitled to a refund, you would subtract that amount from withholding to reach total taxes paid. By repeating the same process on state returns, you now will have a picture of all taxes paid. Social Security should be included in your expense calculations at this stage as well. The figures can be obtained from the tax return, if self-employed, or from a paycheck stub.

TABLE 34. EXPENDITURES

	AMOUNT
1. Housing	
Mortgage or rent	$_____
Property taxes	_____
Insurance	_____
Utilities	_____
Yard maintenance	_____
Other housing costs	_____
Subtotal, housing	_____
2. Food	_____
Home	_____
Restaurant	_____
Subtotal, food	_____
3. Clothing	
You	_____
Spouse	_____
Children	_____
Subtotal, clothing	_____
4. Transportation	
Installment payments	_____
Insurance	_____
Fuel	_____
Maintenance	_____
Other transportation	_____
Subtotal, transportation	_____
5. Phone	_____
6. Household purchases and supplies	_____
7. House cleaning and household help	_____
8. Education	_____
9. Recreation/club membership	_____
10. Personal care and improvements	_____
11. Medical and dental, health and disability insurance and expenses	_____
12. Life insurance	_____
13. Other insurance	_____
14. Contributions	_____
15. Entertainment and eating out	_____
16. Vacations/travel	_____
17. Hobbies	_____
18. Gifts	_____

TABLE 34—*Continued*

	AMOUNT
19. Support of relatives/others	_____
20. Home improvements	_____
21. Retirement plans (IRA/Keogh)	_____
22. Debt reduction	_____
23. Other	_____
Subtotal, expenditures	_____
24. Taxes	
Federal income tax	_____
State income tax	_____
Social Security/FICA	_____
State disability/unemployment	_____
Subtotal, taxes	_____
TOTAL EXPENDITURES	$_____

Computing Income

With a summary of your expenses in hand, it is now time to turn to your income. Calculating your annual income should be easier than taking inventory of your expenses, unless you are in business for yourself.

For income, assemble paycheck stubs, invoices for your work, bank statements, savings statements, and any other documentation, including contracts. Write down your total pre-tax income, whether weekly, monthly, or annually. If your income is other than monthly, make the necessary calculation so that you will have an average monthly income.

It is important to use your full income figure rather than just your take-home pay. Remember: your amount taxed is not written in stone; through utilizing the tax saving strategies outlined throughout this book, you may be able to have more of your income for yourself. Also, we have included taxes as an expense on the outgo side of our ledger, so gross income, not take-home, needs to be listed on the income side.

If you have income other than from a monthly paycheck, such as dividends, rents, and interest, write these down as well.

If you belong to a credit union with a savings plan that

amount separately on your expenses rather than deduct it from
the amount of income you list. List your total income in full
rather than the amount you take home, which includes this
expense deducted.

If your earnings are irregular and not guaranteed, be conservative. Include a margin of error.

Adapt the income summary here to fit your own case.

		TABLE 35. INCOME		
		YOU	SPOUSE (IF APPLICABLE)	TOTAL
1. Income from employment				
	Salary	$_____	$_____	$_____
	Commissions	_____	_____	_____
	Self-employment	_____	_____	_____
	Other	_____	_____	_____
Subtotal, employment		_____	_____	_____
2. Investment income				
	Taxable interest	_____	_____	_____
	Nontaxable interest	_____	_____	_____
	Dividends	_____	_____	_____
	Rents	_____	_____	_____
	Investment partnerships	_____	_____	_____
	Social Security	_____	_____	_____
	Pension	_____	_____	_____
	Trust fund	_____	_____	_____
	Other	_____	_____	_____
Subtotal, investments		_____	_____	_____
TOTAL		$_____	$_____	$_____

Statement of Annual Income and Expenditure

Now it is time to consolidate all the information into one summary statement of annual income and expenditures. This statement is called a "summary of cash receipts and disbursements
for the year," or a "cash-flow statement."

The value of an annual figure is that it smooths out cyclical differences in spending and gives you a total picture. If you spend more than you make, you'll obviously have to make changes. The budget you prepare will be based, in good part, on these past annual expenses.

TABLE 36.   ANNUAL STATEMENT OF INCOME AND EXPENDITURES (CASH-FLOW STATEMENT)

Income	$_____
Expenditures	_____
Total	$_____

SETTING GOALS

Cash-flow analysis is not a budget. To move from income and expenditures to budgeting, you must set specific goals for growth and establish plans with targets and dates to meet your goals.

While gathering information, you have made some preliminary assessments. Now the time has come for serious planning. You must identify goals. Once goals are set, specific targets or benchmarks can be established.

TABLE 37.   GOALS

OBJECTIVE	DATE	TOTAL	HOW TO ACHIEVE
House down payment	Jan. 1992	$20,000	Save $500/mo.

These goals, when committed to paper, should serve as guidelines for your budgeting. For example, if your goal is to save for a house down payment, you will have to set the money aside each month.

ALLOCATING AND TRACKING RESOURCES

You know your current behavior, and you have set new goals for future behavior. Now what? The next step is to decide how to allocate your resources so that these new goals can be met.

If all your income is being used to meet expenses, you won't have room to set aside money for your new goals. Assuming steady income, what changes in spending patterns do you need to make to meet these new objectives? Figuring out these changes and adjusting expenditures is allocating resources through a spending budget.

You can establish an expenditure budget, by category, to plan and monitor performance for control and evaluation. When it is reviewed at the end of a given period, this budget will also serve as an aid in making new plans, thus closing the loop by providing feedback for future undertakings.

For example, if you decide to cut expenditures by $100 a month, your budget should indicate exactly where. Say you sacrificed restaurant meals: each month you would show your budgeted amount, how much you actually spent, and the variation between the budgeted amount and what you spent. Provided you took time to track actual expenses, you would know if you met your target. If not, you would make necessary adjustments— either cutting back or changing your target if your plan wasn't workable. This final checking and adjusting is the feedback you need to complete the process.

How Much Should I Spend?

SET A REALISTIC SAVINGS GOAL

Save from 5 to 10 percent depending on your income and debts. Pay yourself first through payroll savings plans or U.S. Savings Bonds, just one kind of bond available from the U.S. government (see pages 186–88).

WHERE TO CUT BACK

Vacations. No more than 3 or 4 percent of your total income should go to vacations. If you haven't purchased a home, redirect vacation funds to a home down payment fund. Vacation at home; vacation closer to home. Try camping. Exchange homes with relatives or friends in other locales. If on vacation, make breakfast or lunch in your room and use bargain guides to locate interesting inexpensive restaurants in other cities. If you must go to resorts, go during the off-season.

Eating Out. If dining out has put your food bill at 10 percent of your gross income or above, cut back. Even though it's hard for working women to find time to cook, and too few husbands share family chores, try these tips: order out (eliminate the tip); choose neighborhood restaurants; order off the low end of the menu; share entrées; don't add extras such as drinks, desserts, and side dishes.

Clothing. Women annually spend five times as much on clothing as men. If your clothing expenses exceed 5 percent of your income, shift the remainder to savings. Resist fashion pressure; shop discount stores and sales; pay cash. Buy basics, borrow frills.

Cars. Don't ever buy a new car if you haven't bought a home. New cars go down in value the minute you drive off the showroom floor. The best car bargain is a two- to three-year-old one-owner used car (Mercedes calls them "pre-owned"). Manufacturers have stretched car payments on new cars to sixty months, while used-car loans usually run thirty-six months. As you comparison shop, add up the difference two more years of payments would make to your savings portfolio. Remember: Cars, *at best, retain* their value. They *rarely appreciate.*

Insurance. Carry life insurance only if you need it. Certainly single people with no dependents can pass. If you are the sole breadwinner and you have no children, do not insure your non-earning spouse. Recheck your policy. You can save 1 to 2 percent of your income by eliminating unnecessary insurance. (For more information, see Appendix 9.)

Housing. If you can stretch and get into real estate, do. If you watch all other expenditures and cut debt, you can afford to exceed the 33 to 40 percent of income that is recommended for housing expenditures. (*Note:* Remember that national averages of 15 percent on housing costs include people who already own their homes.) But not for rent—stretching for ownership may be worth the sacrifice. Stretching on rent—unless you are in an urban area that offers no choice at your income level—wastes money that should go toward savings.

It's hard to resist societal messages to spend. But by using these techniques and others you can develop, your budgeting, no matter how informal, can pay off.

Budget Formats

Exactly how to set up the budget is a bookkeeping detail that should flow logically from the data you have gathered so far. A convenient way to keep track is to use the income and expenditure categories you have established and add two more columns, the amount to be budgeted and the amount spent.

Each column of the budget would now look like this:

BUDGET			
ITEM	BUDGETED	SPENT	DIFFERENCE

Now comes the part requiring time and discipline: doing the bookkeeping necessary to see whether actual expenses match projected ones. This step is the hardest part of budgeting. Practically speaking, this task may be one that you can accomplish only for a limited time. Once you have gained control, the process may become second nature, a running tote board you keep in your mind.

For your actual tools, you might pick a ledger or a computer spread sheet. Fill in the ledger when you pay your bills, then take time to log other expenses from your checkbook and cash receipts at the same time.

Of course, not every penny can be tracked. Give yourself some slack with a petty cash or miscellaneous fund.

COMPUTERIZED BUDGETING

With a personal computer, you can create an electronic version of the budget ledger and make it as simple or complicated as you like. To make it work, you have to have the inclination to toy with the computer and the time to input your records.

If you wish, use a computer program such as Lotus 1-2-3, VisiCalc, a home accounting package, or other electronic spread sheet. Be aware that computerized systems are only as good as the data put into them. For many people, time constraints make everyday computer bookkeeping impractical. Posting data may turn into a barrier. If you are in the habit of throwing your receipts into shoe boxes, think carefully about whether you will make the commitment required for computerized bookkeeping.

On the positive side, computers save time in the long run for those with sufficiently complicated financial lives. If you use an accountant at tax time, you can take her your already computerized records, saving time and money.

A computerized or written budget will be too complicated for many people. If you have made up and dropped many budgets, the answer may lie in instituting controls through a simplified "accounts" system using more than one bank account.

Bank accounts can serve two broad budget categories: current expenses and long-term investments. With a checking account for monthly bills and a money-market or interest-bearing fund for longer-term goals, you can budget by depositing to one account the amount you plan to spend on current expenses. Segregate the rest of your funds in the interest account and leave it there.

Caution: you will need discipline, because having investment funds liquid can provide a temptation should overspending occur in the expense account.

A slightly more complicated version of the same arrangement can work for a couple. In addition to the current expense account for bills and the investment account, each spouse will need an individual account for personal expenses. Even though it might seem complicated for a couple to have four accounts, this way each person has discretionary funds that leave the family expense account intact.

PURCHASE ORDER BUDGETING

If you cannot bring yourself to budget (or have very little room to change most expenses), but want to cut back on your cash outgo, try purchase order budgeting. Prepare a form and use it for all your planned purchases.

To use the form, fill in what you intend to purchase and the price. Think about the purchase and get approval from yourself,

TABLE 38.   PURCHASE ORDER

Date _____
Item _____
Purpose _____
Date needed _____
Estimated cost _____
Discussed with _____
Agreed upon? _____

as if you worked for a business where the order would have had
to be approved by a controller or financial officer.

Reviewing and Readjusting

No matter what format you use, if you budget, eventually the
time will come in your budgeting process for a review. The review provides a chance to see how you have done and to set goals
for succeeding months or years. You may want to graph debt
repayment and savings so you can actually see the debt line fall
and the savings line rise. Or you may simply adjust plans for
expenditure categories that exceeded their limits. But, before
you leave budgeting behind, take time to check how you per-
formed against your original plans. Even if you complete the
cycle only once, you will have a better sense of how your spending compares to your plans.

CONCLUSION

A budget is an acknowledgment of a businesslike approach to the
management of money. Written plans provide an opportunity to
make and record annual spending plans. Once the budget is
prepared, it can help communicate these plans to the entire
family.

If you have a family, a budget can help motivate members
to act together to achieve the goals set.

During the period for which the budget has been created, the
document provides a benchmark for controlling ongoing ex-

penses. At the end of the budget period, the figures provide a basis for evaluating your performance.

Whether you choose a stationer's ledger, a computer, or a checkbook tally, the main objective involves having a process that fits your needs so that you can bring your cash flow to bear on your growth.

CHAPTER 8

YOUR

TAXES

This chapter is designed to help you improve your tax situation. First we shall look at the basic tax return, the 1040, and see how yours can be improved. Second, you will not only learn how to maximize tax savings annually but how to organize your financial life around tax savings. We shall show you why tax experts understand that only after-tax dollars are a meaningful measure of income.

Because there is no substitute for hands-on experience, we shall work with your own 1040 to see how tax theory meets practice. In many instances, with careful work you can save tax preparer fees and do the work yourself, reserving your expert team member for consultation on complicated issues. However, if your financial life is less simple, you should have a CPA—not simply an "accountant"—prepare your return. Then use your knowledge to make sure she did it right and took advantage of all the tax saving opportunities. Finally, never take tax advice from a commission-based tax adviser or financial planner. Pay your tax adviser by the hour—the advice you get "for free" can be very expensive in costly mistakes.

Becoming a "Long-Form" Filer

If you are among the majority of taxpayers who file the short form 1040EZ or 1040A, you may be able to save by filing the 1040 long form. Your first challenge will be to investigate whether using this form is to your advantage.

Tax reform increased the number of short-form filers by 6 percent in the first full year. But even though the short form may seem to be the easy way out, it may be an expensive option. If you are eligible for enough of the deductions, big money can be saved (and earned) by taking the time to figure your tax position and file a long form. Do not let form-phobia prevent you from getting the most out of your tax savings.

Although spending time with the 1040 may seem to be a hassle, weigh this hassle against the value of your time. If you earn $2,500 a month, which works out to approximately $15 per hour before taxes, then for each $2,500 you can save in taxes you are saving yourself a month's earnings—legally diverting this money from Uncle Sam toward your own use.

CONQUERING YOUR OWN 1040

Glance back over the case histories in Chapters 4, 5, and 6. Do any of these situations parallel or resemble your own?

Do you have uncharted employee business expenses, as did Melissa Hilton, that could add up to significant deductions? Do you have child-care tax credits that are not being used? Do you qualify for an IRA or 401(k) plan? Are your business expenses properly accounted? Once you have started thinking along these lines, turn your attention to your previous tax returns. Have them near you and work with them as you read through this chapter.

Using your latest return, start by filling out the first column of the tax overview worksheet in table 39 showing last year's actual taxes. Take the information from last year and fill it in under the appropriate line in the worksheet for the last year's amounts. *Note:* The numbers on the worksheet do not correspond to 1040 line numbers because each year the forms change slightly to reflect revisions in the law; however, the items will be in approximately the same location on the 1040. Look for the items by name, not number.

Tax Planning: Projecting Before the End of the Year

In order to save money on taxes, you must take action during the tax year in question. (One of the very few exceptions to this rule is the IRA, which can be set up as a savings vehicle after the end of the tax year, up to April 15 of the next year.) Therefore, you need to project your taxes long before December 31.

Optimizing tax savings cannot be done once a year under the pressure of a filing deadline. Strategic thinking has to occur all year long. Even if you file your own return, you should have a competent CPA on your team to question. You should see your tax adviser for year-end planning, certainly no later than November, or do a year-end review yourself.

Also check with your tax adviser before making any major investment move.

Next, use table 39, the tax overview worksheet, on pages 158–59, and estimate this year's income and deductions. Don't worry about digging out every single scrap of paper documenting your deductions right now, although you will eventually need to do this. For now just use an estimate on each line that applies to you under the column for this year. It should be fairly easy to estimate your income.

Unless you have had an unusual year with many changes, such as starting a new business or selling a home, your spending and thus your deductions will remain fairly stable. However, the tax treatment of items may change—for example, medical expense deductions—thus changing your amount of deduction. Double-check your deductions and exemptions and make the calculations necessary to predict your taxable income for the coming year.

SCHEDULE A

Now consider "Schedule A, Itemized Deductions" (see table 40, p. 160). In order to take full advantage of filing on the long form,

TABLE 39.   TAX OVERVIEW WORKSHEET

	LAST YEAR (ACTUAL)	THIS YEAR (PROJECTED)
Income		
1. Earned income (wages, salaries, tips, etc.)	$_____	$_____
2. Taxable interest	_____	_____
3. Dividends	_____	_____
4. Business income	_____	_____
5. Capital gains	_____	_____
6. Income (or deductible losses) from limited partnerships or rental property	_____	_____
7. Other income, including alimony, or spousal support, but excluding child support	_____	_____
8. Total income (add lines 1–7)	$_____	$_____
Adjustments to Income		
9. Alimony, or spousal support, paid	$_____	$_____
10. IRA contributions	_____	_____
11. Keogh contributions	_____	_____
12. Total adjustments (add lines 9–11)	_____	_____
13. Adjusted gross income (line 8 minus line 12)	$_____	$_____
Taxable Computation		
14. Write in amount of total itemized deductions or standard deduction, whichever is higher*	$_____	$_____
15. Exemptions	_____	_____
16. Total deductions plus exemptions (line 14 + line 15)	_____	_____
17. Taxable income (line 13 minus line 16)	_____	_____
18. Tax before credits†	$_____	$_____
Credits		
19. Child care or other credit	$_____	$_____
20. Net income tax (line 18 minus line 19)	_____	_____
21. Self-employment or other taxes	_____	_____

TABLE 39—*Continued*

	LAST YEAR (ACTUAL)	THIS YEAR (PROJECTED)
22. Total tax		
23. Effective tax rate: (line 22 divided by line 17) as a percentage‡	$	$

*If you filed on the long form 1040, check the amount on last year's Schedule A deductions. If you filed on the short form 1040EZ or 1040A, take the standard deduction listed there. This deduction is subject to adjustment for inflation, so in subsequent years, check with the IRS directly for current amounts. If your estimate of personal deductions exceeds the standard amount, you should file on the long form. See table 40 to estimate.

†In order to figure your taxes, you will need to look at a tax rate chart. The tax rate chart for 1989 is provided in Appendix 2 (for later years, check directly with the IRS if you do not have a tax form). Your actual tax liability for last year is listed on your return. Or, without a rate chart, to estimate next year's tax, go through the calculations on the form and then pick out your rate from Appendix 2. Multiply your taxable income (line 17) by your tax rate to get line 18, tax before credits.

‡To get a more exact estimate for planning purposes, if you have last year's return, figure your marginal tax rate from there. To find the marginal rate (for example, the rate at which your next dollar will be taxed) check your *taxable* income against the rate table in Appendix 2. This figure will allow you to determine your prospective tax savings on your next deduction, assuming your tax picture was the same as last year. If not, add or subtract income.

If you are self-employed, you can use line 17 instead of line 20 to find your true effective rate; however, the self-employment tax is on earned income, not taxable income.

Remember that your effective tax rate is your tax liability divided by your taxable income. Take the figure from line 22, total tax, and divide it by the figure on line 17, taxable income. Convert to a percentage and you will have your effective rate.

you will want to itemize your deductions. The term "Schedule A, Itemized Deductions," is misleading because it does not list all itemized deductions that are available to you by using the 1040— for example, alimony paid.

A better way to think of Schedule A is as itemized personal deductions. (Remember, if you are in business for yourself, deductions are itemized on Schedule C, or if you are in a partnership, Schedule E.) Your Schedule A deductions primarily include the seven items listed on the schematic Schedule A in table 40. These items are medical and dental expenses, taxes you paid, interest you paid, contributions you made, casualty and theft losses, and miscellaneous deductions. Many miscellaneous deductions are now subject to a 2 percent floor. To take the deduction, only the total amount exceeding 2 percent of your adjusted

TABLE 40.   SCHEDULE A WORKSHEET (REPORTED ON 1040 LINE 33A)

	LAST YEAR (ACTUAL)	THIS YEAR (PROJECTED)
1. Medical expenses*	$_____	$_____
2. State and local income and property taxes	_____	_____
3. Mortgage interest†	_____	_____
4. Other deductible interest	_____	_____
5. Charitable contributions	_____	_____
6. Miscellaneous deductions and employee business expenses‡	_____	_____
7. Casualty and theft losses	_____	_____
8. Total itemized deductions (add lines 1–7)	$_____	$_____

*Must exceed 7.5 percent of adjusted gross income in order to receive a deduction. To estimate, look at last year's adjusted gross income at the bottom of page one of your tax return.
†For acquisition mortgage interest not exceeding one million, principal residence and one vacation home; interest on equity credit lines of up to $100,000 is also deductible. See Chapter 2.
‡Must exceed 2 percent of adjusted gross income in order to receive a deduction. Even if it does exceed 2 percent, only the portion over 2 percent counts.

gross income counts (the amount on the bottom line of page one of the 1040 or on line 13 of the tax overview worksheet).

If you have filed a Schedule A in the past but had your return prepared by a tax professional, you might want to review the schedule carefully to see if there are other deductible items that you have but forgot to give your tax preparer. For example, many people forget to include medical transportation and parking: what it costs traveling to and from your doctor's office or clinic for treatment.

Note: If you are in business for yourself, 25 percent of medical insurance expenses and miscellaneous deductions limits on Schedule A do not apply if you file these instead on Schedule C. In fact, if you are a self-employed businessperson, you can deduct 25 percent of your health insurance on your business return, but you must provide the same coverage for any employees. Therefore, if you meet the test, you will be better off taking that portion of your medical insurance on Schedule C. Likewise, many of your miscellaneous deductions will be better taken on the business return where they will not be subject to the 2 percent limit.

If you have not itemized or filed a Schedule A, use the worksheet in table 40 to see whether your potential deductions would be enough to warrant filing on the long form.

Where We Stand

If you have been working along with the chapter as directed, you should have a completed tax overview worksheet showing your taxes for last year on one simplified page, and alongside that, your projected income picture for this year (table 39). In addition, your personal deductions have been recorded for last year and estimated for this year on the Schedule A worksheet (table 40).

Finally, if you have not done so already, figure your projected tax on the taxable income you have estimated. Use the rate table in Appendix 2 or estimate your projected tax bill by multiplying your taxable income by your marginal tax rate.

Now for the real work—using the information gathered in the first part of the chapter to think prospectively about your taxes. This means looking at possible areas for tax exclusions, deductions, credits, or deferrals and taking advantage of these savings.

FIVE WAYS TO SAVE ON YOUR TAXES

Although the trade-off for lower tax rates was a restriction on tax preferences or loopholes, saving on taxes still involves our five friends—exclusions, deductions, rates, credits, and deferrals. Review the five now to find additional tax breaks.

Exclusions

Wherever possible, take advantage of exclusions since tax-free dollars are always worth more than taxable dollars.

TAX-EXEMPT BONDS

If your income is decent, why invest in an activity that will produce taxable income? Look instead to solidly rated municipal and state bonds, which often earn interest free of federal and state income taxes. Buy bonds issued by your home state (or local governments in your state) so that the interest income is exempt from state income taxes. If you are subject to the alternative minimum tax (AMT), note that some but not all tax-exempt bonds are subject to AMT. Taxpayers subject to AMT must be careful which tax-exempt bonds they buy.

CAPITAL GAINS

As of this writing, all gains are taxed at regular income rates, but Congress was near passage of a lower capital-gains rate (see Appendix 7 for information on ordering a tax update). If you have made profits in any investment, whether real estate or stocks, think carefully about cashing, or "realizing," your gains. Even with lower rates, considering commissions and fees, you might be better off staying in a slightly lower-earning investment than in taking your profit and paying taxes.

Remember too that the previous $200-dividend exclusion has ended. If you want tax-free income, you will have to look elsewhere. In addition, stock market loss deductions are limited to $3,000 per year.

FRINGE BENEFITS

Most fringe benefits still remain excluded from tax. Examples of excluded noncash benefits are: employee-provided health and life insurance, tuition reductions, employee discounts, and small or *de minimis* (minimal) benefits such as free parking and small holiday gifts.

If you are now working part-time, rather than asking for a raise you might see if you can get on your employer's benefit rolls. This way you will receive tax-free benefits that you are now paying for in after-tax dollars.

Watch for further changes in tax treatment of fringe benefits, which have been increasingly regarded as taxable compensation. In fact, employers must now consider personal use of the company car or airplane as taxable income.

SCHOLARSHIPS

Scholarships and fellowships are still tax excluded if for tuition, fees, books, and supplies. But now scholarship monies covering room and board are considered taxable income. If your college-bound child receives a full scholarship, be aware that either you or your student could be stuck paying hundreds of dollars in taxes on the portion that goes to room and board.

Graduate students with teaching stipends—often awarded in lieu of outright financial aid—will also be adversely affected. At a state university where in-state tuition is $2,800, a graduate student receiving a yearly stipend of $8,300 will pay $974 in federal taxes, up from $524, an increase of 86 percent.

SOCIAL SECURITY

Earlier reform changed the treatment of Social Security benefits, part of which may be taxed. The calculations are complicated. Make sure you are familiar with the rules as outlined on pages 190–92 if you are drawing Social Security benefits.

DEPENDENT CARE

The structure of Dependent Care Assistance Plans (DCAPs) was not affected by reform, but a new cap of $5,000 for total benefits was added. As we saw in Leslie and Andrew Carlson's case, this exclusion is an alternative to a tax credit for dependent care. According to this plan, employees can voluntarily take a lower salary and receive the difference of up to $5,000 in nontaxable child- or dependent-care benefits. This option must be carefully outlined for employees according to the new laws.

OTHERS

Life insurance proceeds, most damages from personal injury lawsuits, and interest earned on tax-exempt bonds, to mention a few, remain excluded and untaxed. When applicable, take advantage of these exclusions.

Deductions

Deductions are vehicles for subtracting expenses from your income before taxes. Their worth to you depends on your tax bracket: the higher your bracket the more useful the deduction. Thus, with rates generally lower, deductions don't save as much. However, careful tracking of available deductions can save many tax dollars.

Make sure that you are taking all the personal deductions to which you are entitled. Then see how you can add more deductions through structuring your tax life along lines to improve your access to new deductions.

PERSONAL DEDUCTIONS

Most personal deductions are found on Schedule A, as we saw above. Review the key items to see whether you are getting your full tax break.

Mortgage Interest: The interest on the mortgages for home acquisitions, construction, or substantial improvement remains fully deductible under 1987 revisions on your first and second home provided the combined mortgages do not exceed $1 million. Interest on home equity loans of up to $100,000 is also deductible, provided your original mortgage and your home equity line do not exceed the fair market value of the home. You cannot refinance your home beyond your original acquisition indebtedness and take the deduction. In other words, you cannot take additional cash out of the refinance and have it count as acquisition (deductible) indebtedness. Provided you follow these rules, every allowable dollar of interest that you pay to a bank to secure your property also gets taken off your taxable income.

To see how home ownership would affect your own taxes, try the exercise in table 41 (this analysis is the same that Melissa Hilton completed in Chapter 6).

Miscellaneous Deductions. These deductions, such as employee business expenses and tax preparation fees, must exceed

---

TABLE 41.   EXERCISE: ANALYSIS OF HOME
OWNERSHIP COSTS

Basic Facts

1. Purchase price of home $_____
2. Cash required   _____
3. Loan   _____
4. Monthly payments, principal, and interest   _____
5. Monthly deposit for property taxes   _____
6. Maintenance for cooperative*   _____
7. Monthly deposit for insurance, approximately   _____
8. Total monthly payment (lines 4, 5, 6, and 7)   _____

Expense Items for Income Tax Purposes

9. First month's interest†   _____
10. Monthly property tax deposit   _____
11. Total deductions (line 9 + line 10)   _____
12. Tax bracket   _____
13. Tax savings per month (line 12 x line 11)   _____

Total After-Tax Cost

14. Total monthly payment (line 8)   _____
15. Less estimated tax savings (line 9)   _____
16. Effective monthly cost in cash, after taxes (line 14   _____
    minus line 15)
17. Subtract equity,† which is being gained monthly   _____
    (line 4 minus line 9)

Actual Monthly Cost $_____

*Or homeowner's association fees for condominium.
†Interest amount decreases by a small amount each month and equity increases by the
same amount.

---

2 percent of adjusted gross income. Business meals, which factor
into this 2 percent pool, are limited to 80 percent of the meal
rather than the full cost. Qualified educational expenses are still
fully deductible, but only under this miscellaneous category.

State and Local Real Estate and Income Taxes. These remain deductible; however, state and local sales taxes are no
longer deductible.

Medical Expenses. Those expenses not covered by health

insurance plus the cost of medical insurance (if not provided by your employer) are deductible to the extent they exceed 7.5 percent of adjusted gross income, up from a pre-reform 5 percent.

Credit card and other personal interest deductions are being phased out.

PASSIVE LOSS RULES

Sheltering income from taxes is much more difficult because of the passive loss rules. These rules impose a new standard of involvement in activities to create a tax savings.

To deduct a loss, you must meet three tests. First, you must prove that you are actively involved in the business. Second, the IRS will ask how often you were on the premises of the business. Third, you must have a certain knowledge or experience regarding the business activity. The burden of proof to show that you qualify for passive loss deductions is on you. If you find an investment that meets these passive loss rules, you can still shelter your losses. But—it's difficult. As to rental activities, even if you meet all three tests, the losses are still passive (except for the $25,000 exception discussed below and certain rules on rehabilitation and low-income housing).

RENTAL REAL ESTATE

With real estate, the new rules are a bit more complex, but conquering them is worthwhile because real estate still offers significant tax savings. Real estate is blessed with a lesser standard than the passive loss rule, the so-called active standard. This active standard is aimed at helping middle- and upper-middle-income earners. It is important to review these key deductions. Even if you cannot afford to invest in rental real estate now, you should think about working toward this goal.

THE GENERAL RULE FOR RENTAL PROPERTY

Taxpayers with less than $100,000 adjusted gross income can deduct up to $25,000 of rental losses, provided they are actively involved. For example, if you owned a duplex and you oversaw the renting and maintenance, but the building stood empty for six months during refurbishing, you could deduct up to $25,000 of loss against active (for example, salary) income.

Interest and depreciation are also fully deductible for tax-payers in this category, provided that the total deduction, including losses, does not exceed $25,000.

In general, depreciation was stretched out from 19 years to 27.5 years for residential real property. This deduction can be worth a bundle. With a $200,000 rental residential property, for example, you would have a depreciation deduction of $7,272 per year for 27.5 years. In the 28 percent bracket, you would rack up another $2,036 in tax savings a year.

An additional rule requires that you be "at risk" to get the deductions, but here again, in writing the law Congress had middle-income small real estate investors in mind. Even "non-recourse" mortgages, in which only the property itself will be forfeited in the event of default, qualify if they actually finance the property itself and are from a qualified lender.

By contrast, you could not meet the active and at risk standards were you to put your money in a real estate limited partnership. By definition, the risk would be limited, and the general partner, not you the limited partner, would be the only "active" participant.

Two Exceptions to the Rule. Low-income housing and rehabilitation of older and historic buildings are not subject to the active standard, and the income requirement for deductions is higher. With an adjusted gross income of $200,000, a person can invest in these two specialized types of property and receive both deductions and credits (described under "Credits" on page 170). There is a phaseout from $200,000 to $250,000, meaning the amount of the deduction decreases as income increases. However, the low-income credits ended on January 1, 1990. Seek professional advice if you are interested in these areas.

Do not get involved in a complicated real estate business merely for the tax breaks alone. If you do not understand the investment, if it is not economically productive apart from tax considerations, or if it involves too much of a hassle factor, stay away.

SIDE-BUSINESS DEDUCTIONS

If a salaried individual starts a legitimate income-producing business on the side and participates in that business regularly, continually, and substantially, and if the business does not show a profit, the taxpayer can use the losses to offset salaried income. But be careful. Reform stiffened the performance rules for small businesses. To prove you have a legitimate business and not a hobby, you may have to show a profit three out of every five years, up from two out of five.

Remember, too, as we saw in Leslie Carlson's case, you cannot use a home office deduction—that is, deducting a portion of your rent or mortgage—to create a loss for an otherwise profitable business.

STOCK DEDUCTIONS

There is no depreciation deduction on stock market investments. Interest paid to carry stock investments can be deducted only to the extent of your investment income (such as dividends and interest). If you invest in securities, only $3,000 in losses can be deducted in a single year. During the October 1987 stock market plunge of 508 points, $3,000 would not have been much of a deduction if you had had a substantial position in the market.

So, if your tax position needs improvement, you may want to consider switching from the stock market to real estate.

TWO-EARNER FAMILIES

You may be among those who lost a two-earner deduction, designed to level the notch effect for families whose second income pushed them into a higher bracket. In general, tax experts projected that most two-earner families would find that lower tax rates would blur the impact of this change, but your experience may differ.

If your two-earner family found itself paying more in taxes after reform, there is not much action you can take on an individual level. But watch for further reform efforts and lobby to get this break reinstated.

Rates

Rates are commonly referred to as tax "brackets." The percentage of income paid in taxes varies with each rate. Changes in rates were a key factor in tax reform. Regrouping tax rate levels has had several effects, at least in theory.

LOWER RATES

The rates overall were lowered. The top rate, which stood in 1981 at 70 percent before it was lowered to 50 percent in 1984, was lowered to 33 percent with the 1986 reform. The range, which was formerly 11 percent to 50 percent, now stands at 15 percent, 28 percent, and 33 percent.

However, studies suggest that lower- and middle-income people may find themselves paying higher—not lower—taxes. If you can find your 1986 tax return, compare it to your 1988 results. See whether reform delivered for you by calculating your effective rate pre- and post-reform.

FEWER RATES

The rates were also condensed to three rather than fourteen levels. In theory, the effect was to lower the probability of being pushed into a higher tax bracket because these rates are now fewer; in practice, the main result has been to lower top rates.

The theory is that two-earner households in particular are affected since the "second" income will no longer push the household up a rate notch. If you had the two-earner deduction before, did your taxes go up or down?

ALTERNATIVE MINIMUM TAX

Another provision strengthened by reform is the 21 percent flat rate, or the alternative minimum tax (AMT). This flat rate tax is due only when certain deductions exceed a threshold set out in a formula in the tax manual. If your income and deductions are high and your taxes are low, check to see if you will owe the alternative minimum tax.

Calculate your taxes both ways if you're not sure. The instructions come with your tax form or you can find current rules in the library as well as from the IRS.

Credits

Tax credits—which are subtracted from your tax itself and therefore are worth their face value—are hard to locate in today's tax code. All credits involving investments in machinery, automobiles, or airplanes for business purposes were excluded. The only easily accessible remaining tax credits in the individual investment arena are in low-income housing or older building rehabilitation.

The child- and dependent-care credit is also still available, as is the earned-income tax credit.

SPECIAL REAL ESTATE CREDITS

Credits for older building rehabilitation and Certified Historical Structures remain. These credits are available even for passive investors. These investments are not for everyone, however, so proceed with caution.

DEPENDENT-CARE TAX CREDIT

Congress did not raise qualifying expenses for the child- and dependent-care credit, which is designed to help working parents. Although this credit still exists, it is at a low 30 percent of qualified costs and can go down to 20 percent, depending on your income. (See Chapter 2 for further discussion and Appendix 3 for a chart of credit amounts by income.)

If you pay for more in child care than you can apply toward the credit, then monitor further tax reform efforts to ensure that this credit is strengthened in the future. In the meantime, consider switching to a DCAP, an exclusion that is equal in value to a deduction.

To decide which plan makes most sense for you—provided you have the option to take either—you want to compare the two by dividing the amount of the credit by your tax bracket. For example, if your credit, a dollar-for-dollar reduction, amounts to

$200 right off your tax bill, then your break-even point would be a $714 deduction in the 28 percent bracket ($200 divided by .28) and a $1,333 deduction in the 15 percent bracket. If your child-care costs exceed your break-even point, then you should try to get a DCAP. *Note:* A new 1989 rule requires that you write the taxpayer identification number of your day-care provider on your return Form 2441 (Child and Dependent Care Expense Form) to receive either credits or deductions. If you use an in-home baby-sitter, you will need the Social Security Number (SSN); a day-care center will give you an Employee Identification Number (EIN).

You must choose between the credit and the exclusion, as you can only take advantage of one or the other.

EARNED INCOME TAX CREDIT (EITC)

The earned income tax credit has been designed to reward people who work for a living, have dependents, but don't earn a great deal of money.

The credit is refunded to you even if you owe and have paid no taxes. If your adjusted gross income is less than $17,000 and you have one or more dependents, you may be eligible for the credit. Even if you do not currently file taxes because your income is so low, check the EITC table included with the tax instruction booklet and file to receive cash credit of $170 to $800. (If you know someone in this position who is otherwise qualified, tell her about this credit. Only a small portion of people currently receive it.)

Deferrals

Deferrals are an accounting strategy for delaying tax payments. Anytime you delay taking income or gains, you are taking advantage of the principle of deferral.

REAL ESTATE DEFERRALS

A home is uniquely qualified to circumvent capital-gains rules. With a residence, as we have seen, you can roll over or defer paying tax on the profits. The only catch is you must buy a new home with equal or greater value within two years of the sale of your original home.

Another option, if you are a homeowner and need cash, is to borrow against the equity in your home rather than selling it. While any borrowing should always be done with care, if you find yourself in a high-earnings bracket one year, but know that you will be in a lower-earnings bracket the next, you might want to borrow against your stocks or your home to cover current cash needs. Any money borrowed, even though it might be tapping into profits, is not taxed until the underlying item providing the security for the loan is sold.

For example, look at the options if you are about to sell a piece of property. Any profit will be taxed as straight income, not gain. If you can do a trade (of an investment property) or roll over a home, you will get a tax deferral. In tax terms, a dollar paid later is better than a dollar paid today. Presumably, unless severe deflation occurs, you will be paying later in cheaper dollars and you will be able to keep your gain for yourself.

IRAS

The Individual Retirement Account is another easily accessible form of deferral. If you are qualified for the full IRA deduction of $2,000, you essentially defer taxes on that amount until retirement, when presumably your tax bracket will be lower.

Anyone not an active participant in a company pension plan or Keogh plan is qualified. In addition, those with adjusted gross incomes under $25,000, if single, and $40,000, if married filing jointly, can take the full IRA deduction.

With incomes between $25,000 and $30,000, if single ($40,000 and $50,000 if married), you can take a reduced IRA tax-deferred deduction. The exact amount can be calculated from the worksheets provided with the tax forms.

For those not qualified for deferral of tax on the $2,000 principal, the interest earned on an IRA is still deferred.

Two other forms of deferral are the 401(k) and Keogh, as discussed for the Carlsons. If you select a 401(k) plan, your IRA contribution counts toward the $7,000 base limit. See Chapter 9 for more details on these plans.

The ultimate deferral, of course, is delaying taxes until after your death. Although your heirs don't have to pay your income taxes, unfortunately, many upper-middle-class people struggle to cut their income tax bills by a few thousand dollars, only to have their estates pay many thousands in easily avoidable estate taxes at the time of their death.

A full discussion of estate tax planning is beyond the scope of this book. Here's a rule of thumb: if your assets, your spouse's assets, and your life insurance are close to $600,000, get tax-oriented estate advice. (See Appendix 8 for more on estate planning.)

THREE TIERS TO TAX ACCESS

Using exclusions, deductions, rates, credits, and deferrals will not happen overnight. Now that you have a clear understanding of the five tax principles and how they apply to your own present taxes, use a three-tiered approach to tax savings. This approach is similar to the three stages of growth, in that you start first with conquering the basics before moving to more complicated strategies. By following these guidelines, you should soon benefit from tax savings.

Tier 1

At the first tier you should try to access nontaxable items such as extra fringe benefits and tax-free income such as municipal bonds. Access any exclusions that fit your situation as a beginning point for tax savings.

Tier 2

At the second tier you should find ways to lower the amount of taxes you must pay by adding deductions and credits. Check to be sure that you are taking all available deductions and credits to which you are already entitled. Keep better records and don't overlook provisions you haven't utilized before.

Once you have taken advantage of tax-free income in tier 1, and have utilized all the possible itemized deductions in tier 2, the next step is tier 3.

Tier 3

At the third tier of tax strategy, you should decide how to restructure your affairs around tax issues. This means looking at alternatives to present or planned financial endeavors in order to receive tax benefits. For example, if you have high income but don't own a home, you should pick real estate over the stock market to gain deductions. Or, if your salaried position could legitimately be structured as a consultancy or independent business, explore this option. If you have profits on appreciated property, consider bypassing turnover in favor of lower taxes. Or, you may want to organize your estate so that it will pass to your heirs with the lowest possible taxes. Another option: employ deferrals.

Restructuring activity takes time, but whenever you consider a new financial undertaking, ask yourself: "Is there a better way to go to reduce taxes? Are there alternative paths to follow?"

CONCLUSION

As you consider your tax strategy, note the extent to which you previously relied on exclusions, deductions, credits, and deferrals last year and figure out ways to add new treatments this year. Once you understand your existing tax pattern, the next step is to design your finances to minimize taxes.

It is not a matter of filing strategy—although changes such as choosing the long form over the short form help—but of choosing financial activities with a favorable tax component.

Finally, once you have used the information presented to help you think about taxes, you will need to keep up-to-date annually. Updating your information should be easier now that you understand the basic tax principles. When you read news stories about proposed tax changes, mentally fit each provision under the five-point scheme. To order an annual tax supplement to this book, please see Appendix 7.

Keep taxes in their place. Though you want to avoid them as much as you legitimately can, one of the smartest entrepreneurs I know said, "I'm always glad when I owe a lot of taxes—it means I made a lot of money."

CHAPTER 9

YOUR

GROWTH

Achieving growth—at least to the point of financial security—is the goal of all your financial efforts. Our strategy consists of developing your own step-by-step plan resting on the three stages of growth, each with different goals, and each with a different entry level.

In stage 1 you begin saving and accumulating cash for future, higher-earning investments. In stage 2, you secure your retirement, including three key components: Social Security, a home, and an IRA or other retirement funds. Finally, at stage 3, you consider investing in high-earning vehicles.

The best investment philosophy is "keep it simple." Unless you are very sophisticated financially, it is easy to lose your way in a maze of investments. As a starting point only, this chapter is designed to provide you with an overview of the investment arena. To prepare your finances for analysis, you will first create your own balance sheet to establish your present position. Next you will focus on your financial goals and the preparation of your own plan. Finally, you will consider investment vehicles according to where you are in the three-stage growth process.

The various investment possibilities are discussed in the following sections.

Stage 1. "Institutional Savings" and "Government Bonds."

Stage 2. "Social Security," "A Home or Rent-Replacement Fund," and "Retirement Plans."

Stage 3. "Corporate Bonds," "Stocks," "Other Real Estate Investments," "High-Risk Investments," and "New Business Ventures."

When you finish the materials presented here, you should stop by the library to look at books and articles devoted to the investments that interest you most. Talk to friends and experts. Take time to get advice from a CPA and an attorney if substantial sums are involved or if contracts need to be drawn or signed. Learn all you can before putting your money in investments that are new to you.

WHERE YOU ARE NOW: YOUR BALANCE SHEET

The key to creating growth is first to recognize what you have by outlining your present position. You need to make up a balance sheet: a summary of what you own (your assets) minus what you owe (your liabilities). (Our character Sherry Marshall did the same.) By putting your facts on paper you can take stock of your financial situation.

Using table 42 on pages 178–79, fill in your assets, including cash and cash equivalents, personal property, real estate, and investments. Then list all of your liabilities by category, including current bills, amount owed on loans, taxes due, and any other debts. At this point, you're ready to obtain your net worth by subtracting your total liabilities from your total assets. Once you know your "worth," you have a realistic starting point for financial goal-setting.

WHERE YOU WANT TO BE: YOUR PLAN

To ensure growth you must first plan. In contrast to budgeting for cash flow, which involves setting and meeting short-term

TABLE 42.   BALANCE SHEET

What You Own (Assets)

Cash and cash equivalents
   Cash on hand $_____
   Cash in checking accounts   _____
   Cash in savings accounts   _____
   Life insurance cash value   _____
   Savings Bonds   _____
   Money owed you   _____
Personal property*
   Household furnishings   _____
   Special items (car, boat, jewelry, furs,
      antiques, tools, art, etc.)   _____
   Miscellaneous personal property   _____
Real estate*
   Your house   _____
   Other properties   _____
Investments
   Stocks   _____
   Bonds   _____
   Government securities   _____
   Mutual funds   _____
   Other investments   _____
   Equity interest in your own business _____
   Vested interest in pension or profit
      sharing (money now owed you, even if you
      leave your firm)
   IRA, Keogh, or 401(k) retirement savings _____

Total Assets $_____

What You Owe (Liabilities)

Current bills
   Charge account balances $_____
   Credit cards
   Utilities   _____
   Rent   _____
   Insurance premiums   _____
   Taxes
   Other bills   _____
Amount owed on loans
   Mortgage
   Auto loan   _____

TABLE 42—*Continued*

Personal loans	_____
Installment loans	_____
Life insurance loans	_____
Taxes due	_____
Other	_____
Total Liabilities	$_____

Net Worth

Total assets	$_____
Total liabilities	_____
Net worth (assets minus liabilities)	$_____

*Estimated currnet market value.

---

goals, financial planning is concerned with longer time periods, from three years to a lifetime.

Map out your goals for next year, then for the next five years, ten years, and for retirement. Keep in mind that at each point in your financial life, goals are dependent on what has been previously accomplished. For example, if you already have savings in the bank, a good retirement plan, and own a home, now is the time to branch out and investigate new ways of making money. However, if you have accomplished none of these primary goals, then your initial goal is to start the necessary saving to reach these three basics.

If you are part of a couple, your spouse will also need to be involved in the goal setting. If you decide to set aside $1,000 a month while your spouse is thinking of buying a new stereo, your plans will not work. Mutual goal setting is a must.

The next step is to write down a growth plan that works for you, given the long-term goals you have set (see table 43). Data gathering as well as accruing the necessary funds are both key parts of the planning process. For instance, if you have decided that you'd like to own a home in five years, find the means to raise enough funds for your down payment target. If one of your goals is to open an IRA, your plan should include finding a bank or brokerage house where you'd like to open the account, as well as gathering information about fees and deposits required.

TABLE 43.   GROWTH PLAN

Name _____

Date _____ Age _____

Planned retirement date _____
Years to retirement   _____
Current net worth   _____

1. Four goals for this year:

   A. _____
   B. _____
   C. _____
   D. _____

2. In 5 years, my ideal financial position will include.

   A. _____
   B. _____
   C. _____
   D. _____

3. My desired net worth:

   A. In 1 year _____
   B. In 5 years _____
   C. In 10 years _____
   D. In 15 years _____
   E. At the end of my earning career _____

4. My goals for retirement:

   A. Personal _____
   B. Financial _____

5. What I need to retire: (70% of current life-style is standard)

   A. Pension _____
   B. Financial security _____
   C. Home or rental property _____

6. What I must do to reach my goals:

   A. Amount to save/invest _____
   B. Number of years until retirement _____
   C. Amount needed per year _____

A Note on Experts. Before we start the exercises, a word about professional advisers is in order. Anna Seaver found herself in trouble by listening to poor expert advice, while Kate English failed to seek it soon enough. You need to become as expert as you are able yourself to take control of your financial affairs. Even if you hire topflight advisers, to get the best use out of them, you must have command of the basics.

Expert misadventure is all too common. Let's take the case of financial planners. Consumers Union—the prestigious consumer-research outfit—has concluded that most consumers would be better off doing their own plans and avoiding these often sales-oriented professionals. Consumers Union recommends that you resort to a paid planner only if you are unable to create and follow a workable plan for yourself.

Although there are individual planners who are competent, the planning industry is not well regulated and the credentials are not so impressive as they sound. A planning credential involves—at most—several hours of undergraduate instruction and an examination. A bachelor's degree is often held but is not a requirement, according to the Institute of Certified Financial Planners. By comparison, attorneys complete three years of graduate school and take a bar examination; CPAs undergo rigorous examinations as well.

Many planners earn their money from commissions they make from products they sell to clients, creating potential conflicts of interest between the client's needs and their own. Conflicts of interest are diminished with fee-only planners.

People turn to planners because the number of products on the market makes it difficult to choose among competing alternatives. Scattershot reference books and articles leave us with more information but not the analysis necessary.

To help you order your investments, use the three stages developed here. Don't tantalize yourself or waste your energy on complicated investment alternatives until you have brought the basics under control. Work through these stages, and when you are ready to make an investment, use the guidelines here to make your choices.

Once you have made your own plan, you can then turn to a broker or other salesperson to make your purchase. But reserve the basic planning choices for yourself.

The best approach to experts is to assemble a team for yourself. The team should be put together carefully, using business and personal contacts to find people whose outlooks and investment philosophies fit your own. Most important, your team should be composed of people that you trust, and that trust should be built upon a pattern of involvement over time.

Start by selecting a general business attorney and a CPA whose practices match your needs. If you are a small consumer with simplified affairs, you don't need a major national law or accounting firm—and the associated fees. On the other hand, if your affairs are complex and you are a person with great resources, you will need more sophisticated (and expensive) advice.

Once you have built a working relationship with these two basic team members, you can branch out and add a planner or other general adviser should you still feel the need for additional points of view.

Keep in mind that any advice will be useful only if it fits your needs. Likewise, any investment—whether a multimillion-dollar real estate development or a $25 Savings Bond—ultimately involves a person exercising a judgment, in consultation with her team, about what is right for her.

Stages of Growth

The key to successful investing is to start with what is practical for your situation and then build from there. Thus, you should not enter stage 3 of investment without completing stages 1 and 2. At stage 1, you will start on a solid savings program. At stage 2, you will begin building a well-rounded retirement base. Finally, at stage 3, you will explore riskier investments offering higher rewards. But remember, greater chances for loss often accompany greater potential earnings.

To summarize, the three stages of growth are:

Stage 1. Saving for Future Investments. Begin savings. Accumulate a minimum of $5,000 (the basic entry ticket to many higher-earning investments) or more, depending upon your monthly cash-flow needs in case of emergency.

Stage 2. Securing Your Retirement. The three-pillared plan includes Social Security, a home or other real estate, and an IRA, pension, or other retirement fund.

Stage 3. Investing for Maximum Growth. Now turn to considering higher risk/higher growth investments.

STAGE 1: SAVING FOR FUTURE INVESTMENTS

If you have not already begun to save, start a savings program. Your target should be between 5 and 10 percent of your income, including any voluntary pensions or retirement funds. Until you have accumulated funds in the $5,000 to $15,000 range, it is difficult to begin serious investing. Also, if you experience a financial emergency, as the average person does once every five years, you will have nothing to fall back on unless you save now. Thus if you don't have any capital saved, invest in low-risk savings vehicles that will help you build funds for future investments.

Institutional Savings

Keep your initial investment dollars in cash and cash convertibles until you have enough to move into less liquid but more profitable alternatives. Savings accounts, money-market accounts, and similar funds provide modest to competitive interest. Financial institutions' requirements vary in terms of initial deposit, interest rates, and account services.

SAVINGS ACCOUNTS

A savings account can be in an investment bank, savings and loan, or credit union on which single or compound interest is paid. The account is insured up to a statutory limit (now $100,000) by the Federal Deposit Insurance Corporation (FDIC), the Federal Savings and Loan Insurance Company (FSLIC), or the National Credit Union Administration (NCUA).

Although these accounts offer modest earnings and, ordinarily, little risk, watch how often interest is paid. Daily is best because that interest earns interest through compounding. Banks and savings and loans have maximum interest set by law, while credit unions usually offer a point or two higher. Although a savings account is a good entry point, you should choose one only if you have small amounts to save, because other accounts offer higher interest rates.

NOW AND SUPER NOW ACCOUNTS

If you routinely keep the required minimum in checking accounts, review whether you would be better off earning interest.

Open a NOW (Negotiable Order of Withdrawal) Account, an interest-earning checking account. As a result of bank deregulation, federal law mandates no maximum interest-rate ceilings if a minimum balance is kept. Interest-bearing checking accounts are federally insured up to $100,000 by FDIC and FSLIC institutions. Super NOW accounts offer higher minimum and interest than regular NOW accounts, but lower than money-market bank accounts.

Transfers and service fees are set by institutions, so check the details. And, don't forget this interest earned when tax time comes.

MONEY-MARKET BANK (DEPOSIT) ACCOUNTS

Both banks and brokerage houses offer "money-market" vehicles. Banks offer money-market bank accounts that provide high interest rates but require larger minimum deposits than a savings account. Your money is invested in highly secured, short-term investments such as certificates of deposit, bankers' acceptances, and government acceptance notes. The funds are insured up to the FDIC or FSLIC maximum of $100,000. Your money is pooled with that of other investors so you earn higher interest than you would acting alone.

Bank money-market accounts pay more competitive interest than savings accounts, riding three to four points above prime, although rates vary constantly. While your money compounds in the accounts, your funds are liquid. You may withdraw limited funds with a check, and you must maintain a minimum balance set individually by the institution.

Institutions offering money-market accounts also set their own rates, so compare rates and frequency of compounding. Remember, the more often your money compounds, the better.

CERTIFICATES OF DEPOSIT

For a minimum deposit of as little as $500 at most banks and savings and loans, you can purchase a Certificate of Deposit, or "CD." CDs are like interest-bearing savings account but have a set time before which the money can be withdrawn without a penalty. The benefit of this account is that the interest yield is generally higher than a regular savings account so you earn more.

If you have already saved a substantial amount, higher entry-ticket vehicles are an option for you.

GOVERNMENT SECURITIES

Some investment choices are government-backed mortgage securities and Treasury bills, which offer high yield and low risk. However, like all interest-bearing investments, their value is limited to the cash flow they generate. Government securities, offered by federal corporations in $25,000 certificates, can be purchased on a partial participation basis through a broker for $1,000.

Government and government-created agencies purchase mortgages on homes from individual borrowers and banks. The agencies then repackage such mortgages in groups, or "pools," for resale to investors. When the mortgagee makes his or her payment each month, the investor receives interest and principal on the original investment.

Popular securities are the "Ginnie Mae" for the GNMA, or Government National Mortgage Association; the "Freddie Mac," for the FHLC or Federal Home Loan Corporation; or "Sallie Mae," for the SLMA or Student Loan Marketing Association.

The GNMA and the FHLC are almost identical agencies. Although both were created by an act of Congress, only the Ginnie Mae is insured by the federal government and based on federal government securities. It is considered a safe investment because Uncle Sam guarantees a monthly payment of interest and principal. The Freddie Mac, in essence, is backed by the U.S. housing market and based on conventional securities.

The main difference in safety between the two is considered academic by experts. If the U.S. housing market were to collapse, causing widespread defaulting on mortgages, the federal government would have to take unusual steps to cover all its debts. The government does not insure a constant market value for your Ginnie Mae or Freddie Mac, as the safety of either investment is affected by fluctuating interest rates. You can lose money if you sell your Ginnie Mae or Freddie Mac at a lower market value (because of high interest rates) than when you bought it. Conversely, your investment will appreciate if the economy's interest rates are lower than the rate you locked in when you bought it.

Also, if interest rates in the economy drop, the mortgagee, who can pay back his or her mortgage anytime, may choose to take advantage of the low rates and pay off his or her mortgage loan. This early repayment forces investors to get their capital back faster than they expected and gives earnings less interest than planned.

Other differences between the two are superficial and can vary. Freddie Macs may sometimes have a slightly higher yield. It is best to examine the market when you are ready to invest and choose the option that is most affordable at that time.

Bonds

A bond is a loan to a corporation or government, whereas a stock is an ownership interest. As a creditor, a bondholder's worth is almost always more secure than that of a shareholder owner.

Corporate bonds are a loan to a company offering to pay back the capital along with interest. Government bonds—whether to the Treasury, an independent agency, or a municipal government—are a similar loan backed by a government entity.

The borrower (for example, the issuing entity) pays the lender a specific amount of interest (rate of return) over a set period of time and repays the principal investment at an agreed-upon date ("maturity"). The interest rate is generally a fixed percentage of the bond's face value, and the interest on most bonds is paid twice a year. The trading price of bonds may vary with the economy.

If you want interest or cash flow rather than an equity growth investment and you are in a position to have your money in place for a time, then look at bonds. For example, if your prime concern is to supplement your earnings, then bond income would make sense. During a deflationary period, bonds are attractive because they offer a fixed rate of interest that, if prices are dropping, would remain higher than the market.

By contrast, in a highly inflationary period, bonds—like all fixed equity investments—would decline in value relative to the price of money. Bonds make sense for their security and predictability in a long-term investment setting where cash flow rather than growth is key.

In this section, we shall review the safer bond investments such as U.S. Savings Bonds and municipal bonds. Riskier investments such as corporate and junk bonds will be discussed in stage 3.

U.S. SAVINGS BONDS

If you have only a little money to invest, try a U.S. Government Savings Bond. Sold in $25 denominations at banks and through payroll deductions, the series EE bond matures in ten years and pays full interest only at maturity. With $25 you can purchase a bond with a face value of $50; after ten years, the bond will be worth the full face value. You cannot cash the bond during the first six months, but thereafter you can get your money back, losing some of your interest. However, if you hold the bond for at least five years you are guaranteed a minimum return. As an added bonus, EE bonds give you the option at maturity to "roll over" your earnings to a new series of bonds (HH bonds, which further defer taxes until they are mature), which provide higher interest and are only available to previous bondholders.

Rates of U.S. Savings Bonds vary but usually stand near those for passbook savings, which makes their after-tax yield higher considering deferral.

OTHER GOVERNMENT BONDS

Other government bonds are issued at the state, regional, or local levels. Often called municipal bonds ("muni bonds" or "munis" for short), you earn interest that is usually exempt from federal taxes. If the bond was issued by your home state, you may be exempt from state or local taxes, depending on the type of bond. When the bonds are exempt at both state and local levels, they are known as "double-tax-exempt bonds." Municipal bonds' yields are low compared to taxable bonds with similar maturities, but you must evaluate these bonds in light of your tax position to find the better buy for you. For example, in the 15 percent tax bracket, you would have to yield 10 percent in a non-tax-advantaged bond to equal 8.5 percent in a double-tax-exempt bond.

Muni bonds are offered in $1,000 and $5,000 denominations. They are widely traded and are generally considered low-risk investments.

Yet, different types of muni bonds have varying risks, and a government entity in trouble can create risk. *General obligation* bonds are backed by the taxing power of the issuer. That is, if the issuer is the state of California, the state's ability to collect money through taxes backs the general obligation bond. This bond is sold to generate capital for the issuer. A riskier muni bond is the *revenue bond,* which is backed only by the projected money made from the project they are sold to finance. Thus it is a good idea to check which kind of bond you are acquiring.

For a slightly lower interest rate you can "insure" your muni bond and protect its safety for no additional cost. You do not pay a separate fee for insurance; rather, the issuer pays the premium and makes up the cost by offering you a somewhat lower (usually one-tenth to one-third) interest rate than on uninsured bonds.

Likewise, Treasury bills offer a safe investment through a loan to the federal government that accrues interest until the date of the bill's maturity (a year or less). The purchase price for Treasury bills fluctuates with the economy, but is usually offered at a discount rate a few hundred dollars less than the bill's $10,000 face value price. T-bills are auctioned off weekly at branches of the Federal Reserve Bank and can be purchased through the Federal Reserve Bank and its branches, or through commercial banks or brokerage houses (a small fee is common at banks and brokerage houses).

Formerly sold only in $10,000 increments, T-bills were out of reach for smaller investors. Now, however, you can invest in them through a money-market fund, which usually requires a minimum investment of only $1,000.

Besides security and higher rates, the major advantage T-bills have over conventional savings is their exemption from state and local income taxes. You still owe federal taxes, but a T-bill's income is deferred until maturity, making it a good source of income deferral for short-term tax planning purposes.

Be aware, however, that currently available investments like T-bills may not be available in the future. The Social Security fund is required by law to invest its assets solely in government securities. Some analysts predict that with the current surplus in the Social Security fund, the market availability of Treasury securities will be severely limited because the mandatory Social Security investment will use all available government funds. This prediction is a good reminder that even the most routine investment is affected by a variety of economic forces.

As a general rule, you should pay off your debts before you save. The interest paid on credit cards is double or triple what you would make through savings. However, if your investments earn more than the amount you pay for credit or if you would be tempted to reuse your credit, then combine saving and debt reduction. If you do not have the discipline not to overuse your cards, consider retiring them to a safe place and pay cash, using and paying off your cards only occasionally to keep them active.

Once you get into the habit of saving, you should build a cushion of at least three months' expenses. If your income varies, your line of work is insecure, or your health unsteady, you will need an even larger cushion. With these funds in hand, you will be able to move to the next step, that of securing your future retirement.

STAGE 2: SAVING FOR A SECURE RETIREMENT

Stage 2 is divided into three parts—all important to securing your retirement. The three components are Social Security benefits; home ownership; and a pension, an IRA, or another type of retirement plan. Unless you have taken care of these, there is no point advancing to more complex investment strategies.

Unfortunately, statistics suggest that very few women have managed to attain these fundamental prerequisites to advanced investing. Although a high percentage of women are joint homeowners with their husbands, of the 64 percent of Americans living in owner-occupied residences, the number of women owning homes (without a husband present) remains a low 13 percent. Most unmarried women and single women who head households remain renters. Only 21.5 percent of women are entitled to any kind of pension, compared to 45.2 percent of men. Of all taxpayers, in 1986 only 15 percent had opened an Individual Retirement Account; with tax reform and accompanying changes in eligibility rules, the number dropped to 6.8 percent in 1987.

Component 1: Social Security

If like many women you will receive Social Security benefits for retirement, you have completed component 1 of stage 2. Although the income will not be sufficient to live on, it does offer support to the other two retirement pillars.

Your benefit level as an individual retiree will be calculated based on your earnings and the number of years you have been employed. If you are married, under current law, you will get half the benefit of your spouse, if your spouse earned more than you did. Or, you can choose to take your benefit in full and your spouse will get half of your payment.

If you are divorced after having been married for ten years or more, you are entitled to draw on your former spouse's account (formerly, twenty years of marriage were required). If you have earned your own Social Security through employment, you have a choice of the higher benefits—your own or half your former spouse's. More than one spouse can claim retirement benefits; your former spouse's remarriage will not affect this right.

With some 205 million Social Security accounts, there are bound to be mistakes. To ensure that you are receiving credit for the income you have earned, periodically check that your earnings are being correctly reported. To check your account, request a "statement of earnings" form (No. SSA7004) from your local Social Security office or from the Commissioner of Social Security, 6410 Security Boulevard, Baltimore, Maryland 21235. A few weeks after you return the completed form, you should receive a review of your work life and earnings as recorded by the Social Security Administration.

Depending on your age and what new policies government sets, retirees in the future could face uncertainties with the system. People who retired at age sixty-five in 1986 could expect a maximum benefit of $760 a month, depending on their employment and earnings record. However, 60 percent of current retirees chose early retirement at age sixty-two and thus received 80 percent of the benefit they would have received had they waited till age sixty-five.

Benefits are always under review. For example, budget discussions frequently look at the possibility of reducing cost-of-living allowances and shifting the age at which payment commences. In addition, the 1983 reforms in the Social Security system provided that for retirees born after 1938, the retirement age will be increased by two months for each year up to the new maximum benefit retirement age of sixty-seven for those born after 1960. Early retirement at age sixty-two will still be an option, but the benefit will be decreased to 70 percent of the maximum paid at age sixty-seven.

Under current law, if you reach age sixty-five in 1994 or later, you will need to have been employed for ten years or forty quarters to collect your full retirement benefit. If you are age fifty-five and have not been contributing fully to the Social Security system (by deducting Social Security taxes from your paycheck), you should make a point of doing so, even if you must pay additional self-employment tax.

If you are drawing Social Security benefits, a portion of them may be taxable. The formula is best explained by reference to an example.

Your base amount is (1) $32,000 if your filing status is married filing jointly, (2) zero if married filing separately, and (3) $25,000 for any other filing status.

Look at Janet and George Jones's taxes for an illustration of this calculation. They have an adjusted gross income of $25,000 for 1988. Janet, who is retired, receives Social Security benefits of $7,200 per year. The couple also receives $8,000 per year from a mutual fund that invests solely in tax-exempt municipal bonds. On their joint return for 1988, the couple would make the following computation to determine if any of Janet's Social Security benefits must be included in their gross income:

TABLE 44.   JONES'S SOCIAL SECURITY TAX COMPUTATION

1. Adjusted gross income*	$25,000
2. Plus all tax-exempt interest†	8,000
3. Modified adjusted gross income	33,000
4. Plus half of Janet's Social Security benefits	3,600
5. Combined income	36,600
6. Minus base amount‡	32,000
7. Excess above base amount	4,600
8. Half of excess above base amount	2,300
9. Half of Social Security benefits	3,600
10. Amount includible in gross income (lesser of 8 or 9)	$ 1,300

*Includes taxable interest.
†For the purpose of calculating this tax, interest from sources such as nontaxable municipal bonds is included in income. This prevents people with large nontaxable investments from having a loophole on this tax.
‡The base amount is (1) $32,000 if your filing status is married filing jointly, (2) zero if married filing separately, and (3) $25,000 for any other filing status.

In order to keep this part of your retirement solid, keep abreast of the changes in retirement rules such as selecting the age at which you will retire. In so doing, you will receive full benefit from this cornerstone of your retirement plan.

Component 2: Investing in a Home- or Rent-Replacement Fund

Component 2 for building a solid retirement is purchasing a home. In terms of future security and growth, purchasing property is the most significant investment you can make. Real estate outperforms other investments. Residential real estate provides the classic trade-off between tax shelter and growth. The interest is by and large deductible as are property taxes. As for capital gains, with a residence you can roll over or defer paying tax on the profits as long as you buy a new home of equal or greater value within two years of the sale of your original home.

Most real estate investments require a cash down payment. The down payment feature creates one of real estate's attractions—leveraging. A *leveraged* transaction uses a small amount of money plus borrowed funds to produce a potentially large gain or loss. In corporate takeover, a leveraged buyout is the taking over of a company by means of borrowed funds with the target company's funds serving as collateral for loans. Likewise, in real estate, the asset itself—the property—becomes the collateral for the real estate loan.

With real estate, normally you pay 20 percent down, but deals with 10, 5 percent, or even nothing down are possible depending on market conditions, interest rates, and your credit. If the market grows, you earn equity appreciation on the bank's money as well as on your own.

Yet another plus to buying real estate is that it offers steady growth, especially in inflationary times. If you purchase a home, your rent won't rise. As the cost of living goes up, your home mortgage will stay the same (or be adjusted slightly if you have a variable interest mortgage).

As a key part of retirement planning, a secure living space is critical. But not all of us will be able to afford to purchase our own homes. If you have been permanently priced out of the housing market, it is critical that you take active steps to ensure you can afford to be a renter by retirement time.

You will need to set aside enough to cover your rent today plus inflation, assuming you would want to continue at your current life-style level. Although there isn't an exact correlation between rents and inflation, rents, in general, rise parallel to the inflation rate. To figure the amount of rent money you would need in the future, you would have to estimate the affect of inflation.

Inflation levels cannot be predicted with certainty. Over the last decade, inflation rose by 84 percent. Assuming the past decade is a reasonable guide, if your rent in 1990 stands at $1,000, by the year 2000 the equivalent rent would be $1,840 and by 2010, $3,680. Among your investments, savings, pensions, and Social Security, you have to conserve enough resources to pay your future inflation-adjusted rent—a "home-replacement fund."

With these numbers, such a task can seem overwhelming. A key strategy is to put your home-replacement fund in investments that do have growth potential so that they, too, will rise with inflation and keep pace with rising rents.

Figuring zero inflation, for $12,000 rent a year (or $1,000 a month) at 10 percent interest (that's high), you would need a fund of $120,000 on top of all other living expenses to defray your annual rent of $12,000. If the home-replacement fund is in an equity-growth investment, you could figure on this target amount.

To reach a fund of $120,000, you need to set aside $12,000 a year to retire in ten years (not counting compounding interest).

Depending on your age, the number of years to retirement, and your expectations about retirement life-style, you need to add a target for rent replacement to your current growth strategy. Obviously, if retirement is years off, this component can be a small amount. But if retirement is near, you must make this an absolute priority. (Of course, in the unlikely event of steady deflation between now and your retirement, you will be that much better off, because your savings will be worth more.) Reaching this level of savings will obviously be impossible for many women. The alternative is to live in reduced circimstances for an unknown number of retirement years or to purchase property.

Above all else, if necessary, sacrifice savings liquidity to buy a home. Even though you may violate the recommended savings level of three to six months of income, if these savings are the only source of your down payment and you can get into a home of your own, in almost all cases, you should buy the house. Even though your liquidity will be low, you will have assets to fall back on and you can build your savings again.

These benefits make purchasing a home a very attractive investment. Once you have the funds for a down payment, you will watch your equity grow as you pay off your mortgage and approach retirement. But again, if you cannot purchase, engage in the rent-replacement strategy.

Component 3: An IRA, Pension, or Other Retirement Fund

A secure retirement fund is retirement component 3. If you qualify for a company pension with sufficient vested benefits (meaning you will receive the funds even if you change jobs, usually after a minimum of five years), then you have this base covered.

IRAS

If you qualify for full tax breaks and if you have no pension or a small one, funding an Individual Retirement Account (IRA) is the best option to begin building retirement funds.

By utilizing an IRA, you can trade current cash flow for tax savings and future growth. IRAs allow you to set aside funds for retirement while permitting you to defer taxes. Currently, you can qualify for tax deferment if you are not actively involved in a company pension or even with a pension, if your taxable income is below $25,000, if single, or $40,000, if married. (Note: Reinstating IRAs for all income levels has substantial political support; check for possible changes in the law.) The maximum IRA contribution is $2,000 annually for an individual earner, $4,000 per two-earner couple, or $2,250 where only one person in a couple is employed. At higher incomes, the tax-deferred contribution will be reduced on a sliding scale up to an adjusted gross income of $50,000 for married filers, or up to $35,000 for single-income earners or heads of household. Even if you do not qualify for deferral on the contributions, the interest earned is deferred.

IRA accounts can range from interest-only savings accounts, to equity-based investments like mutual funds and stocks, but an IRA grows much more quickly than monies put away with after-tax funds because of the tax-shelter feature. If you invest the same amount of money in an IRA for thirty years that you put in a non-tax-advantaged account, for the 15 percent bracket you will gain almost $100,000 more in the IRA. In the 20 and 30 percent brackets, your funds will gain even more by comparison.

TABLE 45.   IRA GROWTH TABLE

YEARS	IRA* (NO TAX)†	NON-IRA/TAX BRACKET‡		
		15%	28%	33%
10	$ 31,875	$ 27,363	$ 21,531	$ 19,390
20	114,550	89,231	64,683	56,476
30	328,998	229,114	151,171	127,410

*$2,000 per year at 10 percent interest.
†Taxed upon retirement at the then prevailing rates.
‡Investment of $2,000 reduced by tax each year: for example, at 15 percent, $1,700; 28 percent, $1,440; 33 percent, $1,340. All interest at 10 percent.

Withdrawals from IRAs must begin by age seventy and a half and a penalty fee is charged for withdrawal before age fifty-nine and a half. You can take money out of the account and pay a penalty if funds are needed early.

If you are considering investing in an IRA, but are afraid early withdrawal penalties will outweigh gains, consider that there is a crossover point at which you can actually come out ahead even with the penalty. Because the crossover point depends on interest rates, if you earn 8 percent interest on your monies in the IRA the first year and must make an early withdrawal with a penalty of 10 percent, you will lose 2 percent. But, after two years, you will have made 16 percent on the capital, not compounded, and with a 10 percent penalty for early withdrawal, you will have crossed over into a gain of 6 percent.

Remember, however, that taxes must be paid on the withdrawn sum according to your bracket. For example, a $2,000 withdrawal the second year would incur a 10 percent penalty of $200 plus $560 in taxes if you are in the 28 percent bracket. So you pay $760 to withdraw $2,000, leaving you with $1,240 cash and the balance in the account to continue to accrue tax-deferred interest. However, you would have had the use of the money tax-free for two years.

Given the tax and growth advantages, funding an IRA makes sense even for people with fairly low liquidity.

PENSION PLANS

A pension plan is an investment made over time in which the earnings are reinvested and are then released in a series of payments after retirement.

Pension plans vary. In some plans, both employees and employers contribute regularly to the investment, but the usual is an employer-sponsored *defined-benefit* pension program. The employer promises to pay the employee a specified amount per year at retirement. Most fall into two categories regardless of the yield.

Another choice is the *defined-contribution* plan, which sets the size of the contribution and pays out whatever yield the investment has accrued.

These pension benefits are insured up to $25,000 even if the company goes bankrupt. A *self-directed* program, however, makes the employee responsible for the investment decisions, and the employer is not required to insure it. Take time to learn the details of your fund.

The major benefit of a pension plan—apart from the retirement security it provides—is the income tax shelter it provides for both the employer and the employee. The employer's contributions are deductible, and the employees defer tax payment on pension income until the monies are received. Thus, an individual may well choose to take a lower-paying position that offers a higher pension benefit.

Three points particularly concern women. Federal law requires that pensions must vest (you own it) and be portable (even if you move jobs) after five years. This provision protects women, whose work lives often involve interruptions.

Second, in the past wives found themselves left with pension choices made by spouses. Since most women outlive men, in general if you are dependent on a husband's pension, you will want longer, lower payments keyed to your expected longevity rather than shorter, higher payments geared to his. By law, wives now must be given the option for informed consent.

Finally, upon divorce, some pension benefits may still be yours. Check federal and state law and make sure you don't lose your rightful share.

401(к)

As a supplement or an alternative to the company pension, consider a "401(k) plan" (named after the section of the IRS code that defines it) if your company offers one. These *salary-reduction* plans involve employees' voluntarily diverting pre-tax salary to retirement or other employee benefit programs. Salary reduction is an excellent solution if you will not be with an employer long enough to qualify for full regular pension benefits from the company plan.

Although only a small number of employers currently offer 401(k) plans, they do report high employee participation rates (according to the Association of Private Pension and Welfare Plans). In fact, workers in the $10,000 to $25,000 annual earnings range who are offered the option of participating in salary-reduction plans do so at double the rates of IRA participants.

People employed by IRS code 501(c)(3) organizations—public school systems and certain nonprofit educational, charitable, literary, scientific, or religious organizations—are eligible for a similar salary-reduction plan under IRS code 403(b). The plan for nonprofit employees offers tax benefits similar to those in the 401(k). In addition, the employer has the option to contribute an additional amount in the employee's name to increase the employee's retirement benefit.

Both salary-reduction plans offer tax benefits to the employer as well as to the employee. However, antidiscrimination provisions limit an employer's contributions to 125 percent of his or her employee's voluntary contributions. Your maximum reduction is $7,000, indexed for inflation annually. (In 1988, the indexed amount stood at $7,313; in 1989, the figure was $7,627. The IRS announces the indexed amount during each tax year —therefore, check annually for the current figure. See also Appendix 7.) Every dollar you take out of your salary for these plans is a dollar less that you will be able to contribute to your IRA. For instance, if you have a $500 401(k), your maximum IRA contribution would be $1,500 rather than $2,000. Likewise, your IRA contribution reduces your 401(k); the combined total for the two cannot exceed the indexed maximum 401(k) limit.

KEOGHS

If you are self-employed and can afford to save more than the $2,000 upper limit on an IRA, take advantage of a Keogh plan.

A Keogh plan is a pension fund for any person who reports earnings from self-employment, regardless of how small. Generally, there are three situations where you might encounter a Keogh—as an employee, as a self-employed person, or as partner or member of a board of directors.

If you are employed by someone else, your employer may contribute to your Keogh plan. If so, he or she is required by antidiscrimination laws to contribute the same percentage of your income to your Keogh as your employer contributes to his or her own Keogh. Usually, this contribution comes from the employer and not from your salary.

If you are not self-employed, this is the only way a Keogh may apply to you.

If, however, you are the sole proprietor of a business, you may set up a Keogh for yourself. There are two basic types of Keogh plans: *defined-contribution* plans and *defined-benefit* plans. With defined-contribution plans (discussed below), you contribute a certain amount of your income, which is fixed by law. On the other hand, a defined-benefit plan allows annual payments according to your predetermined retirement income needs. This plan works best if you have ample discretionary funds and are fairly close to retirement.

Defined-contribution plans are the most common types of Keoghs. They offer two options, depending on your payment plan. If you fix an annual percentage of income to be contributed when you first open the account, you may contribute up to 20 percent of your earned income with a $30,000 maximum. However, if you want to have the option of paying differing percentages each year, you may contribute up to 13 percent of your earned income.

Partners and members of boards of directors (and self-employed people who employ others) may also open Keoghs. However, remember, if you employ others, you must match percentages with their salaries, potentially making a Keogh very expensive.

With Keogh plans, no matter what type, you determine

whether the funds will be released in a lump sum or in installments. You also decide how you want the funds invested—in a money market, mutual fund insurance policy, an interest-bearing bank account, or any combination of these. However, you do have certain limitations with your Keogh such as those on IRAs. For instance, you are generally not allowed to withdraw money without a penalty until age fifty-nine and a half or until you become disabled. And, you must begin withdrawing money from your Keogh plan when you reach age seventy and a half, even if you have not yet retired.

The calculations in Keoghs are complex, so it is a good idea to seek professional advice if you are considering this plan.

ANNUITIES

If you have a minimum of $2,500, you may want to consider an annuity as a supplement to retirement. An annuity is an insurance plan under which the holder pays a set sum of money to a life insurance company. This money (plus interest) is then paid back at a predetermined date either for a set period of time or for the life of the policyholder.

You can cash in an annuity at any time, although there is a penalty for early withdrawal. The smallest annuity available is usually $2,500. The insurance company will apply charges that include a sales fee.

You receive a tax break with a deferred annuity as the interest accrues with taxes deferred until withdrawal at retirement. This option is a good supplementary retirement plan.

Whatever type of fund you choose to round out your retirement plan, make sure that it fits into your personal plan. Once you have established your retirement through this three-component plan, you are ready for the third and final stage of growth—advanced investing.

STAGE 3: INVESTING FOR MAXIMUM GROWTH

At growth stage 3 you can begin putting some of your savings into higher-yield investments. Though these investments are either riskier and/or require a higher entry fee, they can provide you with great financial growth because your capital earns more income. You should not begin advanced investing until you have built up solid savings and retirement plans.

The decision about which investment to make depends on economic factors such as inflation, deflation, interest rates, and tax laws. The general rules of thumb are as follows:

> If you are betting on *inflation,* pick real estate, stocks, and items such as collectibles, art, and antiques. Use credit for buying now and paying later.

> If you project *deflation,* invest in bonds, mortgages, or other fixed-rate investments. Because of falling interest rates, real estate will not be an attractive option.

Keep in mind the direction of the economy when choosing from among the investment vehicles. Be prepared to shift your strategies depending on changing economic circumstances. Never overlook personal preferences. Your investment must fit you.

A simplified way of approaching advanced investing is to look at the opportunities by category. If you see investments that interest you, then the real work starts. Use the overview here to indicate directions for intensive self-education. Use the library. Talk to experts and follow business page coverage of investments that tempt you. At each step of the way, keep an open but critical attitude as well as a healthy dose of realism. Underestimate any returns promised, overestimate any costs. Keep in mind that every investment is subject to changing conditions. If returns were a sure thing, we would not need money and investment advice.

Corporate Bonds

Corporations, like the government, issue bonds. Industrial, manufacturing, transportation, and utility companies are a few examples of corporations that issue bonds. Trading prices of bonds may vary according to fluctuations in the economy. With most bonds, the purchaser earns both "yield," or cash-flow payment, and appreciation.

Corporate bonds come in several types. *Registered* bonds automatically pay every six months, whereas *coupon* bonds are sent in by the bondholder (investor) in order to receive payment. Both pay interest on a regular basis. Most bonds today are registered.

A third type, *zero-coupon bonds,* are sold at a discount to the face value (much the same procedure as U.S. government EE bonds, discussed above) rather than paying periodic or fixed interest.

Corporate bond yields are often higher than those of federal bonds, but they are also riskier because the investor's security rests on the fortune of the company that issued the bond. It is important to check bond ratings before investing. Bonds are rated by two agencies, Moody's and Standard & Poor's, whose ratings books are in most public libraries. The best rating is AAA and the worst is D+. The "safe" range is considered AAA to BAA (for Moody's) or AAA to BBB (for Standard & Poor's). The agencies rate the bonds according to the issuer's perceived ability to make the required yearly interest payments and to repay the investor's principal when it comes due.

A bond's rating may significantly affect its market value. If the issuer's bond rating goes up, it means the bond is less risky but will therefore have a lower yield than before. This does not affect the bondholder, because the issuer cannot reduce the interest on its outstanding debts, but another investor will be willing to buy your bond for more than you paid, even with a lower current yield, as the risk of default is lower. Thus, the market value of your bond increases if the bond rating goes up.

Conversely, if the issuer's bond rating goes down, the market value of your bond would drop as buyers would require a higher yield to offset the higher risk.

Pay careful attention to the requirements surrounding your corporate bond. If your bond has a *call* option, issuers may require you to sell back your bond before it matures, making it a *callable* bond.

If your bond is callable, it will include a *call provision* in its contract. This provision contains the *call price,* which is the set number the issuer must pay you when he calls the bond back. The price is either face value or face value plus premium. Corporations may exercise their call option to reduce their debt or to refinance a debt at a lower interest rate.

Stocks

A stock represents a share in the ownership of a company. The size of the share is determined by the number of shares the company has offered. In theory, a stock's value is set by dividing a company's net assets by its outstanding shares. In practice, the value of the stock depends on both the success of the company and the perception of its success by the stock-buying public. If a company's stock is in demand, the stock's value increases. If a company's fortunes are perceived to be dwindling, investors will not want to buy shares, and the stock's value will decrease, even though objectively the company might offer solid earnings and assets.

To make a successful investment in the stock market, it is best to pick one or several stocks where you have personal knowledge of the marketplace. Your expertise relieves you from investigating and researching stocks about which you have no firsthand knowledge.

If you use a broker to do the actual trading, you will be charged. The commission varies: some charge a flat rate for all transactions, whereas others have a sliding scale based on the numbers and/or the price of the shares.

Despite the risk, stock ownership offers certain advantages. Widely traded stocks are very liquid (naturally, however, you run the risk of loss if you need to pull your money out when the stock is down). Banks will take stock as collateral for a loan.

Stocks are a good investment in inflationary periods when the market as a whole tends to rise in value parallel to inflation. Conversely, stocks ordinarily drop in value during deflationary times, and bonds become more attractive.

Many advisers suggest staying away from the stock market unless you have substantial assets and the time to follow the market. With institutional investors using computerized trading programs, it is difficult for small players to compete effectively.

DIVIDENDS, YIELD, AND APPRECIATION

Dividends are a percentage of a company's earnings paid out at regular intervals to its shareholders; appreciation is the amount a stock's value has risen. Yield is the annual dividend by the purchase price.

While there are many ways to categorize stocks, a useful distinction rests on the emphasis of income versus appreciation. *Income stocks* pay dividends on a regular basis, an advantage if you want a steady income from your investment. If you are looking for an investment emphasizing appreciation, choose *growth stocks*.

Taxation on stocks rests on the same basis as other income. (The previous exclusion for $200 in dividend income has been abolished.) Capital gains are also fully taxed with no exclusion. In addition, *capital losses* are limited to $3,000 over taxable gains per year, although you can carry stock losses over until the next tax year. In contrast to real estate, stocks offer no special treatment or depreciation deductions.

Real Estate Investments

Once you have a home you should consider investing in nonresidential real estate, which could range from a duplex to a multimillion-dollar office building. Real estate is an attractive investment because of leveraging and steady equity growth. However, you must feel comfortable with the extra work that may be involved with property. Even if you hire managers, property always involves maintenance, dealing with tenants, and the uncertainties of problems such as fire and flood.

Rental real estate offers the same growth and leverage advantages as residential real estate, and depending on your income and the amount invested, it offers tax breaks as well.

If you are interested in real estate, but want to limit your cash, time, and some of the hassles, look at a real estate partnership. Because the cost of the investment is shared, partnerships offer a low entry price, but fees and overhead can also reduce growth potential as well.

Remember that passive loss rules will limit the real estate

tax breaks with nonresidential real estate. With *residential* rental real estate, special rules state that an investor must meet specific income criteria in order to deduct amounts that in turn have ceilings set by law. As discussed below, special rules apply, so if you are interested in this investment, check the rules carefully.

VACATION HOME

Many of the same growth and tax benefits apply to a secondary or vacation home as to a primary residence. Certain special rules apply: the vacation home can only be rented to nonowners two weeks a year to qualify for a full tax break. Since you cannot rent it more often, you must carry the mortgage without much rental income to meet costs.

RENTAL AND COMMERCIAL REAL ESTATE

Rental and commercial real estate, like residential real estate, offers steady growth and leverage. Depending on your income and the amount invested, rental real estate offers additional tax breaks.

Rental real estate involves a much more complex set of factors than buying personal residential real estate. These include dealing with tenants, vacancies, and maintenance.

If you have the temperament to cope with the hassles, rental real estate can be a good source of appreciation and later income. Time and energy put into acquiring even one or two rental properties can assure a steady income later, provided you select locations that hold their value. At the opposite end of the investment spectrum, large real estate holdings offer greater growth potential and professional management, but also more risk.

Rental, residential, and commercial real estate count on a steady stream of renters, so you are betting on the economic prospects for a given geographic area. Before getting involved in rental real estate you want to examine the property market in the area.

No matter the size of the rental property, look at cash-flow projections and rental records. With any projections proposed by the seller, check assumptions about occupancy rates (85 to 95 percent would be standard) and proportional rent increases.

If statutory limits such as rent control apply, confirm that projected rises do not exceed the legally allowed amounts. Remember that any area can be subject to high vacancies in times of economic downturn, particularly those rentals in areas dependent on one or two industries.

In a tax context, real estate is by definition a *passive* investment and generally does not offer deductions against salaried incomes. But, for those whose incomes qualify, *active* investors can still get a tax deduction.

Taxpayers with less than $100,000 adjusted gross income can deduct up to $25,000 in rental losses, including interest and depreciation, provided they are actively involved in overseeing a *residential* rental property. For example, if a person owned a duplex and oversaw the renting and maintenance and the building stood empty for six months during refurbishing, she could deduct up to $25,000 of loss. (For those with adjusted gross incomes from $100,000 to $150,000 a sliding scale or "phaseout" applies, with the $25,000 limitation being reduced by 50 percent of the amount that your AGI exceeds $100,000.)

An additional rule requires that an investor be *at risk* to get deductions. At risk investments threaten a loss not only of initial outlay, but of additional assets. For instance, if you buy rental real estate property and the property is condemned, you will lose more than your initial investment if you signed a *recourse* mortgage (one that allows the mortgage holder to reach your other nonmortgaged assets if you default). However, in real estate, a special rule applies so that even nonrecourse notes count if they financed the property directly and are from a qualified lender.

The exception applies only for *residential* rental property. For commercial or office property, the passive loss rules mean that "passive" losses can only offset other "passive" gains, not salaried income.

REAL ESTATE PARTNERSHIPS

A real estate partnership involves two or more people investing in real estate together. A partnership can be as simple as two friends getting together and buying a home and as complicated as a multimillion-dollar public offering of limited partnership interests. In theory, real estate partnerships offer access to additional capital and property management to help allay the hassles of individual property ownership. Because the cost of the investment is shared, partnerships offer a low entry price, but as the size of the partnership grows, so does the overhead. Within a partnership, any income or tax deduction will pass to the individual partner and be taxed on the individual (in contrast to the corporate) level. Although passive loss rules expressly limit the use to which partnerships losses can be applied, partnerships offer growth and some tax shelter.

Disadvantages of partnerships include the necessary cooperation with partners, paying someone to organize the offering, managing both the partnership and the property, and low liquidity.

(Be certain that you check carefully how you take title. If you want your heirs to receive your share, take the title as *tenants in common.* If you want your partners to inherit your shares, take the title as *joint tenants,* which provides a "right of survivorship" or automatic inheritance to your partners, leaving your other heirs nothing.)

HISTORIC PROPERTIES / LOW-INCOME HOUSING

Congress has temporarily provided for tax breaks for investors in both rehabilitation housing and historic properties.

The rehabilitation of a historic property carries a tax credit of 20 percent of rehabilitation costs for property listed on the Regional Register of Historic Places and a $25,000 allowable deduction on losses if the active standard net adjusted gross income is below $200,000. The property must be listed on the National Register of Historic Landmarks. This tax shelter encourages renovation and preservation of landmarks.

Older properties built before 1936 that are not historic landmarks also offer renovation credits. These low-income properties offer a tax credit of 10 percent of the qualified rehabilitation expenditures, as well as the $25,000 deduction for interest and depreciation, for qualified investors.

Remember three key points about these or any unusual opportunities. First, make sure to address the question of whether such an investment will appreciate and provide equity growth; no investment should be made because of its tax incentives alone. Second, do not forget about the "hassle factor" of such investing. Third, be on the lookout for the next opportunity. Congress has historically added provisions such as the rehabilitation and historic credits when investment funds are needed or desired in a particular sector of the economy.

High-Risk Investments

High-risk investments, which put capital on the line in exchange for equity growth, offer you potentially high but uncertain returns. From aggressive mutual funds, which include stocks of young and unproven companies, to penny stocks, which offer a low entry price of one dollar, the hallmark of high-risk investing is the chance of great loss as well as great gain. Other high-risk investments include junk bonds, oil and gas drilling, precious metals, foreign currencies, stock options, commodities futures, and new business ventures.

Whatever the high-risk investment, never put money into it that you are not absolutely ready to lose. Allocate only a limited portion—10 percent to a maximum 20 percent—of your investment funds, and then only after your security is protected.

High-risk investing requires a stomach as well as a pocketbook. There is absolutely no point in putting a penny of your funds at risk if the result will be constant worry. Ironically, those who can best afford high-risk investing—the very wealthy—need it least. The rest of us who cannot afford to lose our hard-won equity should not place it in jeopardy. Even with these cautions, some of us will "take a flyer." For the record, so you'll know what generally to *avoid*, here is a look at several commonly available high-risk opportunities.

AGGRESSIVE MUTUAL FUNDS

Aggressive mutual funds invest in the stock of young and unproven companies. The prospectus or even the fund's name itself will usually incorporate the words *aggressive* and *volatile* in its description. Share values fluctuate far more widely than for traditional mutual funds, creating higher risk.

Although aggressive funds do not pay a monthly dividend, they do offer the possibility of a high quarterly or annual yield as well as appreciation. But buy this sort of fund only in your risk pool, as it does not offer the safety usually sought with mutual funds.

JUNK BONDS

Junk bonds are undercollateralized corporate loan obligations put on the market for the specific purpose of creating takeover capital. Issued by corporations and groups of investors to finance acquisition of target corporations, junk bonds pay higher rates to compensate buyers for greater risk. Prices tend to be volatile and marketability lower than those of better collateralized bonds with higher ratings.

To speculate in junk bonds, you must follow the market carefully and be ready to move swiftly to respond to rapidly changing circumstances.

OIL AND GAS DRILLING

Oil and gas remain the primary source of energy in the industrialized world, but despite their central economic role, oil and gas represent high-risk investments.

The profitable production of oil or gas involves the two processes of exploration and development. Of the two, the preliminary step of exploration is the riskiest and, correspondingly, the most potentially profitable oil investment. Even with the best geological information, exploration undertakings offer no guarantees that oil or gas will be found in quantities that justify further development.

Development, the next step, yields a lower return but has a more certain chance of success. By this phase, exploration has shown there is a reasonable chance oil or gas will eventually be located or pumped.

Once a deposit has been found and developed, profitability depends on global economic supply and demand. Factors ranging from OPEC pricing to the weather greatly affect the world price of oil and competing sources of energy.

Although the Tax Reform Act of 1986 did not remove all oil

exploration and development tax incentives, investing in oil or gas should be undertaken only with a sound knowledge of this complex, politically vulnerable market. Nevertheless, if you are otherwise inclined to invest in oil, make sure your choice meets the criteria that bypass the passive loss restrictions.

PRECIOUS METALS

Small investors can enter the precious metals market by buying gold, platinum, silver, and other metals' shares in mining companies, or buying shares in mutual funds that specialize in one or more of the metals or forms. All share the risk of volatile prices and are dependent on global economic factors.

Nevertheless, precious metals have always attracted a following, especially among those with depression or doomsday concerns. If precious metals appeal to you, invest after learning the details carefully. Remember, if you buy the actual metal, you have the additional costs of safe storage and, at sale, reproving your quantities.

FOREIGN CURRENCIES AND OVERSEAS INVESTMENTS

Foreign currencies offer high-yield profit. But to trade foreign currencies successfully requires sophistication and up-to-the-minute knowledge of global economies.

Besides direct currency speculation, another way to invest in a foreign currency is to buy overseas money funds or bonds. When the bonds mature, many pay a considerably higher rate of interest than do domestic bonds of equal price. But rates are inversely related to the stability of the country's currency. For instance, if the stability of a country's currency decreases, interest rates on bonds will go up in order to compensate for the additional risk. Foreign currency funds, like domestic money markets, spread the investment among a variety of instruments but reward and risk potential remain high.

PENNY STOCKS

These stocks are shares in new ventures, which can be purchased for one dollar or less per share. The entry ticket is low because they are usually offered for new and unproven companies. They are usually considered too uncertain for heavy investors.

STOCK OPTIONS AND FUTURES

Stock options and futures provide one of the most visible and accessible risk investments. An option gives you the right to buy or sell a specific stock at a specified price—termed the *strike price*—at a predetermined date within a limited time period, usually about ninety days. At that time you can either exercise your option (provided you can put up the cash for the stock) and get the stock at a bargain price or sell your option (which you hope will have increased in value). If not, you will have to make up the difference out of your own pocket—hence the risk.

The great appeal of options is that, in theory, since you need not buy or sell the expensive shares themselves, a relatively small amount of money spent can allow you to realize substantial profit. Options buy you the option to buy or sell shares, but you never actually need to exercise them. You can take your profit by selling the options themselves, always assuming there *is* a profit. But options are more like bets than investments. Unlike stocks, an option has no book value and, unless exercised or sold at a profit, becomes valueless when it expires.

With futures you sell commodities under the same risky conditions as options. You offer to buy or sell commodities at a specified price and time in the future, hoping that the product increases in value while your price remains fixed. These products include agricultural commodities, industrial products, financial products, and metals. You eventually sell your futures at a profit or at a loss, depending on the relationship between the market price and the futures price on the date specified.

Futures, like options, constitute a bet that depends on many unpredictable factors for a successful outcome, from the weather to international trade agreements.

Remember, futures and options are investments for people who can devote the time and energy to tracking trends and who are prepared to take losses as a price of possible high gain. Stay away from them unless you meet the criteria of time, resources, and stomach.

NEW BUSINESS VENTURES

Investing in business—whether your own or someone else's—offers the chance for great rewards as well as great loss.

Statistics on business failures should discourage any rational person from setting up shop, but entrepreneurs are optimists and their dreams are fueled by media reports of billionaires who started empires in their garages. The more likely and frequent outcome of these ventures is losing the garage rather than making a million.

With these cautions, starting a business to some extent makes more sense than other high-risk investments. You can bet on yourself and create opportunity because doors in corporate settings are closed to women even today. Business owners enjoy tax breaks as well as the potential for growth.

If you decide to try business, do your homework. Think the project through strategically. Consult specialized books on the subject of business planning and talk to successful businesspeople in your potential field to learn from their experience. Ask your accountant, lawyer, or other business adviser to review your proposed plan and its tax advantages, which can be considerable. (For resources, see Appendix 6.)

But remember, your cash flow and ultimately your growth will suffer if the business turns sour. To protect yourself, do not bet your basic security funds. As tempting as you may find putting yourself on the line for your dreams, let your home and savings stay on the warm-up bench. Do not pledge these essential personal assets for any investment undertaking and certainly not for one of the riskiest—starting up a business. Do not put your basic security at risk to start or fund a business, no matter how appealing the prospects.

CONCLUSION

Now that you have worked through the three stages of growth, look back again at your initial plan. Decide whether or not you have reached your goals. If not, tighten your budget, make needed investment changes, or even revise your goals now that you have a different outlook. If you have reached your goals, begin to set new ones.

The proper goal of growth should be security, not riches. Once you have adequate resources, don't stretch yourself trying to get yet another dollar. Not only may you lose money you have worked hard to accrue, but at some point the value of your time and your peace of mind outweigh the value of more money. Although expectations tend to rise with income, if you keep the understanding of "enough is enough" in mind, you will be able to accept and enjoy what you have already gained.

THE MYTHS
AND REALITIES
OF MONEY MANAGEMENT

Although it is true that a woman can improve her financial life through conserving cash flow, saving taxes, and creating personal growth, there are systemic limits to the changes that can occur in personal pocketbooks without alteration in public policy.

The policy debates in the coming decade will take place in the "male" context of guns, rather than the "female" context of butter, unless women find a way to shape the discussion. The 1988 election demonstrated the difficulty of getting women's concerns on the agenda. Ironically, the only two areas that drew much attention were abortion and child care. While the mounting national debt will to some extent limit our policy options in the coming decade, room for maneuvering clearly exists.

The unwelcome fact is that women generally are not well off. To change our status, two principles must be followed: individual responsibility and political action.

First, you must take responsibility for yourself and your family if you have one. Examine, learn, and utilize the information presented in this book. Do not be lulled into thinking someday someone else—from a financial adviser to a spouse—will take care of your financial needs.

TEN RULES FOR PROSPERING IN THE COMING DECADE

Reflecting on the lessons from our characters in this book, here are ten rules to follow for prospering in the next decade.

1. Save money each month, if only $5.
2. Secure your retirement—Social Security, home, and pension or other cash fund.
3. Buy residential real estate in the best location you can afford.
4. Choose your investments according to your stage of growth. Do not try complicated investments unless you have covered the basics.
5. Keep up with changes in the tax laws.
6. Choose your advisers carefully. Do not seek or take financial advice from people who earn a commission for sales. Do not rely on a certified financial planner or a stockbroker if you need an accountant or a lawyer.
7. Analyze investments with an understanding that the world-wide economy and global markets can offset any financial undertaking.
8. If you play the stock market, go back to number 7. Remember that while you sleep, other markets are trading.
9. If in doubt, keep your money in cash instruments.
10. Know when enough is enough.

When you have mastered these ten rules, you will be ready for the next stage, taking steps to change policies that undermine your efforts to follow these rules.

POLITICAL ACTION

As a labor force, women constitute an enormous component of contributions to both gross national product and government tax revenues, yet we are not adequately rewarded by policies that address our needs. Your personal cash flow, taxes, and prospects for future growth are closely tied to public policy. After reading the examples that follow, of widespread discrimination present in our public policy, it should become clear that the ultimate solution to women's financial security lies in combining personal financial growth with political support for change to benefit women and children.

CASH FLOW: EQUAL PAY AND MORE

Concerns over equal pay for women date back to World War I and World War II, when efforts to place women in jobs previously reserved for men focused attention on the issue. But it was not until 1963 that Congress mandated equal pay for equal work through the Equal Pay Act. The goals of equal pay for the same job and equality of income for similar jobs still have not been achieved, although the gap is growing smaller.

According to the Census Bureau, the average earnings of men rose by 3.7 percent in 1987 (the latest year for which figures are available), to over $26,000 per annum, while women's earnings went up by 4.2 percent, to just under $17,000. But women's earnings peak at an earlier age and flatten out, rather than rising later into life, as do men's. Even when adjustments are made for all the factors that might impinge on women's earning ability—including interruptions for maternity, part-time employment, and education—a significant, measurable gap between women's and men's earnings remains, a gap that can only be explained by discrimination.

Education does not close the gap. Women college graduates working full time earn only 20 percent more than male high school dropouts. Even in professional fields where education counts the most, women encounter barriers to employment equality. A 1986 study found that seven years after graduating from Harvard Law School, 25 percent of the men and only 1 percent of the women were partners in law firms. Although the outlook has improved slightly, the Los Angeles Women's Law Association found that, in law firms containing twenty or more attorneys, only 8 percent of partners were women. In terms of paychecks, the average salaries of graduates from the Harvard School of Public Health were $37,800 a year for men and only

$21,300 a year for women. A difference of that size can translate into the difference between buying or renting a home.

With employment offering limits to advancement, women have turned in record numbers to entrepreneurship. Having been attracted by the possibility of greater economic rewards and being their own bosses, many women find that once in business, the rosy picture dims. Gross receipts for women-owned sole proprietorships (which account for two-thirds of all women-headed businesses compared to the men's pattern—59 percent operate corporations or partnerships) averaged just over $16,000 in 1983. But the average net income for such businesses was very low. While male-operated sole proprietorships netted $6,330 in 1982 (the last year complete figures were available), the average woman-owned sole proprietorship netted only $1,995. Even accounting for the extra tax benefits available to women who own businesses, these figures suggest that income equality in business may prove as elusive as in paid employment.

Comparable Worth

Occupational segregation still continues, contributing significantly to the earnings differential between men and women. Workers in predominantly female occupations averaged $4,000 a year less in 1987 than those in predominantly male occupations. Even after considering such variables as education, continuity of employment, and work experience, between one-half and one-third of the occupational and earnings differences between men and women cannot be accounted for. When faced with these statistics, many women's rights advocates have turned their attention to comparable worth as a solution to the earnings gap.

In a nutshell, the concept of *comparable worth* entails establishing the intrinsic worth of a job and paying according to other jobs equally valued, even if the jobs are seemingly different. The government has been regularly making such assessments for years; all civil service jobs are routinely rated on a point basis. Having industry do the same could help women break out of job ghettos.

But opponents of comparable worth argue that job evaluations are unwieldy, and if implemented, they would represent undue governmental interference with the free-market setting of prices, including wages. Proponents counter that the government intervenes in free markets continually, and that a market guided by ideologies about "women's work" has artificially dampened the value of jobs held predominantly by women.

A TAX SYSTEM THAT VALUES "WOMEN'S WORK"

The foundation of the income tax system was laid at a time when the majority of women were expected to stay at home and care for children. When the Sixteenth Amendment, allowing Congress to tax income, was ratified in 1913, women couldn't even vote in federal elections. The Nineteenth Amendment, providing universal suffrage, was not ratified until 1920, so those women who did pay taxes, whether directly on their own earnings or indirectly through their husband's incomes, experienced the very taxation without representation that the American Revolution was supposed to end.

With its beginnings at such a point in history, the tax system is built on a foundation of biases. The seventy-five years that have passed have not changed the fundamental assumptions of the system. As one tax theorist noted, "The federal tax policy has . . . frozen into economic and social law the philosophy that women belong in the home, not in the work place; any concessions to the reality of working women have been viewed as concessions rather than as acceptance of changed circumstances."

The treatment of both minor and major issues illustrates how the system favors traditionally male concerns at the expense of female needs.

Take the tax code's allowances for business entertainment. Until the Tax Reform Act of 1986, expensive luxury "sky boxes" for sports entertainment were fully deductible, even if no immediate business activity was involved. By contrast, taxpayers who wished to engage child care so that they could volunteer for community service could not deduct such costs because they were not related to earning an income. Although reform has added some qualifiers to sports and entertainment deductions—

business must be discussed just before or just after to take the deduction—child-care tax breaks are still strictly related to producing an income or seeking employment.

The rationale for these differences lies in a fundamental principle of the system that expenses necessary to create income in a business are almost always deductible, whereas expenses for wage earners and personal expenses usually are not. The tax system favors business expenses over income earners, and income earners over nonearners.

The rule is that "ordinary and necessary" expenses in connection with producing income in a trade or business are deductible. Such expenses are not usually figured into tax debates because they are removed from gross income before the income even finds its way to the 1040. Just as the tax forms relegate these expenses to backup schedules, the government does not include them as "tax expenditures" when tax loopholes are under review. By contrast, items of concern to women, such as the child-care tax credit, the two-earner deduction, and even IRAs are counted as "tax expenditures"—that is, a shift of money directly back to the person or corporation that receives the tax break. When revenue negotiations occur in Congress, items so categorized become the subject of debate and trade-off, while "ordinary and necessary" business expenses are left untouched.

But even "business" is defined along traditionally male lines. An employer may hire any number of workers, including personal secretaries, the costs of which are fully tax deductible. Yet, if a working woman wants to hire a housekeeper, the costs are not deductible. The rationale is that the tax system supports business activities because it contributes to people earning incomes, whereas personal activities are left up to the family. In reality, if a businessman decides to hire fifty employees through his company to do his company work while he goes on personal fishing trips, the salaries are all tax deductible without limitation (as long as the employees continue with company business), whereas a housekeeper doing replacement work for a working woman earning an income in outside employment is not. The result: working women do their paid labor and continue to do the housework as well.

For example, a business owner who has the use of a company

car can deduct a good portion of the costs of the car. By contrast, a wage earner who uses her car for business purposes will face limits on taking a deduction for such use.

Or, look at the treatment of housework—still mostly women's work—in our economic and tax system: housework is not paid, its contribution to the gross national product is not credited, and its value is treated as "imputed income" by the tax system. The "recipient" of the "imputed" income, usually a husband, is not taxed for this nonpaid income. While the issue of how to treat such a large volume of unpaid activity raises many complex issues, the point illustrates the differing roles and treatment of work traditionally done by women for the benefit of men.

An equitable system might acknowledge that work occurs inside and outside the home, that such work should be paid and taxed, and that the distinction between personal secretaries—which are deductible for businesspersons—and household workers—which are not deductible—is arbitrary and based on outmoded ways of thinking about women's roles.

Think about restaurant meals. Many two-earner couples eat out not to indulge or treat themselves but to solve the structural problem of family maintenance when both spouses work. Two businesspersons out for a business meal can deduct 80 percent of a meal's cost as a business expense. Making the two-earner couple's restaurant meal deductible might seem excessive. Yet the line must be redrawn between the "ordinary and necessary" business expense and today's necessities when yesterday's homemakers work outside the home.

To take another example, compare the effect of alimony on the payor (usually a man) and the payee (usually a woman). Even though alimony is in reality a "personal" expense, as we saw, alimony is treated differently in the tax system, with alimony being given a favored position on page 1 of the 1040. The person who pays alimony receives a deduction, and there is no upper limit on the amount (assuming it is in line with a person's income) as there is on other "personal" deductions such as the child-care tax credit. Alimony recipients must pay tax on the alimony income. One rationale is that allowing the presumably higher-earning male obtain the deduction helps women who receive alimony, since the dollars their former spouses pay are cheaper as a result of the tax break. But the hard-pressed woman who receives alimony must pay taxes on what is already a reduced income.

As in the case of the tax treatment of housework—from which the treatment of alimony flows as a corollary—finding equitable answers involves a complex discussion. But clearly the treatment of alimony revolves around a model favoring the traditional male payor.

Consider the child-care tax credit. From the inception of the income tax in 1913 until 1954, no deductions were allowed for child care. With a major overhaul of the tax system that year, a $600 deduction was allowed for a gainfully employed "taxpayer who is a woman or a widower." The code also placed upper income limits on a married woman's deduction. Gradually, the deduction was widened to include other categories of working persons, and in 1976 the current credit system was introduced. In 1989, the child-care tax credit stands exactly as it did in 1981, including the limits on the cost of care, which is used to figure the credit.

Just look at the idea of spending limits alone. While the rationale is that the government should not "subsidize" high-priced, top care for those who can afford it, it would be unthinkable for Congress to tell an executive how much to spend on secretaries or assistants.

By creating a tax credit rather than a deduction, supposedly to benefit those in lower income brackets, government underscores treatment of the entire category as personal rather than "ordinary and necessary" business expense.

The tax system incorporates a hidden agenda and is often used to encourage particular behavior as well as raise revenue. Opponents of allowing higher child-care tax deductions believe that such deductions would encourage women to abandon their children in favor of their work place. Yet 53 percent of families already include working women, validating the need for child care and fuller tax treatment.

The decision that a certain item will be left untaxed or be treated as a tax deduction represents a policy choice made by Congress. And, every tax deduction is a tax expenditure, representing a shift of resources—or in this case, an absence of interference—back to the taxpayer taking the deduction.

For example, homeowners who take the mortgage interest deduction are being "subsidized" by all those who do not take such a deduction. Nationally, 64 percent of female-headed households rent rather than own, compared to 36 percent of renters in the total number of households. Thus, the decision to offer a mortgage interest tax deduction to homeowners means that these already better-off persons are subsidized at the expense of those who cannot afford to own, of which women form a larger proportion. Even as we have urged individual readers to take advantage of these policies, we must also recognize that women as a group are adversely affected by the decision to make such tax expenditures.

A leading tax text has noted that "at bottom, every tax structure . . . is an assembly of value judgments on scores of issues that plausibly could have been decided differently." The value judgments that underlie the tax system must be questioned and adjusted to reflect women's changed economic participation.

GROWTH

Ensuring women's access to higher incomes and beneficial tax treatment provides the basis on which women can begin to undertake greater personal savings and create capital for equity growth. Currently, statistical indicators show that women are doing worse than men in terms of their access to wealth or even financial security.

Elderly Women

Ironically, because women live longer than men, we are left with longer lives to be lived on fewer resources. The average woman will live seventy-eight years, seven years longer than the average man. Although the age gap between women and men is narrowing, women find they must stretch their life resources further. In excess of seventeen million elderly women are poor. Many live solely on Social Security and do not have pension benefits. Seventeen percent of American women over sixty-five have incomes below the poverty line, in comparison to 10 percent of men. Almost half of older women have median incomes of less than $5,000 a year, according to the Congressional Caucus for Women's Issues.

Policies can be put into place that will improve older women's lives. From making pension coverage more widely available—only 42 percent of working women have pensions now—to passing laws to provide affordable housing and to protect women's financial security during and after marriage, it is clear that older women need special attention and special protections.

The Shrinking Middle Class

Headline after headline confirms the downward mobility of the middle class. Despite media attention to the "yuppies," newspapers report that "Middle Class Wages Are Vanishing" and tell the distressing news of "The Downwardly Mobile Baby-Boomers." In an Urban Institute study comparing the five years prior to 1983, disposable income of poor people fell by 9.4 percent while disposable income of affluent families fell by only 0.05 percent. (*Disposable income* consists of cash income plus food stamps, minus taxes—after adjustments for inflation.)

A 1987 Congressional Budget Office study found that in 1978, 55 percent of the population fell in the middle part of the middle class. By 1983, this figure had dropped to 42 percent. In comparison, the richest 10 percent saw an average income increase of 16 percent, and the top 5 percent saw an average 23 percent rise. In fact, the richest 1 percent of families saw their income grow by 50 percent during this period.

According to the same study, tax reform shifted the burden of tax from wealthy taxpayers to middle-income and poor taxpayers. The poorest 10 percent of taxpayers paid 20 percent more of their income in taxes in 1987 than they did in 1977, while the richest 10 percent of taxpayers paid 20 percent less. Although poor taxpayers were expected to pay lower taxes as reform took full effect, Social Security and excise taxes caused a net increase in the federal tax burden at this level.

Again, women find themselves at the bottom of the income ladder, so that women heads of household and two-earner families find themselves with expanded responsibilities and shrinking resources.

At the opposite end of the scale, at the very top, women are not found in great numbers. In the 1987 *Forbes* listing of the 400 wealthiest Americans whose worth ran into the millions, even billions, of dollars, only 55 of the 400 (about 13.75 percent) were women. (Interestingly enough, of these women, almost 20 percent were du Ponts.)

Nor does the cultural imagery for women include archetypes such as Horatio Alger or even a Ted Turner. As more women enter high-earning professions, certainly opportunities for more women to create capital will appear. But financial success is still not as emphasized a goal for women as it is for men, and some would argue that this is positive. However, think for a moment about the differences in the way wealthy women and wealthy men are perceived. Jane Fonda has made a tremendous amount of money from various undertakings, yet her media image centers on her film, political, and exercise contributions rather than her wealth. Contrast that mental picture with the Donald Trump success story, where his entrepreneurial successes are highlighted.

While endless individual financial growth may not be desirable, our imagery about desirable roles for women and men does affect women's opportunities to create wealth. As we have seen, the results of the last few years have been exactly the opposite of what is needed: while the poor pay more taxes and earn less income, the wealthy are earning more income and paying fewer taxes. But women aren't proportionately among their number.

As feminists, we must determine where we want to see our society put its priorities and work to achieve these goals. We may decide that the only ethical choice for bringing equality to all is to reverse the trend of transferring wealth from the bottom to the top. In a society in which wealth plays such a critical role, women must have access to making it and manipulating it, and perhaps redistributing it.

Globalization of Markets

We must also remain aware that what happens in other countries directly and often immediately affects our own economic lives. National economies are interdependent today. All of us are familiar with the effect of OPEC on oil prices and our economy at home, a relationship that was amply demonstrated in the 1970s.

But less obvious is the effect of an international marketplace on women's lives. Women workers in the world today have become an economic underclass. The gaps between men's and women's wages at home are magnified abroad. The 1975–85 United Nations Decade on Women highlighted women's global economic disadvantages. If the position of women and the structure of their work are inferior throughout the world, then it is difficult for American women to advance because our economy links directly with these other economies.

It is hard for an Olivia Wong, struggling with her budget concerns, to recognize that she is a rich woman by most of the world's standards. It is also difficult for a person as privileged as Melissa Hilton to see how her position relates to a woman farmer in Kenya seeking credit. Yet both share being first-generation participants in their economic systems, and despite their successes, both must face hurdles that men, equally positioned, do not.

One American woman executive tells of going to Japan and being shown the "executive" (male) bathroom rather than the women's room. The Japanese perception was that because she was an executive she must be treated like a man. But the anecdote is a chilling reminder of how our lives are constrained by our sisters' limits. Increased international economic links will play a more important role in women's lives in the future, and we must be prepared to understand how other cultures' perceptions affect our own economic positions.

MAKING CHANGES

As you have studied the characters in this book, becoming familiar with how growth works on a personal level, it is my hope that you have come to the realization that you can improve your own position. Take the steps outlined in this book and do just that.

An equally important realization, however, is that each of us must recognize when enough is enough, both within the context of our own lives and within the context of society. How rich does a person have to be? No single individual can use more than a certain amount of money, and even the richest person can't take it with her.

Personal economics can carry an individual or group only so far. In order to lift people out of economic deprivation, we must create a commitment to change. The knowledge we gain about personal finance becomes one more basis for informing ourselves about policy.

Politics has been defined as the allocation of scarce resources in our society. These resources can be reallocated through one of four mechanisms: an individual's ethical code; the persuasion of ideology, indoctrination, or education; the market system; or the authority of a social or governmental institution.

To some extent, each of us can change the allocation of resources in our society simply by one's own individual actions. If all of us make personal changes, the sum total is a new societal result.

Beyond that, we can convince others through the use of *ideology* and education, specifically, through information about women.

To some extent the *market* system helps improve women's lot. For example, rather than denying women credit, as was the case in the past, marketers have actively aimed their advertising campaign toward women, who are now perceived as lucrative customers.

Credit also provides a perfect example of why none of the three nongovernmental tools can be totally relied on to produce new political realities. Neither the marketplace, ideology, nor individual action provided the mechanism for wide access to credit for women. The advent of the government's influencing the course of the economy is one of the most significant developments of the twentieth century, and it took federal legislation to accomplish full credit access for women. When I had the opportunity to work on the Equal Credit Opportunity Act, appeals had been made to the market system, to ideology, and to individuals' moral codes. But to achieve widespread quick success, legislation was the key.

Although government cannot solve every problem and legislative intervention is not always feasible or desirable, the cases in this book have highlighted some issues that need to be on the feminist economic agenda and given further consideration. As we have reviewed potential policy changes under the three familiar categories of cash flow, taxes, and future growth, you have seen concrete ways in which policy changes could make a difference.

Other Basic Issues

The influence on women's finances of these issues is immediately apparent. There are other issues that relate to finances that do not fall neatly under cash flow, taxes, and future growth. These include affordable child care and parental leave, so women can keep their jobs.

And, there are some issues that, although not directly dealing with finance, actually do have repercussions for women's financial well-being. These issues range from privacy rights to the selection of justices for the Supreme Court. These indirectly affect the finances of women by affecting how women are viewed by society as well as individual women's opportunities.

As an example of an issue that must be addressed before women can gain full financial equality, take a look at child care.

As the cost of raising children increases, societywide relief must be provided for parents. In the early 1970s, the women's movement fought for quality day care, but today, with the enormous rise in the number of working mothers, just finding *available* day care often proves difficult. In 1948, only 10.8 percent of married women with children under six participated in the labor force; today the number stands at almost 60 percent. Yet, according to a congressional study, "there are no comprehensive data on need for or uses made of child care services in the U.S. . . . [or] on the number, types, or quality of child day care facilities." As the Children's Defense Fund notes, "it is a measure of the national inattention to these issues that we do not even have current, reliable numbers about the known forms of child care."

A 1982 federal survey on the subject of child-care arrangements found that only 30.6 percent of children are cared for in their own homes. The rest are cared for outside their homes, with 40.2 percent in other people's homes, and only 15 percent in group day care. Much of this "day care" occurs in someone's private home, without licensed quality-controlled settings. A wide range of literature suggests that children who go even to informal care outside their homes show no adverse affects, and some children present better adjustment than those who stay at home. Therefore, for educational as well as economic reasons, day care is urgently required.

The dearth of day care also contributes to the growing number of women and children in poverty because day-care costs are sufficiently high to serve as a deterrent to work. Statistics show the continual rise in poverty for households headed by women. According to the House of Representatives Select Committee Report on Children, Youth and Families, one-third of all households maintained by women were poor in 1978, while the number rose to 40 percent by 1984. A Census study showed that among mothers of young children who are not in the labor force, 36 percent with families with an income under $15,000 would look for work if child care were available at a reasonable cost.

TEN ECONOMIC AND POLICY CHANGES WOMEN NEED NOW

From job-training programs to better assistance, we must find creative answers. Reflecting on the top ten trends for women in the introduction of this book, here are ten opportunities to create ten policy solutions women need now.

1. Women as a group continue to earn less than men.
    Solutions: Support continued educational and job opportunities for women. Patronize women-owned businesses and women professionals. Expand women's access to traditionally male occupations.

    Create a new national consensus supporting comparable worth. This change will help women transcend job ghettos and create cross-occupational pay equality.
2. Women's participation in the professions has increased dramatically, yet women still meet resistance in making it to the top.
    Solutions: Shatter the so-called glass ceiling, which

puts women within sight of—but excludes them from—top positions in their fields. From changing laws to ensuring access to private clubs to providing leadership from government, we must work to ensure that women occupy positions of leadership.

3. Women are the fastest-growing segment of entrepreneurs, but their profits remain low.

   Solutions: Provide economic development assistance with public/private participation to women-owned businesses. Create business consultation firms and business loan guarantee programs that combine local control with national sharing of successful business strategies.

4. The two-earner family now provides the predominant lifestyle, yet work-place accommodations have not been fashioned to reflect changed demographics.

   Solutions: Create fringe benefits for part-time employees, maternity and paternity leaves, flex-time, and incentives for employers to allow workers with families to mix work and family life.

5. Tax provisions give only partial recognition to the special working expenses women bear.

   Solution: Create new tax treatments for child care and allow some deductions for homemaker-replacement costs.

6. Marriage offers little economic security today.

   Solutions: Pass legislation allowing equal control of assets in marriage, including businesses in which marital partners are engaged. Provide more equitable divorce arrangements for women whose long-term earning potential is limited as a result of interrupting careers to raise children and/or provide homemaking services.

7. Women comprise over 63 percent of the poor.

   Solutions: Provide education and training programs for women to obtain and retain jobs. Create public-housing incentives and low-income housing.

8. Children remain women's primary responsibility both in and after marriage, with the result that almost one-fourth of American children live in poverty.

   Solution: Provide universal public day care so that parents and children are assured of both care and educational opportunities. Working women will benefit because current child-care provisions are woefully inadequate. Poor women and children will benefit in the long run as quality education helps break the cycle of poverty by allowing children to start regular school on a more equal footing.

9. Many women depend entirely on Social Security for retirement.

Solutions: Increase private pension opportunities for women. Encourage private retirement savings through continued and expanded tax incentives as well as higher pay.

10. Personal savings are at an all-time low, with many middle-income people slipping down the economic ladder.

Solution: Create a strong economy with tax and business incentives to help middle-income and working-poor Americans, rather than providing further breaks for the wealthy.

CONCLUSION

Money management has two ultimate goals. The first objective in learning how money works is to improve one's own financial position. By mastering the magic formula of cash flow, tax savings, and future growth and by putting the formula to work in your own finances, you should be able to improve your lot.

Second, learn how the system works so that you can join others to change policies that deprive women of their full share of the economic pie. By using our characters to illustrate the differences between people at varying income levels, we have attempted to give concrete, understandable evidence of how personal finance policies affect women and men.

Recognizing that there is only so much you can do as an individual, I hope you feel motivated to join with others and work for institutional change to better the lives of women and all those who have been left out or given a lesser place in our system.

TAX

FORMS

Form **1040EZ**

Department of the Treasury · Internal Revenue Service

Income Tax Return for Single Filers With No Dependents **1989**

OMB No. 1545-0675

Name & address

Use the IRS mailing label. If you don't have one, please print.

L A B E L / H E R E

Print your name above (first, initial, last)

Home address (number and street). (If you have a P.O. box, see back.) Apt. no.

City, town or post office, state, and ZIP code

Please print your numbers like this:

Your social security number

Instructions are on the back. Also, see the Form 1040A/ 1040EZ booklet, especially the checklist on page 14.

Presidential Election Campaign Fund
Do you want $1 to go to this fund?

Note: *Checking "Yes" will not change your tax or reduce your refund.*

Yes No

Dollars **Cents**

Report your income

1 Total wages, salaries, and tips. This should be shown in Box 10 of your W-2 form(s). (Attach your W-2 form(s).) **1**

Attach Copy B of Form(s) W-2 here.

2 Taxable interest income of $400 or less. If the total is more than $400, you cannot use Form 1040EZ. **2**

3 Add line 1 and line 2. This is your **adjusted gross income.** **3**

Note: You must check Yes or No.

4 Can your parents (or someone else) claim you on their return?

☐ **Yes.** Do worksheet on back; enter amount from line E here.

☐ **No.** Enter 5,100. This is the total of your standard deduction and personal exemption. **4**

5 Subtract line 4 from line 3. If line 4 is larger than line 3, enter 0. This is your **taxable income.** **5**

Figure your tax

6 Enter your Federal income tax withheld from Box 9 of your W-2 form(s). **6**

7 **Tax.** Use the amount on **line 5** to look up your tax in the tax table on pages 41-46 of the Form 1040A/1040EZ booklet. Use the **single** column in the table. Enter the tax from the table on this line. **7**

Refund or amount you owe

Attach tax payment here.

8 If line 6 is larger than line 7, subtract line 7 from line 6. This is your **refund.** **8**

9 If line 7 is larger than line 6, subtract line 6 from line 7. This is the **amount you owe.** Attach check or money order for the full amount, payable to "Internal Revenue Service." **9**

Sign your return

(Keep a copy of this form for your records.)

I have read this return. Under penalties of perjury, I declare that to the best of my knowledge and belief, the return is true, correct, and complete.

Your signature   Date

X

For IRS Use Only—Please do not write in boxes below.

For Privacy Act and Paperwork Reduction Act Notice, see page 3 in the booklet.

Form 1040EZ (1989)

1989	**Instructions for Form 1040EZ**

Use this form if:
- Your filing status is single.
- You do not claim any dependents.
- You were under 65 and not blind at the end of 1989.
- Your taxable income (line 5) is less than $50,000.
- You had **only** wages, salaries, tips, and taxable scholarships or fellowships, and your taxable interest income was $400 or less. **Caution:** *If you earned tips (including allocated tips) that are not included in Box 14 of your W-2, you may not be able to use Form 1040EZ. See page 23 in the booklet.*

If you are not sure about your filing status or dependents, see pages 15 through 20 in the booklet.

If you can't use this form, see pages 11 through 13 in the booklet for which form to use.

Completing your return

Please print your numbers inside the boxes. Do not type your numbers. Do not use dollar signs. You may round off cents to whole dollars. To do so, drop amounts under 50 cents and increase amounts that are 50 cents or more. For example, $129.49 becomes $129 and $129.50 becomes $130. If you round off, do so for all amounts. But if you have to add two or more amounts to figure the amount to enter on a line, include cents when adding and round off only the total.

Name & address

Please use the mailing label we sent you. It can help speed your refund. After you complete your return, put the label in the name and address area. Cross out any errors. Print the right information on the label (including apartment number). **If you don't have a label,** print your name, address, and social security number. If your post office does not deliver mail to your home and you have a P.O. box, show your P.O. box number instead of your home address.

Presidential campaign fund

Congress set up this fund to help pay for Presidential election costs. If you want $1 of your tax to go to this fund, check the "Yes" box. If you check "Yes," your tax or refund will not change.

Report your income

Line 1. If you don't get your W-2 by February 15, contact your local IRS office. You must still report your wages, salaries, and tips even if you don't get a W-2 from your employer. Students, if you received a scholarship or fellowship, see page 23 in the booklet.

Line 2. Banks, savings and loans, credit unions, etc., should send you a Form 1099-INT showing the amount of taxable interest paid to you. You must report all your taxable interest even if you don't get a Form 1099-INT. If you had tax-exempt interest, such as on municipal bonds, write "TEI" in the space to the left of line 2. After "TEI," show the amount of your tax-exempt interest. **Do not** add tax-exempt interest in the total on line 2.

Line 4. If you checked "Yes" because someone can claim you as a dependent, fill in this worksheet to figure the amount to enter on line 4.

Standard deduction worksheet for dependents who checked "Yes" on line 4	**A.** Enter the amount from line 1 on front.		**A.** _____	
	B. Minimum amount.		**B.** _____ 500.00	
	C. Compare the amounts on lines A and B above. Enter the LARGER of the two amounts here.		**C.** _____	
	D. Maximum amount.		**D.** _____ 3,100.00	
	E. Compare the amounts on lines C and D above. Enter the SMALLER of the two amounts here and on line 4 on front.		**E.** _____	

If you checked "No" because no one can claim you as a dependent, enter 5,100 on line 4. This is the total of your standard deduction (3,100) and personal exemption (2,000).

Figure your tax

Line 6. If you received a Form 1099-INT showing income tax withheld (backup withholding), include the amount in the total on line 6. To the left of line 6, write "Form 1099." If you had two or more employers and had total wages of over $48,000, see page 35 in the booklet.

If you want IRS to figure your tax, skip lines 7 through 9. Then sign and date your return. If you paid too much tax, we will send you a refund. If you didn't pay enough tax, we will send you a bill. We won't charge you interest or a late payment penalty if you pay within 30 days of the notice date or by April 16, 1990, whichever is later. If you want to figure your own tax, complete the rest of your return.

Amount you owe

Line 9. If you owe tax, attach your check or money order for the full amount. Write your social security number, daytime phone number, and "1989 Form 1040EZ" on your payment.

Sign your return

You must sign and date your return. If you pay someone to prepare your return, that person must sign it and show other information. See page 40 in the booklet.

Mailing your return

Mail your return by **April 16, 1990.** Use the envelope that came with your booklet. If you don't have that envelope, see page 49 in the booklet for the address.

Form **1040** Department of the Treasury—Internal Revenue Service
U.S. Individual Income Tax Return 19**89**

For the year Jan.–Dec. 31, 1989, or other tax year beginning _____ , 1989, ending _____ , 19 ___ | OMB No. 1545-0074

Label

Use IRS label. Otherwise, please print or type.

LABEL HERE

Your first name and initial | Last name | Your social security number

If a joint return, spouse's first name and initial | Last name | Spouse's social security number

Home address (number and street). (If a P.O. box, see page 7 of Instructions.) | Apt. no.

City, town or post office, state and ZIP code. (If a foreign address, see page 7.)

For Privacy Act and Paperwork Reduction Act Notice, see Instructions.

Presidential Election Campaign ▶ Do you want $1 to go to this fund? . . . . Yes ▨ No
If joint return, does your spouse want $1 to go to this fund? . Yes ▨ No

Note: Checking "Yes" will not change your tax or reduce your refund.

Filing Status

Check only one box.

1 ☐ Single
2 ☐ Married filing joint return (even if only one had income)
3 ☐ Married filing separate return. Enter spouse's social security no. above and full name here. _____
4 ☐ Head of household (with qualifying person). (See page 7 of Instructions.) If the qualifying person is your child but not your dependent, enter child's name here. _____
5 ☐ Qualifying widow(er) with dependent child (year spouse died ▶ 19___). (See page 7 of Instructions.)

Exemptions

(See Instructions on page 8.)

6a ☐ **Yourself** If someone (such as your parent) can claim you as a dependent on his or her tax return, do not check box 6a. But be sure to check the box on line 33b on page 2 .
b ☐ **Spouse** . . . .

No. of boxes checked on 6a and 6b _____
No. of your children on 6c who:

c **Dependents:**

(1) Name (first, initial, and last name)	(2) Check if under age 2	(3) If age 2 or older, dependent's social security number	(4) Relationship	(5) No. of months lived in your home in 1989
		⋮ ⋮		
		⋮ ⋮		
		⋮ ⋮		
		⋮ ⋮		
		⋮ ⋮		
		⋮ ⋮		

If more than 6 dependents, see Instructions on page 8.

● lived with you _____
● didn't live with you due to divorce or separation (see page 9) _____
No. of other dependents on 6c _____

d If your child didn't live with you but is claimed as your dependent under a pre-1985 agreement, check here ▶ ☐
e Total number of exemptions claimed . . . .

Add numbers entered on lines above ▶ ☐

Income

Please attach Copy B of your Forms W-2, W-2G, and W-2P here.

If you do not have a W-2, see page 6 of Instructions.

Please attach check or money order here.

7 Wages, salaries, tips, etc. (attach Form(s) W-2) . . . . | 7 |
8a Taxable interest income (also attach Schedule B if over $400) . . . . | 8a |
b Tax-exempt interest income (see page 10). DON'T include on line 8a | 8b | ▨
9 Dividend income (also attach Schedule B if over $400) . . . . . . | 9 |
10 Taxable refunds of state and local income taxes, if any, from worksheet on page 11 of Instructions . | 10 |
11 Alimony received . . . . | 11 |
12 Business income or (loss) (attach Schedule C) . . . . | 12 |
13 Capital gain or (loss) (attach Schedule D) . . . . | 13 |
14 Capital gain distributions not reported on line 13 (see page 11) . . . . . . | 14 |
15 Other gains or (losses) (attach Form 4797) . . . . | 15 |
16a Total IRA distributions . . | 16a | 16b Taxable amount (see page 11) | 16b |
17a Total pensions and annuities | 17a | 17b Taxable amount (see page 12) | 17b |
18 Rents, royalties, partnerships, estates, trusts, etc. (attach Schedule E) . . . . | 18 |
19 Farm income or (loss) (attach Schedule F) . . . . | 19 |
20 Unemployment compensation (insurance) (see page 13) . . . . . . | 20 |
21a Social security benefits. | 21a | 21b Taxable amount (see page 13) | 21b |
22 Other income (list type and amount—see page 13) _____ | 22 |
23 Add the amounts shown in the far right column for lines 7 through 22. This is your **total income** ▶ | 23 |

Adjustments to Income

(See Instructions on page 14.)

24 Your IRA deduction, from applicable worksheet on page 14 or 15 | 24 |
25 Spouse's IRA deduction, from applicable worksheet on page 14 or 15 | 25 |
26 Self-employed health insurance deduction, from worksheet on page 15 | 26 |
27 Keogh retirement plan and self-employed SEP deduction . . | 27 |
28 Penalty on early withdrawal of savings . . . . | 28 |
29 Alimony paid. a Recipient's last name _____
and b social security number . . | 29 |
30 Add lines 24 through 29. These are your **total adjustments** . . . . ▶ | 30 |

Adjusted Gross Income

31 Subtract line 30 from line 23. This is your **adjusted gross income.** If this line is less than $19,340 and a child lived with you, see "Earned Income Credit" (line 58) on page 20 of the Instructions. If you want IRS to figure your tax, see page 16 of the Instructions . . ▶ | 31 |

Form 1040 (1989)   Page **2**

Tax Compu- tation	32	Amount from line 31 (adjusted gross income)	32
	33a	Check if: ☐ **You** were 65 or older ☐ Blind; ☐ **Spouse** was 65 or older ☐ Blind. Add the number of boxes checked and enter the total here . . . . ▶ 33a	
	b	If someone (such as your parent) can claim you as a dependent, check here . . ▶ 33b ☐	
	c	If you are married filing a separate return and your spouse itemizes deductions, or you are a dual-status alien, see page 16 and check here . . . . ▶ 33c ☐	
	34	Enter the larger of: { • Your **standard deduction** (from page 17 of the Instructions), **OR** • Your **itemized deductions** (from Schedule A, line 26). If you itemize, attach Schedule A and check here . . ▶ ☐ }	34
	35	Subtract line 34 from line 32. Enter the result here	35
	36	Multiply $2,000 by the total number of exemptions claimed on line 6e	36
	37	**Taxable income.** Subtract line 36 from line 35. Enter the result (if less than zero, enter zero)	37
		Caution: If under age 14 and you have more than $1,000 of investment income, check here ▶ ☐ and see page 17 to see if you have to use Form 8615 to figure your tax.	
	38	Enter tax. Check if from: a ☐ Tax Table, b ☐ Tax Rate Schedules, or c ☐ Form 8615. (If any is from Form(s) 8814, enter that amount here ▶ d _____ .)	38
	39	Additional taxes (see page 18). Check if from: a ☐ Form 4970 b ☐ Form 4972 .	39
	40	Add lines 38 and 39 . . . . ▶	40

Credits (See Instructions on page 18.)	41	Credit for child and dependent care expenses *(attach Form 2441)*	41	
	42	Credit for the elderly or the disabled *(attach Schedule R)* . . .	42	
	43	Foreign tax credit *(attach Form 1116)*	43	
	44	General business credit. Check if from: a ☐ Form 3800 or b ☐ Form (specify) _____	44	
	45	Credit for prior year minimum tax *(attach Form 8801)*	45	
	46	Add lines 41 through 45. Enter the total		46
	47	Subtract line 46 from line 40. Enter the result (if less than zero, enter zero) . . . ▶		47

Other Taxes (Including Advance EIC Payments)	48	Self-employment tax *(attach Schedule SE)*	48
	49	Alternative minimum tax *(attach Form 6251)*	49
	50	Recapture taxes (see page 18). Check if from: a ☐ Form 4255 b ☐ Form 8611 .	50
	51	Social security tax on tip income not reported to employer *(attach Form 4137)* . .	51
	52	Tax on an IRA or a qualified retirement plan *(attach Form 5329)*	52
	53	Add lines 47 through 52. Enter the total . . . . ▶	53

Medicare Premium	54	Supplemental Medicare premium *(attach Form 8808)*	54
	55	Add lines 53 and 54. This is your **total tax** and any supplemental Medicare premium . . ▶	55

Payments Attach Forms W-2, W-2G, and W-2P to front.	56	Federal income tax withheld (if any is from Form(s) 1099, check ▶ ☐)	56	
	57	1989 estimated tax payments and amount applied from 1988 return	57	
	58	Earned income credit (see page 20)	58	
	59	Amount paid with Form 4868 (extension request) . . .	59	
	60	Excess social security tax and RRTA tax withheld (see page 20)	60	
	61	Credit for Federal tax on fuels *(attach Form 4136)* . . .	61	
	62	Regulated investment company credit *(attach Form 2439)* .	62	
	63	Add lines 56 through 62. These are your **total payments** . . . . ▶		63

Refund or Amount You Owe	64	If line 63 is larger than line 55, enter amount **OVERPAID** . . . . ▶	64
	65	Amount of line 64 to be **REFUNDED TO YOU** . . . . ▶	65
	66	Amount of line 64 to be **APPLIED TO YOUR 1990 ESTIMATED TAX** ▶	66	
	67	If line 55 is larger than line 63, enter **AMOUNT YOU OWE.** Attach check or money order for full amount payable to "Internal Revenue Service." Write your social security number, daytime phone number, and "1989 Form 1040" on it	67
	68	Penalty for underpayment of estimated tax (see page 21)	68	

Sign Here (Keep a copy of this return for your records.)	Under penalties of perjury, I declare that I have examined this return and accompanying schedules and statements, and to the best of my knowledge and belief, they are true, correct, and complete. Declaration of preparer (other than taxpayer) is based on all information of which preparer has any knowledge.

Your signature	Date	Your occupation
Spouse's signature (if joint return, BOTH must sign)	Date	Spouse's occupation

Paid Preparer's Use Only	Preparer's signature	Date	Check if self-employed ☐	Preparer's social security no.
	Firm's name (or yours if self-employed) and address		E.I. No.	
			ZIP code	

Form **1040A**	Department of the Treasury – Internal Revenue Service **U.S. Individual Income Tax Return** 1989	

OMB No. 1545-0085

Step 1
Label

Use IRS label. Otherwise, please print or type.

L A B E L   H E R E

Your first name and initial — Last name — Your social security no.

If a joint return, spouse's first name and initial — Last name — Spouse's social security no.

Home address (number and street). (If you have a P.O. box, see page 15 of the instructions.) — Apt. no.

City, town or post office, state and ZIP code. (If you have a foreign address, see page 15.)

For Privacy Act and Paperwork Reduction Act Notice, see page 3.

Presidential Election Campaign Fund

Do you want $1 to go to this fund?. . . . . ☐ Yes ☐ No
If joint return, does your spouse want $1 to go to this fund? ☐ Yes ☐ No

Note: Checking "Yes" will not change your tax or reduce your refund.

Step 2
Check your filing status
(Check only one.)

1 ☐ Single (See if you can use Form 1040EZ.)
2 ☐ Married filing joint return (even if only one had income)
3 ☐ Married filing separate return. Enter spouse's social security number above and spouse's full name here. _____
4 ☐ Head of household (with qualifying person). (See page 16.) If the qualifying person is your child but not your dependent, enter this child's name here. _____
5 ☐ Qualifying widow(er) with dependent child (year spouse died ▶ 19 ____). (See page 17.)

Step 3
Figure your exemptions
(See page 17 of instructions.)

6a ☐ **Yourself** If someone (such as your parent) can claim you as a dependent on his or her tax return, do not check box 6a. But be sure to check the box on line 15b on page 2.

6b ☐ **Spouse**

No. of boxes checked on 6a and 6b ____

c Dependents: 1. Name (first, initial, and last name)	2. Check if under age 2	3. If age 2 or older, dependent's social security number	4. Relationship	5. No. of months lived in your home in 1989

If more than 7 dependents, see page 20.

No. of your children on 6c who:
● lived with you ____
● didn't live with you due to divorce or separation (see page 20) ____

No. of **other** dependents listed on 6c ____

Attach Copy B of Form(s) W-2 here.

d If your child didn't live with you but is claimed as your dependent under a pre-1985 agreement, check here . . . . ▶ ☐
e Total number of exemptions claimed.

Add numbers entered on lines above ☐

Step 4
Figure your total income

Attach check or money order here.

7 Wages, salaries, tips, etc. This should be shown in Box 10 of your W-2 form(s). (Attach Form(s) W-2.) — 7

8a **Taxable** interest income (see page 24). (If over $400, also complete and attach Schedule 1, Part II.) — 8a

b **Tax-exempt** interest income (see page 24). (DO NOT include on line 8a.) — 8b

9 Dividends. (If over $400, also complete and attach Schedule 1, Part III.) — 9

10 Unemployment compensation (insurance) from Form(s) 1099-G. — 10

11 Add lines 7, 8a, 9, and 10. Enter the total. This is your **total income.** ▶ 11

Step 5
Figure your adjusted gross income

12a Your IRA deduction from applicable worksheet. Rules for IRAs begin on page 25. — 12a

b Spouse's IRA deduction from applicable worksheet. Rules for IRAs begin on page 25. — 12b

c Add lines 12a and 12b. Enter the total. These are your **total adjustments.** — 12c

13 Subtract line 12c from line 11. Enter the result. This is your **adjusted gross income.** (If this line is less than $19,340 and a child lived with you, see "Earned Income Credit" (line 25b) on page 37 of instructions.) ▶ 13

1989   **Form 1040A**
                                                                        Page 2

Step 6

14 Enter the amount from line 13.   14

15a Check ☐ **You** were 65 or older ☐ Blind ⎱ **Enter number of**
      if: ☐ **Spouse** was 65 or older ☐ Blind ⎰ **boxes checked** . ▶15a ☐

  b If someone (such as your parent) can claim you as a dependent,
      check here . . . . ▶15b ☐

Figure your standard deduction,

  c If you are married filing separately and your spouse files Form
      1040 and itemizes deductions, see page 29 and check here . . . ▶15c ☐

16 Enter your standard deduction. See page 30 for the chart (or worksheet)
      that applies to you. Be sure to enter your standard deduction here.   16

exemption amount, and

17 Subtract line 16 from line 14. Enter the result. (If line 16 is more than
      line 14, enter -0-.)   17

18 Multiply $2,000 by the total number of exemptions claimed on line 6e. 18

taxable income

19 Subtract line 18 from line 17. Enter the result. (If line 18 is more than line 17,
      enter -0-.) This is your **taxable income.**   ▶ 19

If You Want IRS To Figure Your Tax, See Page 31 of the Instructions.

Step 7

Figure your tax, credits, supplemental Medicare premium, and payments (including advance EIC payments)

Caution: If you are under age 14 and have more than $1,000 of investment
income, check here . . . . ▶ ☐
Also see page 31 to see if you have to use Form 8615 to figure your tax.

20 Find the tax on the amount on line 19. Check if from:
      ☐ Tax Table (pages 41–46) or ☐ Form 8615   20

21 Credit for child and dependent care expenses. Complete and
      attach Schedule 1, Part I.   21

22 Subtract line 21 from line 20. Enter the result. (If line 21 is more than
      line 20, enter -0-.)   22

23 **Supplemental Medicare premium.** See page 35. Complete
      and attach Schedule 2 (Form 1040A).   23

24 Add lines 22 and 23. Enter the total. This is your **total tax** and any
      supplemental Medicare premium.   ▶ 24

25a Total Federal income tax withheld—from Box 9
      of your W-2 form(s). (If any is from Form(s)
      1099, check here ▶ ☐ .)   25a

  b **Earned income credit,** from the worksheet
      on page 38 of the instructions. Also see page 37.   25b

26 Add lines 25a and 25b. Enter the total. These are your **total payments.** ▶ 26

Step 8

Figure your refund or amount you owe

27 If line 26 is more than line 24, subtract line 24 from line 26. Enter the result.
      This is your **refund.**   27

28 If line 24 is more than line 26, subtract line 26 from line 24. Enter the result.
      This is the **amount you owe.** Attach check or money order for full amount
      payable to "Internal Revenue Service." Write your social security number,
      daytime phone number, and "1989 Form 1040A" on it.   28

Step 9

Sign your return

(Keep a copy of this return for your records.)

Under penalties of perjury, I declare that I have examined this return and accompanying schedules and statements, and to the best of my knowledge and belief, they are true, correct, and complete. Declaration of preparer (other than the taxpayer) is based on all information of which the preparer has any knowledge.

Your signature   Date   Your occupation
X

Spouse's signature (if joint return, both must sign) Date Spouse's occupation
X

Paid preparer's use only

Preparer's signature   Date   Preparer's social security no.
X

Firm's name (or yours if self-employed)   Employer identification no.

Address and ZIP code   Check if self-employed ☐

1989 **Schedule 1 (Form 1040A)**   OMB No. 1545-0085

Name(s) shown on Form 1040A | Your social security number

You MUST complete and attach Schedule 1 to Form 1040A only if you:

- Claim the credit for child and dependent care expenses (complete **Part I**)
- Received employer-provided dependent care benefits (complete **Part I**)
- Have over $400 of taxable interest income (complete **Part II**)
- Have over $400 of dividend income (complete **Part III**)

Part I

*Note: If you paid cash wages of $50 or more in a calendar quarter to an individual for services performed in your home, you must file an employment tax return. Get **Form 942** for details.*

Note: See the instructions to find out which expenses qualify.

Child and dependent care expenses (see page 32 of the instructions)

- If you are claiming the child and dependent care credit, complete lines 1 through 12 below. But if you received employer-provided dependent care benefits, first complete lines 13 through 20 on the back.
- If you are not claiming the credit but you received employer-provided dependent care benefits, only complete lines 1 and 2, below, and lines 13 through 20 on the back.

1 Persons or organizations who provided the care. You MUST complete lines 1 and 2. (See page 33.)

a. Name	b. Address (number, street, city, state, and ZIP code)	c. Identification number (SSN or EIN)	d. Amount paid (see instructions)

(If you need more space, attach schedule.)

2 Add the amounts in column d of line 1 and enter the total. | **2**

3 Enter the number of qualifying persons who were cared for in 1989. You must have shared the same home with the qualifying person(s). (See the instructions for the definition of a qualifying person.) | **3**

4 Enter the amount of **qualified** expenses you incurred and actually paid in 1989. See the instructions for the amount to enter. DO NOT ENTER MORE THAN $2,400 ($4,800 if you paid for the care of two or more qualifying persons). | **4**

5 Enter the **excluded benefits**, if any, from line 19 on the back. | **5**

6 Subtract line 5 from line 4. Enter the result. If line 5 is equal to or more than line 4, STOP HERE; you cannot claim the credit. | **6**

7 You **must** enter your **earned income.** (See page 34 of the instructions for the definition of earned income.) | **7**

8 If you are married filing a joint return, you **must** enter your spouse's earned income. (If spouse was a full-time student or disabled, see the instructions for the amount to enter.) | **8**

9 If you are married filing a joint return, compare the amounts on lines 7 and 8. Enter the **smaller** of the two amounts here. | **9**

10 ● If you are married filing a joint return, compare the amounts on lines 6 and 9. Enter the **smaller** of the two amounts here.
 ● All others, compare the amounts on lines 6 and 7. Enter the **smaller** of the two amounts here. | **10**

11 Enter the decimal amount from the table below that applies to the amount on Form 1040A, line 14.

If line 14 is:		Decimal amount is:	If line 14 is:		Decimal amount is:
Over—	But not over—		Over—	But not over—	
$0—10,000		.30	$20,000—22,000		.24
10,000—12,000		.29	22,000—24,000		.23
12,000—14,000		.28	24,000—26,000		.22
14,000—16,000		.27	26,000—28,000		.21
16,000—18,000		.26	28,000		.20
18,000—20,000		.25			

11 ✕

12 Multiply the amount on line 10 by the decimal amount on line 11. Enter the result here and on Form 1040A, line 21. | **12** =

1989   **Schedule 1 (Form 1040A)**

OMB No. 1545-0085

Name(s) shown on Form 1040A. (Do not complete if shown on other side.)

Your social security number

Part I
(continued)

Complete lines 13 through 20 only if you received employer-provided dependent care benefits. Be sure to also complete lines 1 and 2 of Part I.

13 Enter the total amount of employer-provided dependent care benefits you received for 1989. (This amount should be separately shown on your W-2 form(s) and labeled as "DCB.") DO NOT include amounts that were reported to you as wages in Box 10 of Form(s) W-2.   **13**

14 Enter the total amount of **qualified** expenses incurred in 1989 for the care of a qualifying person. (See page 34 of the instructions.)   **14**

15 Compare the amounts on lines 13 and 14. Enter the **smaller** of the two amounts here.   **15**

16 You **must** enter your **earned income.** (See page 34 of the instructions for the definition of earned income.)   **16**

17 If you were married at the end of 1989, you **must** enter your spouse's earned income. (If your spouse was a full-time student or disabled, see page 34 of the instructions for the amount to enter.)   **17**

18 ● If you were married at the end of 1989, compare the amounts on lines 16 and 17 and enter the **smaller** of the two amounts here.
● If you were unmarried, enter the amount from line 16 here.   **18**

Note: *If you are also claiming the child and dependent care credit, first fill in Form 1040A through line 20. Then complete lines 3-12 of Part I.*

19 Excluded benefits. Enter here the **smallest** of the following:
● The amount from line 15, or
● The amount from line 18, or
● $5,000 ($2,500 if married filing a separate return).   **19**

20 Taxable benefits. Subtract line 19 from line 13. Enter the result. (If zero or less, enter -0-.) Include this amount in the total on Form 1040A, line 7. In the space to the left of line 7, write "DCB."   **20**

Part II

Note: *If you received a Form 1099-INT or Form 1099-OID from a brokerage firm, enter the firm's name and the total interest shown on that form.*

Interest income (see page 24 of the instructions)

Complete this part and attach Schedule 1 to Form 1040A if you received over $400 in taxable interest.

1 List name of payer		Amount
	1	

2 Add amounts on line 1. Enter the total here and on Form 1040A, line 8a.   **2**

Part III

Note: *If you received a Form 1099-DIV from a brokerage firm, enter the firm's name and the total dividends shown on that form.*

Dividend income (see page 24 of the instructions)

Complete this part and attach Schedule 1 to Form 1040A if you received over $400 in dividends.

1 List name of payer		Amount
	1	

2 Add amounts on line 1. Enter the total here and on Form 1040A, line 9.   **2**

SCHEDULES A&B (Form 1040) Department of the Treasury Internal Revenue Service	Schedule A—Itemized Deductions (Schedule B is on back) ▶ Attach to Form 1040. ▶ See Instructions for Schedules A and B (Form 1040).	OMB No. 1545-0074 1989 Attachment Sequence No. 07

Name(s) shown on Form 1040

Your social security number

Medical and Dental Expenses (Do not include expenses reimbursed or paid by others.) (See Instructions on page 23.)	**1a** Prescription medicines and drugs, insulin, doctors, dentists, nurses, hospitals, medical insurance premiums you paid, etc . .	1a	
	b Other. (List—include hearing aids, dentures, eyeglasses, transportation and lodging, etc.) ▶	1b	
	2 Add the amounts on lines 1a and 1b. Enter the total here . . .	2	
	3 Multiply the amount on Form 1040, line 32, by 7.5% (.075) . .	3	
	4 Subtract line 3 from line 2. If zero or less, enter -0-. **Total** medical and dental . . ▶		4
Taxes You Paid (See Instructions on page 24.)	**5** State and local income taxes	5	
	6 Real estate taxes	6	
	7 Other taxes. (List—include personal property taxes.) ▶	7	
	8 Add the amounts on lines 5 through 7. Enter the total here. **Total** taxes . ▶		8
Interest You Paid (See Instructions on page 24.)	**9a** Deductible home mortgage interest (from Form 1098) that you paid to financial institutions. Report deductible points on line 10.	9a	
	b Other deductible home mortgage interest. (If paid to an individual, show that person's name and address.) ▶	9b	
	10 Deductible points. (See Instructions for special rules.)	10	
	11 Deductible investment interest. (See page 25.)	11	
	12a Personal interest you paid. (See page 25.) . [12a]		
	b Multiply the amount on line 12a by 20% (.20). Enter the result	12b	
	13 Add the amounts on lines 9a through 11, and 12b. Enter the total here. **Total** interest ▶		13
Gifts to Charity (See Instructions on page 25.)	**14** Contributions by cash or check. (If you gave $3,000 or more to any one organization, show to whom you gave and how much you gave.) ▶	14	
	15 Other than cash or check. (You must attach Form 8283 if over $500.)	15	
	16 Carryover from prior year	16	
	17 Add the amounts on lines 14 through 16. Enter the total here. **Total** contributions . ▶		17
Casualty and Theft Losses	**18** Casualty or theft loss(es) (attach Form 4684). (See page 26 of the Instructions.) . . . . ▶		18
Moving Expenses	**19** Moving expenses (attach Form 3903 or 3903F). (See page 26 of the Instructions.) . . . . ▶		19
Job Expenses and Most Other Miscellaneous Deductions (See page 26 for expenses to deduct here.)	**20** Unreimbursed employee expenses—job travel, union dues, job education, etc. (You MUST attach Form 2106 in some cases. See Instructions.) ▶	20	
	21 Other expenses (investment, tax preparation, safe deposit box, etc.). List type and amount ▶	21	
	22 Add the amounts on lines 20 and 21. Enter the total.	22	
	23 Multiply the amount on Form 1040, line 32, by 2% (.02). Enter the result here	23	
	24 Subtract line 23 from line 22. Enter the result. If zero or less, enter -0-. . . ▶		24
Other Miscellaneous Deductions	**25** Other (from list on page 26 of Instructions). List type and amount ▶ .... ▶		25
Total Itemized Deductions	**26** Add the amounts on lines 4, 8, 13, 17, 18, 19, 24, and 25. Enter the total here. Then enter on Form 1040, line 34, the LARGER of this total or your standard deduction from page 17 of the Instructions . . . . ▶		26

For Paperwork Reduction Act Notice, see Form 1040 Instructions.

Schedule A (Form 1040) 1989

Schedules A&B (Form 1040) 1989   OMB No. 1545-0074   Page **2**

Name(s) shown on Form 1040. (Do not enter name and social security number if shown on other side.)   **Your social security number**

Schedule B—Interest and Dividend Income

Attachment Sequence No. **08**

Part I
Interest
Income

(See Instructions on pages 10 and 27.)

If you received more than $400 in taxable interest income, you must complete Parts I and III. List ALL interest received in Part I. If you received, as a nominee, interest that actually belongs to another person, or you received or paid accrued interest on securities transferred between interest payment dates, see page 27.

Interest Income

1 Interest income from seller-financed mortgages. (See Instructions and list name of payer.) ▶ .... | 1 | | Amount |

2 Other interest income. (List name of payer.) ▶ ....

Note: If you received a Form 1099-INT or Form 1099-OID from a brokerage firm, list the firm's name as the payer and enter the total interest shown on that form.

| 2 | |

3 Add the amounts on lines 1 and 2. Enter the total here and on Form 1040, line 8a. ▶ | 3 | |

Part II
Dividend
Income

(See Instructions on pages 10 and 27.)

If you received more than $400 in gross dividends and/or other distributions on stock, you must complete Parts II and III. If you received, as a nominee, dividends that actually belong to another person, see page 27.

Dividend Income

4 Dividend income. (List name of payer—include on this line capital gain distributions, nontaxable distributions, etc.) ▶ .... | | Amount |

Note: If you received a Form 1099-DIV from a brokerage firm, list the firm's name as the payer and enter the total dividends shown on that form.

| 4 | |

5 Add the amounts on line 4. Enter the total here . . . . | 5 | |
6 Capital gain distributions. Enter here and on Schedule D* . . . | 6 | |
7 Nontaxable distributions. (See the Instructions for Form 1040, line 9.) | 7 | |
8 Add the amounts on lines 6 and 7. Enter the total here . . . . | 8 | |
9 Subtract line 8 from line 5. Enter the result here and on Form 1040, line 9 . . . ▶ | 9 | |

*If you received capital gain distributions but do not need Schedule D to report any other gains or losses, see the Instructions for Form 1040, lines 13 and 14.

Part III
Foreign
Accounts
and
Foreign
Trusts

(See Instructions on page 27.)

If you received more than $400 of interest or dividends, OR if you had a foreign account or were a grantor of, or a transferor to, a foreign trust, you must answer both questions in Part III.   **Yes** | **No**

10a At any time during 1989, did you have an interest in or a signature or other authority over a financial account in a foreign country (such as a bank account, securities account, or other financial account)? (See page 27 of the Instructions for exceptions and filing requirements for Form TD F 90-22.1.) . . . .

b If "Yes," enter the name of the foreign country ▶ ....

11 Were you the grantor of, or transferor to, a foreign trust that existed during 1989, whether or not you have any beneficial interest in it? If "Yes," you may have to file Form 3520, 3520-A, or 926. . . . .

For Paperwork Reduction Act Notice, see Form 1040 Instructions.   Schedule B (Form 1040) 1989

SCHEDULE C
(Form 1040)

Department of the Treasury
Internal Revenue Service

Profit or Loss From Business
(Sole Proprietorship)
Partnerships, Joint Ventures, Etc., Must File Form 1065.
▶ Attach to Form 1040 or Form 1041. ▶ See Instructions for Schedule C (Form 1040).

OMB No. 1545-0074

1989

Attachment
Sequence No. **09**

Name of proprietor | Social security number (SSN)

A Principal business or profession, including product or service (see Instructions) | **B** Principal business code (from page 2) ▶

C Business name and address ▶ .... | **D** Employer ID number (Not SSN)

E Method(s) used to value closing inventory: **(1)** ☐ Cost **(2)** ☐ Lower of cost or market **(3)** ☐ Other (attach explanation) **(4)** ☐ Does not apply (if checked, skip line G)

		Yes	No
F Accounting method: **(1)** ☐ Cash **(2)** ☐ Accrual **(3)** ☐ Other (specify) ▶			
G Was there any change in determining quantities, costs, or valuations between opening and closing inventory? (If "Yes," attach explanation.)			
H Are you deducting expenses for business use of your home? (If "Yes," see Instructions for limitations.)			
I Did you "materially participate" in the operation of this business during 1989? (If "No," see Instructions for limitations on losses.)			

J If this schedule includes a loss, credit, deduction, income, or other tax benefit relating to a tax shelter required to be registered, check here . ▶ ☐
If you checked this box, you MUST attach **Form 8271.**

Part I **Income**

1 Gross receipts or sales	**1**	
2 Returns and allowances	**2**	
3 Subtract line 2 from line 1. Enter the result here	**3**	
4 Cost of goods sold and/or operations (from line 39 on page 2)	**4**	
5 Subtract line 4 from line 3 and enter the **gross profit** here	**5**	
6 Other income, including Federal and state gasoline or fuel tax credit or refund (see Instructions)	**6**	
7 Add lines 5 and 6. This is your **gross income** . . . . ▶	**7**	

Part II **Expenses**

8 Advertising	**8**		**22** Repairs	**22**	
9 Bad debts from sales or services (see Instructions) . . .	**9**		**23** Supplies (not included in Part III)	**23**	
			24 Taxes	**24**	
10 Car and truck expenses . . .	**10**		**25** Travel, meals, and entertainment:		
11 Commissions	**11**		**a** Travel	**25a**	
12 Depletion	**12**		**b** Meals and entertainment		
13 Depreciation and section 179 deduction from **Form 4562** (not included in Part III) . . .	**13**		**c** Enter 20% of line 25b subject to limitations (see Instructions)		
14 Employee benefit programs (other than on line 20) . . .	**14**		**d** Subtract line 25c from line 25b	**25d**	
15 Freight (not included in Part III)	**15**		**26** Utilities (see Instructions) . . .	**26**	
16 Insurance (other than health) .	**16**		**27** Wages (less jobs credit) . .	**27**	
17 Interest:			**28** Other expenses (list type and amount):		
a Mortgage (paid to banks, etc.)	**17a**		....		
b Other	**17b**		....		
18 Legal and professional services	**18**		....		
19 Office expense . . .	**19**		....		
20 Pension and profit-sharing plans	**20**		....		
21 Rent or lease:			....		
a Machinery and equipment . .	**21a**		....		
b Other business property . .	**21b**			**28**	

29 Add amounts in columns for lines 8 through 28. These are your **total expenses** . . . . ▶	**29**	
30 **Net profit or (loss).** Subtract line 29 from line 7. If a profit, enter here and on Form 1040, line 12, and on Schedule SE, line 2. If a loss, you MUST go on to line 31. (Fiduciaries, see Instructions.)	**30**	

31 If you have a loss, you MUST check the box that describes your investment in this activity (see Instructions) . . .
If you checked 31a, enter the loss on Form 1040, line 12, and Schedule SE, line 2.
If you checked 31b, you MUST attach **Form 6198.**

31a ☐ All investment is at risk.
31b ☐ Some investment is not at risk.

For Paperwork Reduction Act Notice, see Form 1040 Instructions. | Schedule C (Form 1040) 1989

Schedule C (Form 1040) 1989   Page **2**

Part III Cost of Goods Sold and/or Operations (See Instructions.)

32	Inventory at beginning of year. (If different from last year's closing inventory, attach explanation.)	32	
33	Purchases less cost of items withdrawn for personal use	33	
34	Cost of labor. (Do not include salary paid to yourself.)	34	
35	Materials and supplies	35	
36	Other costs	36	
37	Add lines 32 through 36	37	
38	Inventory at end of year	38	
39	**Cost of goods sold and/or operations.** Subtract line 38 from line 37. Enter the result here and on page 1, line 4	39	

Part IV Principal Business or Professional Activity Codes (*Caution: Codes have been revised. Check your code carefully.*)

Locate the major business category that best describes your activity (for example, Retail Trade, Services, etc.). Within the major category, select the activity code that most closely identifies the business or profession that is the principal source of your sales or receipts. **Enter this 4-digit code on page 1, line B.** (**Note:** *If your principal source of income is from farming activities, you should file Schedule F (Form 1040), Farm Income and Expenses.*)

Construction

Code
0018 Operative builders (for own account)

General contractors
0034 Residential building
0059 Nonresidential building
0075 Highway and street construction
3889 Other heavy construction (pipe laying, bridge construction, etc.)

Building trade contractors, including repairs
0232 Plumbing, heating, air conditioning
0257 Painting and paper hanging
0273 Electrical work
0299 Masonry, dry wall, stone, tile
0414 Carpentering and flooring
0430 Roofing, siding, and sheet metal
0455 Concrete work
0885 Other building trade contractors (excavation, glazing, etc.)

Manufacturing, Including Printing and Publishing
0638 Food products and beverages
0653 Textile mill products
0679 Apparel and other textile products
0695 Leather, footware, handbags, etc.
0810 Lumber and other wood products
0836 Furniture and fixtures
0851 Printing and publishing
0877 Paper and allied products
1032 Stone, clay, and glass products
1057 Primary metal industries
1073 Fabricated metal products
1099 Machinery and machine shops
1115 Electric and electronic equipment
1883 Other manufacturing industries

Mining and Mineral Extraction
1511 Metal mining
1537 Coal mining
1552 Oil and gas
1719 Quarrying and nonmetallic mining

Agricultural Services, Forestry, Fishing
1933 Crop services
1958 Veterinary services, including pets
1974 Livestock breeding
1990 Other animal services
2113 Farm labor and management services
2212 Horticulture and landscaping
2238 Forestry, except logging
0836 Logging
2246 Commercial fishing
2469 Hunting and trapping

Wholesale Trade—Selling Goods to Other Businesses, Etc.

Durable goods, including machinery, equipment, wood, metals, etc.
2618 Selling for your own account
2634 Agent or broker for other firms— more than 50% of gross sales on commission

Nondurable goods, including food, fiber, chemicals, etc.
2659 Selling for your own account

2675 Agent or broker for other firms— more than 50% of gross sales on commission

Retail Trade—Selling Goods to Individuals and Households
3012 Selling door-to-door, by telephone or party plan, or from mobile unit
3038 Catalog or mail order
3053 Vending machine selling

Selling From Showroom, Store, or Other Fixed Location

Food, beverages, and drugs
3079 Eating places (meals or snacks)
3086 Catering services
3095 Drinking places (alcoholic beverages)
3210 Grocery stores (general line)
0612 Bakeries selling at retail
3236 Other food stores (meat, produce, candy, etc.)
3251 Liquor stores
3277 Drug stores

New car dealers and service stations
3319 New car dealers (franchised)
3335 Used car dealers
3517 Other automotive dealers (motorcycles, recreational vehicles, etc.)
3533 Tires, accessories, and parts
3558 Gasoline service stations

General merchandise, apparel, and furniture
3715 Variety stores
3731 Other general merchandise stores
3756 Shoe stores
3772 Men's and boys' clothing stores
3913 Women's ready-to-wear stores
3921 Women's accessory and specialty stores and furriers
3939 Family clothing stores
3954 Other apparel and accessory stores
3970 Furniture stores
3996 TV, audio, and electronics
3988 Computer and software stores
4119 Household appliance stores
4317 Other home furnishing stores (china, floor coverings, etc.)
4333 Music and record stores

Building, hardware, and garden supply
4416 Building materials dealers
4432 Paint, glass, and wallpaper stores
4457 Hardware stores
4473 Nurseries and garden supply stores

Other retail stores
4614 Used merchandise and antique stores (except motor vehicle parts)
4630 Gift, novelty, and souvenir stores
4655 Florists
4671 Jewelry stores
4697 Sporting goods and bicycle shops
4812 Boat dealers
4838 Hobby, toy, and game shops
4853 Camera and photo supply stores
4879 Optical goods stores
4895 Luggage and leather goods stores
5017 Book stores, excluding newsstands
5033 Stationery stores
5058 Fabric and needlework stores
5074 Mobile home dealers
5090 Fuel dealers (except gasoline)
5884 Other retail stores

Finance, Insurance, Real Estate, and Related Services
5520 Real estate agents or brokers
5579 Real estate property managers
5710 Subdividers and developers, except cemeteries
5538 Operators and lessors of buildings, including residential
5553 Operators and lessors of other real property
5702 Insurance agents or brokers
5744 Other insurance services
6064 Security brokers and dealers
6080 Commodity contracts brokers and dealers, and security and commodity exchanges
6130 Investment advisors and services
6148 Credit institutions and mortgage bankers
6155 Title abstract offices
5777 Other finance and real estate

Transportation, Communications, Public Utilities, and Related Services
6114 Taxicabs
6312 Bus and limousine transportation
6361 Other highway passenger transportation
6338 Trucking (except trash collection)
6395 Courier or package delivery services
6510 Trash collection without own dump
6536 Public warehousing
6551 Water transportation
6619 Air transportation
6635 Travel agents and tour operators
6650 Other transportation services
6676 Communication services
6692 Utilities, including dumps, snowplowing, road cleaning, etc.

Services (Personal, Professional, and Business Services)

Hotels and other lodging places
7096 Hotels, motels, and tourist homes
7211 Rooming and boarding houses
7237 Camps and camping parks

Laundry and cleaning services
7419 Coin-operated laundries and dry cleaning
7435 Other laundry, dry cleaning, and garment services
7450 Carpet and upholstery cleaning
7476 Janitorial and related services (building, house, and window cleaning)

Business and/or personal services
7617 Legal services (or lawyer)
7633 Income tax preparation
7658 Accounting and bookkeeping
7518 Engineering services
7682 Architectural services
7708 Surveying services
7245 Management services
7260 Public relations
7286 Consulting services
7716 Advertising, except direct mail
7732 Employment agencies and personnel supply
7799 Consumer credit reporting and collection services

7856 Mailing, reproduction, commercial art and photography, and stenographic services
7872 Computer programming, processing, data preparation, and related services
7922 Computer repair, maintenance, and leasing
7773 Equipment rental and leasing (except computer or automotive)
7914 Investigative and protective services
7880 Other business services

Personal services
8110 Beauty shops (or beautician)
8318 Barber shop (or barber)
8334 Photographic portrait studios
8532 Funeral services and crematories
8714 Child day care
8730 Teaching or tutoring
8755 Counseling (except health practitioners)
8771 Ministers and chaplains
6882 Other personal services

Automotive services
8813 Automotive rental or leasing, without driver
8839 Parking, except valet
8953 Automotive repairs, general and specialized
8896 Other automotive services (wash, towing, etc.)

Miscellaneous repair, except computers
9019 TV and audio equipment repair
9035 Other electrical equipment repair
9050 Reupholstery and furniture repair
2881 Other equipment repair

Medical and health services
9217 Offices and clinics of medical doctors (MDs)
9233 Offices and clinics of dentists
9258 Osteopathic physicians and surgeons
9241 Podiatrists
9274 Chiropractors
9290 Optometrists
9415 Registered and practical nurses
9431 Other health practitioners
9456 Medical and dental laboratories
9472 Nursing and personal care facilities
9886 Other health services

Amusement and recreational services
8557 Physical fitness facilities
9597 Motion picture and video production
9688 Motion picture and tape distribution and allied services
9613 Videotape rental
9639 Motion picture theaters
9670 Bowling centers
9696 Professional sports and racing, including promoters and managers
9811 Theatrical performers, musicians, agents, producers, and related services
9837 Other amusement and recreational services

8888 Unable to classify

Form **1120**		**U.S. Corporation Income Tax Return**		OMB No. 1545-0123
Department of the Treasury Internal Revenue Service		For calendar year 1989 or tax year beginning _____, 1989, ending _____ 19 ____ ▶ Instructions are separate. See page 1 for Paperwork Reduction Act Notice.		**1989**

Check if a—		Use IRS label. Other-wise, please print or type.	Name	D Employer identification number
A Consolidated return	☐			
B Personal holding co.	☐		Number and street (or P.O. box number if mail is not delivered to street address)	E Date incorporated
C Personal service corp.(as defined in Temp. Regs. sec. 1.441-4T—see instructions)	☐		City or town, state, and ZIP code	F Total assets (see Specific Instructions)

G Check applicable boxes: (1) ☐ Initial return (2) ☐ Final return (3) ☐ Change in address $

Income

1a	Gross receipts or sales	**b** Less returns and allowances _____ **c** Bal ▶	1c
2	Cost of goods sold and/or operations (Schedule A, line 7)		2
3	Gross profit (line 1c less line 2)		3
4	Dividends (Schedule C, line 19)		4
5	Interest		5
6	Gross rents		6
7	Gross royalties		7
8	Capital gain net income (attach Schedule D (Form 1120))		8
9	Net gain or (loss) from Form 4797, Part II, line 18 (attach Form 4797)		9
10	Other income (see instructions—attach schedule)		10
11	**Total** income—Add lines 3 through 10 ▶		11

Deductions (See instructions for limitations on deductions.)

12	Compensation of officers (Schedule E, line 4)		12
13a	Salaries and wages _____ **b** Less jobs credit _____ **c** Balance ▶		13c
14	Repairs		14
15	Bad debts		15
16	Rents		16
17	Taxes		17
18	Interest		18
19	Contributions (**see instructions for 10% limitation**)		19
20	Depreciation (attach Form 4562)	20	
21	Less depreciation claimed on Schedule A and elsewhere on return	21a	21b
22	Depletion		22
23	Advertising		23
24	Pension, profit-sharing, etc., plans		24
25	Employee benefit programs		25
26	Other deductions (attach schedule)		26
27	**Total** deductions—Add lines 12 through 26 ▶		27
28	Taxable income before net operating loss deduction and special deductions (line 11 less line 27)		28
29	**Less: a** Net operating loss deduction (see instructions)	29a	
	b Special deductions (Schedule C, line 20)	29b	29c

Tax and Payments

30	Taxable income—Line 28 less line 29c		30
31	**Total tax** (Schedule J, line 10)		31
32	Payments: **a** 1988 overpayment credited to 1989	32a	
	b 1989 estimated tax payments	32b	
	c Less 1989 refund applied for on Form 4466	32c ( ) **d** Bal ▶ 32d	
	e Tax deposited with Form 7004	32e	
	f Credit from regulated investment companies (attach Form 2439)	32f	
	g Credit for Federal tax on fuels (attach Form 4136)	32g	32h
33	Enter any **penalty** for underpayment of estimated tax—Check ▶ ☐ if Form 2220 is attached		33
34	**Tax due**—If the total of lines 31 and 33 is larger than line 32h, enter amount owed		34
35	**Overpayment**—If line 32h is larger than the total of lines 31 and 33, enter amount overpaid		35
36	Enter amount of line 35 you want: **Credited to 1990 estimated tax** ▶	Refunded ▶	36

Please Sign Here

Under penalties of perjury, I declare that I have examined this return, including accompanying schedules and statements, and to the best of my knowledge and belief, it is true, correct, and complete. Declaration of preparer (other than taxpayer) is based on all information of which preparer has any knowledge.

▶ _____   ▶ _____
Signature of officer   Date   Title

Paid Preparer's Use Only

Preparer's signature ▶	Date	Check if self-employed ☐	Preparer's social security number
Firm's name (or yours if self-employed) and address ▶		E.I. No. ▶ ZIP code ▶	

Form 1120 (1989)   Page **2**

Schedule A   Cost of Goods Sold and/or Operations (See instructions for line 2, page 1.)

1	Inventory at beginning of year	1	
2	Purchases	2	
3	Cost of labor	3	
4a	Additional section 263A costs (see instructions—attach schedule)	4a	
b	Other costs (attach schedule)	4b	
5	Total—Add lines 1 through 4b	5	
6	Inventory at end of year	6	
7	Cost of goods sold and/or operations—Line 5 less line 6. Enter here and on line 2, page 1	7	

8a Check all methods used for valuing closing inventory:

   (i) ☐ Cost (ii) ☐ Lower of cost or market as described in Regulations section 1.471-4 (see instructions)

   (iii) ☐ Writedown of "subnormal" goods as described in Regulations section 1.471-2(c) (see instructions)

   (iv) ☐ Other (Specify method used and attach explanation.) ▶

  b Check if the LIFO inventory method was adopted this tax year for any goods (if checked, attach Form 970) . . . . ☐

  c If the LIFO inventory method was used for this tax year, enter percentage (or amounts) of closing inventory computed under LIFO . . . . | 8c | |

  d Do the rules of section 263A (with respect to property produced or acquired for resale) apply to the corporation? . . ☐ Yes   ☐ No

  e Was there any change in determining quantities, cost, or valuations between opening and closing inventory? If "Yes," attach explanation . . . . ☐ Yes   ☐ No

Schedule C   Dividends and Special Deductions (See instructions.)

	(a) Dividends received	(b) %	(c) Special deductions: (a) × (b)
1 Dividends from less-than-20%-owned domestic corporations that are subject to the 70% deduction (other than debt-financed stock)		70	
2 Dividends from 20%-or-more-owned domestic corporations that are subject to the 80% deduction (other than debt-financed stock)		80	
3 Dividends on debt-financed stock of domestic and foreign corporations (section 246A)		see instructions	
4 Dividends on certain preferred stock of less-than-20%-owned public utilities		41.176	
5 Dividends on certain preferred stock of 20%-or-more-owned public utilities		47.059	
6 Dividends from less-than-20%-owned foreign corporations and certain FSCs that are subject to the 70% deduction		70	
7 Dividends from 20%-or-more-owned foreign corporations and certain FSCs that are subject to the 80% deduction		80	
8 Dividends from wholly owned foreign subsidiaries subject to the 100% deduction (section 245(b))		100	
9 Total—Add lines 1 through 8. See instructions for limitation			
10 Dividends from domestic corporations received by a small business investment company operating under the Small Business Investment Act of 1958		100	
11 Dividends from certain FSCs that are subject to the 100% deduction (section 245(c)(1))		100	
12 Dividends from affiliated group members subject to the 100% deduction (section 243(a)(3))		100	
13 Other dividends from foreign corporations not included on lines 3, 6, 7, 8, or 11			
14 Income from controlled foreign corporations under subpart F (attach Forms 5471)			
15 Foreign dividend gross-up (section 78)			
16 IC-DISC and former DISC dividends not included on lines 1, 2, or 3 (section 246(d))			
17 Other dividends			
18 Deduction for dividends paid on certain preferred stock of public utilities (see instructions)			
19 Total dividends—Add lines 1 through 17. Enter here and on line 4, page 1. ▶			

20 Total deductions—Add lines 9, 10, 11, 12, and 18. Enter here and on line 29b, page 1 . . . . ▶

Schedule E   Compensation of Officers (See instructions for line 12, page 1.)

Complete Schedule E only if total receipts (line 1a, plus lines 4 through 10, of page 1, Form 1120) are $500,000 or more.

(a) Name of officer	(b) Social security number	(c) Percent of time devoted to business	Percent of corporation stock owned		(f) Amount of compensation
			(d) Common	(e) Preferred	
1		%	%	%	
		%	%	%	
		%	%	%	
		%	%	%	
		%	%	%	

2 Total compensation of officers . . . .

3 Less: Compensation of officers claimed on Schedule A and elsewhere on return . . . . ( )

4 Compensation of officers deducted on line 12, page 1 . . . .

APPENDIX 2

TAX RATE TABLES

TABLE 46. INDIVIDUAL TAX TABLES

1989 Schedule X: Single Individuals—No Dependents

TAXABLE INCOME			TAXES	
OVER	BUT NOT OVER	PAY	PERCENTAGE ON EXCESS	OF THE AMOUNT OVER
$ 0	18,550	$ 0	15	$ 0
18,550	44,900	2,782.50	28	18,550
44,900	93,130	10,160.50	33	44,900
93,130	. . . . .	Use IRS worksheet		

1988 Income Tax Rate Schedule for Use by Estates and Nongrantor Trusts

TAXABLE INCOME			TAXES	
OVER	BUT NOT OVER	PAY	PERCENTAGE ON EXCESS	OF THE AMOUNT OVER
$ 0	5,000	$ 0	15	$ 0
5,000	13,000	750	28	5,000
13,000	26,000	2,990	33*	13,000
26,000	. . . . .	7,280	28	26,000

245

TABLE 46—*Continued*

1989 Schedule Y-1: Married Individuals, Joint Returns, and Surviving Spouses

| TAXABLE INCOME | | | TAXES | |
| | BUT NOT | | PERCENTAGE | OF THE AMOUNT |
OVER	OVER	PAY	ON EXCESS	OVER
$ 0	30,950	$ 0	15	$ 0
30,950	74,850	4,642.50	28	30,950
74,850	155,320	16,934.50	33	74,850
155,320	. . . . .	Use IRS worksheet		

1989 Schedule Y-2: Separate Returns, Married Persons

| TAXABLE INCOME | | | TAXES | |
| | BUT NOT | | PERCENTAGE | OF THE AMOUNT |
OVER	OVER	PAY	ON EXCESS	OVER
$ 0	15,475	$ 0	15	$ 0
15,475	37,425	2,321.25	28	15,475
37,425	117,895	8,467.25	33	37,425
117,895	. . . . .	Use IRS worksheet		

1989 Schedule Z: Heads of Households

| TAXABLE INCOME | | | TAXES | |
| | BUT NOT | | PERCENTAGE | OF THE AMOUNT |
OVER	OVER	PAY	ON EXCESS	OVER
$ 0	24,850	$ 0	15	$ 0
24,850	64,200	3,727.50	28	24,850
64,200	128,810	14,745.50	33	64,200
128,810	. . . . .	Use IRS worksheet		

*The 33 percent rate in the above schedule is due to the fact that the benefits of the 15 percent rate are phased out between $13,000 and $26,000.

1989 Tax Table

Use if your taxable income is less than $50,000. If $50,000 or more, use the Tax Rate Schedules.

Example: Mr. and Mrs. Brown are filing a joint return. Their taxable income on line 37 of Form 1040 is $25,300. First, they find the $25,300–25,350 income line. Next, they find the column for married filing jointly and read down the column. The amount shown where the income line and filing status column meet is $3,799. This is the tax amount they must write on line 38 of their return.

At least	But less than	Single	Married filing jointly *	Married filing separately	Head of a house-hold
			Your tax is—		
25,200	25,250	4,652	3,784	5,051	3,833
25,250	25,300	4,666	3,791	5,065	3,847
25,300	25,350	4,680	(3,799)	5,079	3,861
25,350	25,400	4,694	3,806	5,093	3,875

If line 37 (taxable income) is—		And you are—			
At least	But less than	Single	Married filing jointly *	Married filing separately	Head of a house-hold
			Your tax is—		
$0	$5	$0	$0	$0	$0
5	15	2	2	2	2
15	25	3	3	3	3
25	50	6	6	6	6
50	75	9	9	9	9
75	100	13	13	13	13
100	125	17	17	17	17
125	150	21	21	21	21
150	175	24	24	24	24
175	200	28	28	28	28
200	225	32	32	32	32
225	250	36	36	36	36
250	275	39	39	39	39
275	300	43	43	43	43
300	325	47	47	47	47
325	350	51	51	51	51
350	375	54	54	54	54
375	400	58	58	58	58
400	425	62	62	62	62
425	450	66	66	66	66
450	475	69	69	69	69
475	500	73	73	73	73
500	525	77	77	77	77
525	550	81	81	81	81
550	575	84	84	84	84
575	600	88	88	88	88
600	625	92	92	92	92
625	650	96	96	96	96
650	675	99	99	99	99
675	700	103	103	103	103
700	725	107	107	107	107
725	750	111	111	111	111
750	775	114	114	114	114
775	800	118	118	118	118
800	825	122	122	122	122
825	850	126	126	126	126
850	875	129	129	129	129
875	900	133	133	133	133
900	925	137	137	137	137
925	950	141	141	141	141
950	975	144	144	144	144
975	1,000	148	148	148	148
1,000					
1,000	1,025	152	152	152	152
1,025	1,050	156	156	156	156
1,050	1,075	159	159	159	159
1,075	1,100	163	163	163	163
1,100	1,125	167	167	167	167
1,125	1,150	171	171	171	171
1,150	1,175	174	174	174	174
1,175	1,200	178	178	178	178
1,200	1,225	182	182	182	182
1,225	1,250	186	186	186	186
1,250	1,275	189	189	189	189
1,275	1,300	193	193	193	193
1,300	1,325	197	197	197	197
1,325	1,350	201	201	201	201
1,350	1,375	204	204	204	204
1,375	1,400	208	208	208	208

If line 37 (taxable income) is—		And you are—			
At least	But less than	Single	Married filing jointly *	Married filing separately	Head of a house-hold
			Your tax is—		
1,400	1,425	212	212	212	212
1,425	1,450	216	216	216	216
1,450	1,475	219	219	219	219
1,475	1,500	223	223	223	223
1,500	1,525	227	227	227	227
1,525	1,550	231	231	231	231
1,550	1,575	234	234	234	234
1,575	1,600	238	238	238	238
1,600	1,625	242	242	242	242
1,625	1,650	246	246	246	246
1,650	1,675	249	249	249	249
1,675	1,700	253	253	253	253
1,700	1,725	257	257	257	257
1,725	1,750	261	261	261	261
1,750	1,775	264	264	264	264
1,775	1,800	268	268	268	268
1,800	1,825	272	272	272	272
1,825	1,850	276	276	276	276
1,850	1,875	279	279	279	279
1,875	1,900	283	283	283	283
1,900	1,925	287	287	287	287
1,925	1,950	291	291	291	291
1,950	1,975	294	294	294	294
1,975	2,000	298	298	298	298
2,000					
2,000	2,025	302	302	302	302
2,025	2,050	306	306	306	306
2,050	2,075	309	309	309	309
2,075	2,100	313	313	313	313
2,100	2,125	317	317	317	317
2,125	2,150	321	321	321	321
2,150	2,175	324	324	324	324
2,175	2,200	328	328	328	328
2,200	2,225	332	332	332	332
2,225	2,250	336	336	336	336
2,250	2,275	339	339	339	339
2,275	2,300	343	343	343	343
2,300	2,325	347	347	347	347
2,325	2,350	351	351	351	351
2,350	2,375	354	354	354	354
2,375	2,400	358	358	358	358
2,400	2,425	362	362	362	362
2,425	2,450	366	366	366	366
2,450	2,475	369	369	369	369
2,475	2,500	373	373	373	373
2,500	2,525	377	377	377	377
2,525	2,550	381	381	381	381
2,550	2,575	384	384	384	384
2,575	2,600	388	388	388	388
2,600	2,625	392	392	392	392
2,625	2,650	396	396	396	396
2,650	2,675	399	399	399	399
2,675	2,700	403	403	403	403

If line 37 (taxable income) is—		And you are—			
At least	But less than	Single	Married filing jointly *	Married filing separately	Head of a house-hold
			Your tax is—		
2,700	2,725	407	407	407	407
2,725	2,750	411	411	411	411
2,750	2,775	414	414	414	414
2,775	2,800	418	418	418	418
2,800	2,825	422	422	422	422
2,825	2,850	426	426	426	426
2,850	2,875	429	429	429	429
2,875	2,900	433	433	433	433
2,900	2,925	437	437	437	437
2,925	2,950	441	441	441	441
2,950	2,975	444	444	444	444
2,975	3,000	448	448	448	448
3,000					
3,000	3,050	454	454	454	454
3,050	3,100	461	461	461	461
3,100	3,150	469	469	469	469
3,150	3,200	476	476	476	476
3,200	3,250	484	484	484	484
3,250	3,300	491	491	491	491
3,300	3,350	499	499	499	499
3,350	3,400	506	506	506	506
3,400	3,450	514	514	514	514
3,450	3,500	521	521	521	521
3,500	3,550	529	529	529	529
3,550	3,600	536	536	536	536
3,600	3,650	544	544	544	544
3,650	3,700	551	551	551	551
3,700	3,750	559	559	559	559
3,750	3,800	566	566	566	566
3,800	3,850	574	574	574	574
3,850	3,900	581	581	581	581
3,900	3,950	589	589	589	589
3,950	4,000	596	596	596	596
4,000					
4,000	4,050	604	604	604	604
4,050	4,100	611	611	611	611
4,100	4,150	619	619	619	619
4,150	4,200	626	626	626	626
4,200	4,250	634	634	634	634
4,250	4,300	641	641	641	641
4,300	4,350	649	649	649	649
4,350	4,400	656	656	656	656
4,400	4,450	664	664	664	664
4,450	4,500	671	671	671	671
4,500	4,550	679	679	679	679
4,550	4,600	686	686	686	686
4,600	4,650	694	694	694	694
4,650	4,700	701	701	701	701
4,700	4,750	709	709	709	709
4,750	4,800	716	716	716	716
4,800	4,850	724	724	724	724
4,850	4,900	731	731	731	731
4,900	4,950	739	739	739	739
4,950	5,000	746	746	746	746

* This column must also be used by a qualifying widow(er).

Continued on next page

1989 Tax Table—Continued

If line 37 (taxable income) is—		And you are—				If line 37 (taxable income) is—		And you are—				If line 37 (taxable income) is—		And you are—			
At least	But less than	Single	Married filing jointly	Married filing separately *	Head of a household	At least	But less than	Single	Married filing jointly	Married filing separately *	Head of a household	At least	But less than	Single	Married filing jointly	Married filing separately *	Head of a household
		Your tax is—						Your tax is—						Your tax is—			
5,000						**8,000**						**11,000**					
5,000	5,050	754	754	754	754	8,000	8,050	1,204	1,204	1,204	1,204	11,000	11,050	1,654	1,654	1,654	1,654
5,050	5,100	761	761	761	761	8,050	8,100	1,211	1,211	1,211	1,211	11,050	11,100	1,661	1,661	1,661	1,661
5,100	5,150	769	769	769	769	8,100	8,150	1,219	1,219	1,219	1,219	11,100	11,150	1,669	1,669	1,669	1,669
5,150	5,200	776	776	776	776	8,150	8,200	1,226	1,226	1,226	1,226	11,150	11,200	1,676	1,676	1,676	1,676
5,200	5,250	784	784	784	784	8,200	8,250	1,234	1,234	1,234	1,234	11,200	11,250	1,684	1,684	1,684	1,684
5,250	5,300	791	791	791	791	8,250	8,300	1,241	1,241	1,241	1,241	11,250	11,300	1,691	1,691	1,691	1,691
5,300	5,350	799	799	799	799	8,300	8,350	1,249	1,249	1,249	1,249	11,300	11,350	1,699	1,699	1,699	1,699
5,350	5,400	806	806	806	806	8,350	8,400	1,256	1,256	1,256	1,256	11,350	11,400	1,706	1,706	1,706	1,706
5,400	5,450	814	814	814	814	8,400	8,450	1,264	1,264	1,264	1,264	11,400	11,450	1,714	1,714	1,714	1,714
5,450	5,500	821	821	821	821	8,450	8,500	1,271	1,271	1,271	1,271	11,450	11,500	1,721	1,721	1,721	1,721
5,500	5,550	829	829	829	829	8,500	8,550	1,279	1,279	1,279	1,279	11,500	11,550	1,729	1,729	1,729	1,729
5,550	5,600	836	836	836	836	8,550	8,600	1,286	1,286	1,286	1,286	11,550	11,600	1,736	1,736	1,736	1,736
5,600	5,650	844	844	844	844	8,600	8,650	1,294	1,294	1,294	1,294	11,600	11,650	1,744	1,744	1,744	1,744
5,650	5,700	851	851	851	851	8,650	8,700	1,301	1,301	1,301	1,301	11,650	11,700	1,751	1,751	1,751	1,751
5,700	5,750	859	859	859	859	8,700	8,750	1,309	1,309	1,309	1,309	11,700	11,750	1,759	1,759	1,759	1,759
5,750	5,800	866	866	866	866	8,750	8,800	1,316	1,316	1,316	1,316	11,750	11,800	1,766	1,766	1,766	1,766
5,800	5,850	874	874	874	874	8,800	8,850	1,324	1,324	1,324	1,324	11,800	11,850	1,774	1,774	1,774	1,774
5,850	5,900	881	881	881	881	8,850	8,900	1,331	1,331	1,331	1,331	11,850	11,900	1,781	1,781	1,781	1,781
5,900	5,950	889	889	889	889	8,900	8,950	1,339	1,339	1,339	1,339	11,900	11,950	1,789	1,789	1,789	1,789
5,950	6,000	896	896	896	896	8,950	9,000	1,346	1,346	1,346	1,346	11,950	12,000	1,796	1,796	1,796	1,796
6,000						**9,000**						**12,000**					
6,000	6,050	904	904	904	904	9,000	9,050	1,354	1,354	1,354	1,354	12,000	12,050	1,804	1,804	1,804	1,804
6,050	6,100	911	911	911	911	9,050	9,100	1,361	1,361	1,361	1,361	12,050	12,100	1,811	1,811	1,811	1,811
6,100	6,150	919	919	919	919	9,100	9,150	1,369	1,369	1,369	1,369	12,100	12,150	1,819	1,819	1,819	1,819
6,150	6,200	926	926	926	926	9,150	9,200	1,376	1,376	1,376	1,376	12,150	12,200	1,826	1,826	1,826	1,826
6,200	6,250	934	934	934	934	9,200	9,250	1,384	1,384	1,384	1,384	12,200	12,250	1,834	1,834	1,834	1,834
6,250	6,300	941	941	941	941	9,250	9,300	1,391	1,391	1,391	1,391	12,250	12,300	1,841	1,841	1,841	1,841
6,300	6,350	949	949	949	949	9,300	9,350	1,399	1,399	1,399	1,399	12,300	12,350	1,849	1,849	1,849	1,849
6,350	6,400	956	956	956	956	9,350	9,400	1,406	1,406	1,406	1,406	12,350	12,400	1,856	1,856	1,856	1,856
6,400	6,450	964	964	964	964	9,400	9,450	1,414	1,414	1,414	1,414	12,400	12,450	1,864	1,864	1,864	1,864
6,450	6,500	971	971	971	971	9,450	9,500	1,421	1,421	1,421	1,421	12,450	12,500	1,871	1,871	1,871	1,871
6,500	6,550	979	979	979	979	9,500	9,550	1,429	1,429	1,429	1,429	12,500	12,550	1,879	1,879	1,879	1,879
6,550	6,600	986	986	986	986	9,550	9,600	1,436	1,436	1,436	1,436	12,550	12,600	1,886	1,886	1,886	1,886
6,600	6,650	994	994	994	994	9,600	9,650	1,444	1,444	1,444	1,444	12,600	12,650	1,894	1,894	1,894	1,894
6,650	6,700	1,001	1,001	1,001	1,001	9,650	9,700	1,451	1,451	1,451	1,451	12,650	12,700	1,901	1,901	1,901	1,901
6,700	6,750	1,009	1,009	1,009	1,009	9,700	9,750	1,459	1,459	1,459	1,459	12,700	12,750	1,909	1,909	1,909	1,909
6,750	6,800	1,016	1,016	1,016	1,016	9,750	9,800	1,466	1,466	1,466	1,466	12,750	12,800	1,916	1,916	1,916	1,916
6,800	6,850	1,024	1,024	1,024	1,024	9,800	9,850	1,474	1,474	1,474	1,474	12,800	12,850	1,924	1,924	1,924	1,924
6,850	6,900	1,031	1,031	1,031	1,031	9,850	9,900	1,481	1,481	1,481	1,481	12,850	12,900	1,931	1,931	1,931	1,931
6,900	6,950	1,039	1,039	1,039	1,039	9,900	9,950	1,489	1,489	1,489	1,489	12,900	12,950	1,939	1,939	1,939	1,939
6,950	7,000	1,046	1,046	1,046	1,046	9,950	10,000	1,496	1,496	1,496	1,496	12,950	13,000	1,946	1,946	1,946	1,946
7,000						**10,000**						**13,000**					
7,000	7,050	1,054	1,054	1,054	1,054	10,000	10,050	1,504	1,504	1,504	1,504	13,000	13,050	1,954	1,954	1,954	1,954
7,050	7,100	1,061	1,061	1,061	1,061	10,050	10,100	1,511	1,511	1,511	1,511	13,050	13,100	1,961	1,961	1,961	1,961
7,100	7,150	1,069	1,069	1,069	1,069	10,100	10,150	1,519	1,519	1,519	1,519	13,100	13,150	1,969	1,969	1,969	1,969
7,150	7,200	1,076	1,076	1,076	1,076	10,150	10,200	1,526	1,526	1,526	1,526	13,150	13,200	1,976	1,976	1,976	1,976
7,200	7,250	1,084	1,084	1,084	1,084	10,200	10,250	1,534	1,534	1,534	1,534	13,200	13,250	1,984	1,984	1,984	1,984
7,250	7,300	1,091	1,091	1,091	1,091	10,250	10,300	1,541	1,541	1,541	1,541	13,250	13,300	1,991	1,991	1,991	1,991
7,300	7,350	1,099	1,099	1,099	1,099	10,300	10,350	1,549	1,549	1,549	1,549	13,300	13,350	1,999	1,999	1,999	1,999
7,350	7,400	1,106	1,106	1,106	1,106	10,350	10,400	1,556	1,556	1,556	1,556	13,350	13,400	2,006	2,006	2,006	2,006
7,400	7,450	1,114	1,114	1,114	1,114	10,400	10,450	1,564	1,564	1,564	1,564	13,400	13,450	2,014	2,014	2,014	2,014
7,450	7,500	1,121	1,121	1,121	1,121	10,450	10,500	1,571	1,571	1,571	1,571	13,450	13,500	2,021	2,021	2,021	2,021
7,500	7,550	1,129	1,129	1,129	1,129	10,500	10,550	1,579	1,579	1,579	1,579	13,500	13,550	2,029	2,029	2,029	2,029
7,550	7,600	1,136	1,136	1,136	1,136	10,550	10,600	1,586	1,586	1,586	1,586	13,550	13,600	2,036	2,036	2,036	2,036
7,600	7,650	1,144	1,144	1,144	1,144	10,600	10,650	1,594	1,594	1,594	1,594	13,600	13,650	2,044	2,044	2,044	2,044
7,650	7,700	1,151	1,151	1,151	1,151	10,650	10,700	1,601	1,601	1,601	1,601	13,650	13,700	2,051	2,051	2,051	2,051
7,700	7,750	1,159	1,159	1,159	1,159	10,700	10,750	1,609	1,609	1,609	1,609	13,700	13,750	2,059	2,059	2,059	2,059
7,750	7,800	1,166	1,166	1,166	1,166	10,750	10,800	1,616	1,616	1,616	1,616	13,750	13,800	2,066	2,066	2,066	2,066
7,800	7,850	1,174	1,174	1,174	1,174	10,800	10,850	1,624	1,624	1,624	1,624	13,800	13,850	2,074	2,074	2,074	2,074
7,850	7,900	1,181	1,181	1,181	1,181	10,850	10,900	1,631	1,631	1,631	1,631	13,850	13,900	2,081	2,081	2,081	2,081
7,900	7,950	1,189	1,189	1,189	1,189	10,900	10,950	1,639	1,639	1,639	1,639	13,900	13,950	2,089	2,089	2,089	2,089
7,950	8,000	1,196	1,196	1,196	1,196	10,950	11,000	1,646	1,646	1,646	1,646	13,950	14,000	2,096	2,096	2,096	2,096

* This column must also be used by a qualifying widow(er).

Continued on next page

1989 Tax Table—Continued

If line 37 (taxable income) is—		And you are—			
At least	But less than	Single	Married filing jointly *	Married filing separately *	Head of a household
		Your tax is—			
14,000					
14,000	14,050	2,104	2,104	2,104	2,104
14,050	14,100	2,111	2,111	2,111	2,111
14,100	14,150	2,119	2,119	2,119	2,119
14,150	14,200	2,126	2,126	2,126	2,126
14,200	14,250	2,134	2,134	2,134	2,134
14,250	14,300	2,141	2,141	2,141	2,141
14,300	14,350	2,149	2,149	2,149	2,149
14,350	14,400	2,156	2,156	2,156	2,156
14,400	14,450	2,164	2,164	2,164	2,164
14,450	14,500	2,171	2,171	2,171	2,171
14,500	14,550	2,179	2,179	2,179	2,179
14,550	14,600	2,186	2,186	2,186	2,186
14,600	14,650	2,194	2,194	2,194	2,194
14,650	14,700	2,201	2,201	2,201	2,201
14,700	14,750	2,209	2,209	2,209	2,209
14,750	14,800	2,216	2,216	2,216	2,216
14,800	14,850	2,224	2,224	2,224	2,224
14,850	14,900	2,231	2,231	2,231	2,231
14,900	14,950	2,239	2,239	2,239	2,239
14,950	15,000	2,246	2,246	2,246	2,246
15,000					
15,000	15,050	2,254	2,254	2,254	2,254
15,050	15,100	2,261	2,261	2,261	2,261
15,100	15,150	2,269	2,269	2,269	2,269
15,150	15,200	2,276	2,276	2,276	2,276
15,200	15,250	2,284	2,284	2,284	2,284
15,250	15,300	2,291	2,291	2,291	2,291
15,300	15,350	2,299	2,299	2,299	2,299
15,350	15,400	2,306	2,306	2,306	2,306
15,400	15,450	2,314	2,314	2,314	2,314
15,450	15,500	2,321	2,321	2,321	2,321
15,500	15,550	2,329	2,329	2,335	2,329
15,550	15,600	2,336	2,336	2,349	2,336
15,600	15,650	2,344	2,344	2,363	2,344
15,650	15,700	2,351	2,351	2,377	2,351
15,700	15,750	2,359	2,359	2,391	2,359
15,750	15,800	2,366	2,366	2,405	2,366
15,800	15,850	2,374	2,374	2,419	2,374
15,850	15,900	2,381	2,381	2,433	2,381
15,900	15,950	2,389	2,389	2,447	2,389
15,950	16,000	2,396	2,396	2,461	2,396
16,000					
16,000	16,050	2,404	2,404	2,475	2,404
16,050	16,100	2,411	2,411	2,489	2,411
16,100	16,150	2,419	2,419	2,503	2,419
16,150	16,200	2,426	2,426	2,517	2,426
16,200	16,250	2,434	2,434	2,531	2,434
16,250	16,300	2,441	2,441	2,545	2,441
16,300	16,350	2,449	2,449	2,559	2,449
16,350	16,400	2,456	2,456	2,573	2,456
16,400	16,450	2,464	2,464	2,587	2,464
16,450	16,500	2,471	2,471	2,601	2,471
16,500	16,550	2,479	2,479	2,615	2,479
16,550	16,600	2,486	2,486	2,629	2,486
16,600	16,650	2,494	2,494	2,643	2,494
16,650	16,700	2,501	2,501	2,657	2,501
16,700	16,750	2,509	2,509	2,671	2,509
16,750	16,800	2,516	2,516	2,685	2,516
16,800	16,850	2,524	2,524	2,699	2,524
16,850	16,900	2,531	2,531	2,713	2,531
16,900	16,950	2,539	2,539	2,727	2,539
16,950	17,000	2,546	2,546	2,741	2,546

If line 37 (taxable income) is—		And you are—			
At least	But less than	Single	Married filing jointly *	Married filing separately *	Head of a household
		Your tax is—			
17,000					
17,000	17,050	2,554	2,554	2,755	2,554
17,050	17,100	2,561	2,561	2,769	2,561
17,100	17,150	2,569	2,569	2,783	2,569
17,150	17,200	2,576	2,576	2,797	2,576
17,200	17,250	2,584	2,584	2,811	2,584
17,250	17,300	2,591	2,591	2,825	2,591
17,300	17,350	2,599	2,599	2,839	2,599
17,350	17,400	2,606	2,606	2,853	2,606
17,400	17,450	2,614	2,614	2,867	2,614
17,450	17,500	2,621	2,621	2,881	2,621
17,500	17,550	2,629	2,629	2,895	2,629
17,550	17,600	2,636	2,636	2,909	2,636
17,600	17,650	2,644	2,644	2,923	2,644
17,650	17,700	2,651	2,651	2,937	2,651
17,700	17,750	2,659	2,659	2,951	2,659
17,750	17,800	2,666	2,666	2,965	2,666
17,800	17,850	2,674	2,674	2,979	2,674
17,850	17,900	2,681	2,681	2,993	2,681
17,900	17,950	2,689	2,689	3,007	2,689
17,950	18,000	2,696	2,696	3,021	2,696
18,000					
18,000	18,050	2,704	2,704	3,035	2,704
18,050	18,100	2,711	2,711	3,049	2,711
18,100	18,150	2,719	2,719	3,063	2,719
18,150	18,200	2,726	2,726	3,077	2,726
18,200	18,250	2,734	2,734	3,091	2,734
18,250	18,300	2,741	2,741	3,105	2,741
18,300	18,350	2,749	2,749	3,119	2,749
18,350	18,400	2,756	2,756	3,133	2,756
18,400	18,450	2,764	2,764	3,147	2,764
18,450	18,500	2,771	2,771	3,161	2,771
18,500	18,550	2,779	2,779	3,175	2,779
18,550	18,600	2,786	2,786	3,189	2,786
18,600	18,650	2,794	2,794	3,203	2,794
18,650	18,700	2,801	2,801	3,217	2,801
18,700	18,750	2,809	2,809	3,231	2,809
18,750	18,800	2,816	2,816	3,245	2,816
18,800	18,850	2,824	2,824	3,259	2,824
18,850	18,900	2,831	2,831	3,273	2,831
18,900	18,950	2,839	2,839	3,287	2,839
18,950	19,000	2,846	2,846	3,301	2,846
19,000					
19,000	19,050	2,916	2,854	3,315	2,854
19,050	19,100	2,930	2,861	3,329	2,861
19,100	19,150	2,944	2,869	3,343	2,869
19,150	19,200	2,958	2,876	3,357	2,876
19,200	19,250	2,972	2,884	3,371	2,884
19,250	19,300	2,986	2,891	3,385	2,891
19,300	19,350	3,000	2,899	3,399	2,899
19,350	19,400	3,014	2,906	3,413	2,906
19,400	19,450	3,028	2,914	3,427	2,914
19,450	19,500	3,042	2,921	3,441	2,921
19,500	19,550	3,056	2,929	3,455	2,929
19,550	19,600	3,070	2,936	3,469	2,936
19,600	19,650	3,084	2,944	3,483	2,944
19,650	19,700	3,098	2,951	3,497	2,951
19,700	19,750	3,112	2,959	3,511	2,959
19,750	19,800	3,126	2,966	3,525	2,966
19,800	19,850	3,140	2,974	3,539	2,974
19,850	19,900	3,154	2,981	3,553	2,981
19,900	19,950	3,168	2,989	3,567	2,989
19,950	20,000	3,182	2,996	3,581	2,996

If line 37 (taxable income) is—		And you are—			
At least	But less than	Single	Married filing jointly *	Married filing separately *	Head of a household
		Your tax is—			
20,000					
20,000	20,050	3,196	3,004	3,595	3,004
20,050	20,100	3,210	3,011	3,609	3,011
20,100	20,150	3,224	3,019	3,623	3,019
20,150	20,200	3,238	3,026	3,637	3,026
20,200	20,250	3,252	3,034	3,651	3,034
20,250	20,300	3,266	3,041	3,665	3,041
20,300	20,350	3,280	3,049	3,679	3,049
20,350	20,400	3,294	3,056	3,693	3,056
20,400	20,450	3,308	3,064	3,707	3,064
20,450	20,500	3,322	3,071	3,721	3,071
20,500	20,550	3,336	3,079	3,735	3,079
20,550	20,600	3,350	3,086	3,749	3,086
20,600	20,650	3,364	3,094	3,763	3,094
20,650	20,700	3,378	3,101	3,777	3,101
20,700	20,750	3,392	3,109	3,791	3,109
20,750	20,800	3,406	3,116	3,805	3,116
20,800	20,850	3,420	3,124	3,819	3,124
20,850	20,900	3,434	3,131	3,833	3,131
20,900	20,950	3,448	3,139	3,847	3,139
20,950	21,000	3,462	3,146	3,861	3,146
21,000					
21,000	21,050	3,476	3,154	3,875	3,154
21,050	21,100	3,490	3,161	3,889	3,161
21,100	21,150	3,504	3,169	3,903	3,169
21,150	21,200	3,518	3,176	3,917	3,176
21,200	21,250	3,532	3,184	3,931	3,184
21,250	21,300	3,546	3,191	3,945	3,191
21,300	21,350	3,560	3,199	3,959	3,199
21,350	21,400	3,574	3,206	3,973	3,206
21,400	21,450	3,588	3,214	3,987	3,214
21,450	21,500	3,602	3,221	4,001	3,221
21,500	21,550	3,616	3,229	4,015	3,229
21,550	21,600	3,630	3,236	4,029	3,236
21,600	21,650	3,644	3,244	4,043	3,244
21,650	21,700	3,658	3,251	4,057	3,251
21,700	21,750	3,672	3,259	4,071	3,259
21,750	21,800	3,686	3,266	4,085	3,266
21,800	21,850	3,700	3,274	4,099	3,274
21,850	21,900	3,714	3,281	4,113	3,281
21,900	21,950	3,728	3,289	4,127	3,289
21,950	22,000	3,742	3,296	4,141	3,296
22,000					
22,000	22,050	3,756	3,304	4,155	3,304
22,050	22,100	3,770	3,311	4,169	3,311
22,100	22,150	3,784	3,319	4,183	3,319
22,150	22,200	3,798	3,326	4,197	3,326
22,200	22,250	3,812	3,334	4,211	3,334
22,250	22,300	3,826	3,341	4,225	3,341
22,300	22,350	3,840	3,349	4,239	3,349
22,350	22,400	3,854	3,356	4,253	3,356
22,400	22,450	3,868	3,364	4,267	3,364
22,450	22,500	3,882	3,371	4,281	3,371
22,500	22,550	3,896	3,379	4,295	3,379
22,550	22,600	3,910	3,386	4,309	3,386
22,600	22,650	3,924	3,394	4,323	3,394
22,650	22,700	3,938	3,401	4,337	3,401
22,700	22,750	3,952	3,409	4,351	3,409
22,750	22,800	3,966	3,416	4,365	3,416
22,800	22,850	3,980	3,424	4,379	3,424
22,850	22,900	3,994	3,431	4,393	3,431
22,900	22,950	4,008	3,439	4,407	3,439
22,950	23,000	4,022	3,446	4,421	3,446

* This column must also be used by a qualifying widow(er).

Continued on next page

1989 Tax Table—*Continued*

If line 37 (taxable income) is— At least	But less than	And you are— Single	Married filing jointly *	Married filing separately	Head of a household
		Your tax is—			
23,000					
23,000	**23,050**	4,036	3,454	4,435	3,454
23,050	**23,100**	4,050	3,461	4,449	3,461
23,100	**23,150**	4,064	3,469	4,463	3,469
23,150	**23,200**	4,078	3,476	4,477	3,476
23,200	**23,250**	4,092	3,484	4,491	3,484
23,250	**23,300**	4,106	3,491	4,505	3,491
23,300	**23,350**	4,120	3,499	4,519	3,499
23,350	**23,400**	4,134	3,506	4,533	3,506
23,400	**23,450**	4,148	3,514	4,547	3,514
23,450	**23,500**	4,162	3,521	4,561	3,521
23,500	**23,550**	4,176	3,529	4,575	3,529
23,550	**23,600**	4,190	3,536	4,589	3,536
23,600	**23,650**	4,204	3,544	4,603	3,544
23,650	**23,700**	4,218	3,551	4,617	3,551
23,700	**23,750**	4,232	3,559	4,631	3,559
23,750	**23,800**	4,246	3,566	4,645	3,566
23,800	**23,850**	4,260	3,574	4,659	3,574
23,850	**23,900**	4,274	3,581	4,673	3,581
23,900	**23,950**	4,288	3,589	4,687	3,589
23,950	**24,000**	4,302	3,596	4,701	3,596
24,000					
24,000	**24,050**	4,316	3,604	4,715	3,604
24,050	**24,100**	4,330	3,611	4,729	3,611
24,100	**24,150**	4,344	3,619	4,743	3,619
24,150	**24,200**	4,358	3,626	4,757	3,626
24,200	**24,250**	4,372	3,634	4,771	3,634
24,250	**24,300**	4,386	3,641	4,785	3,641
24,300	**24,350**	4,400	3,649	4,799	3,649
24,350	**24,400**	4,414	3,656	4,813	3,656
24,400	**24,450**	4,428	3,664	4,827	3,664
24,450	**24,500**	4,442	3,671	4,841	3,671
24,500	**24,550**	4,456	3,679	4,855	3,679
24,550	**24,600**	4,470	3,686	4,869	3,686
24,600	**24,650**	4,484	3,694	4,883	3,694
24,650	**24,700**	4,498	3,701	4,897	3,701
24,700	**24,750**	4,512	3,709	4,911	3,709
24,750	**24,800**	4,526	3,716	4,925	3,716
24,800	**24,850**	4,540	3,724	4,939	3,724
24,850	**24,900**	4,554	3,731	4,953	3,735
24,900	**24,950**	4,568	3,739	4,967	3,749
24,950	**25,000**	4,582	3,746	4,981	3,763
25,000					
25,000	**25,050**	4,596	3,754	4,995	3,777
25,050	**25,100**	4,610	3,761	5,009	3,791
25,100	**25,150**	4,624	3,769	5,023	3,805
25,150	**25,200**	4,638	3,776	5,037	3,819
25,200	**25,250**	4,652	3,784	5,051	3,833
25,250	**25,300**	4,666	3,791	5,065	3,847
25,300	**25,350**	4,680	3,799	5,079	3,861
25,350	**25,400**	4,694	3,806	5,093	3,875
25,400	**25,450**	4,708	3,814	5,107	3,889
25,450	**25,500**	4,722	3,821	5,121	3,903
25,500	**25,550**	4,736	3,829	5,135	3,917
25,550	**25,600**	4,750	3,836	5,149	3,931
25,600	**25,650**	4,764	3,844	5,163	3,945
25,650	**25,700**	4,778	3,851	5,177	3,959
25,700	**25,750**	4,792	3,859	5,191	3,973
25,750	**25,800**	4,806	3,866	5,205	3,987
25,800	**25,850**	4,820	3,874	5,219	4,001
25,850	**25,900**	4,834	3,881	5,233	4,015
25,900	**25,950**	4,848	3,889	5,247	4,029
25,950	**26,000**	4,862	3,896	5,261	4,043

If line 37 (taxable income) is— At least	But less than	And you are— Single	Married filing jointly *	Married filing separately	Head of a household
		Your tax is—			
26,000					
26,000	**26,050**	4,876	3,904	5,275	4,057
26,050	**26,100**	4,890	3,911	5,289	4,071
26,100	**26,150**	4,904	3,919	5,303	4,085
26,150	**26,200**	4,918	3,926	5,317	4,099
26,200	**26,250**	4,932	3,934	5,331	4,113
26,250	**26,300**	4,946	3,941	5,345	4,127
26,300	**26,350**	4,960	3,949	5,359	4,141
26,350	**26,400**	4,974	3,956	5,373	4,155
26,400	**26,450**	4,988	3,964	5,387	4,169
26,450	**26,500**	5,002	3,971	5,401	4,183
26,500	**26,550**	5,016	3,979	5,415	4,197
26,550	**26,600**	5,030	3,986	5,429	4,211
26,600	**26,650**	5,044	3,994	5,443	4,225
26,650	**26,700**	5,058	4,001	5,457	4,239
26,700	**26,750**	5,072	4,009	5,471	4,253
26,750	**26,800**	5,086	4,016	5,485	4,267
26,800	**26,850**	5,100	4,024	5,499	4,281
26,850	**26,900**	5,114	4,031	5,513	4,295
26,900	**26,950**	5,128	4,039	5,527	4,309
26,950	**27,000**	5,142	4,046	5,541	4,323
27,000					
27,000	**27,050**	5,156	4,054	5,555	4,337
27,050	**27,100**	5,170	4,061	5,569	4,351
27,100	**27,150**	5,184	4,069	5,583	4,365
27,150	**27,200**	5,198	4,076	5,597	4,379
27,200	**27,250**	5,212	4,084	5,611	4,393
27,250	**27,300**	5,226	4,091	5,625	4,407
27,300	**27,350**	5,240	4,099	5,639	4,421
27,350	**27,400**	5,254	4,106	5,653	4,435
27,400	**27,450**	5,268	4,114	5,667	4,449
27,450	**27,500**	5,282	4,121	5,681	4,463
27,500	**27,550**	5,296	4,129	5,695	4,477
27,550	**27,600**	5,310	4,136	5,709	4,491
27,600	**27,650**	5,324	4,144	5,723	4,505
27,650	**27,700**	5,338	4,151	5,737	4,519
27,700	**27,750**	5,352	4,159	5,751	4,533
27,750	**27,800**	5,366	4,166	5,765	4,547
27,800	**27,850**	5,380	4,174	5,779	4,561
27,850	**27,900**	5,394	4,181	5,793	4,575
27,900	**27,950**	5,408	4,189	5,807	4,589
27,950	**28,000**	5,422	4,196	5,821	4,603
28,000					
28,000	**28,050**	5,436	4,204	5,835	4,617
28,050	**28,100**	5,450	4,211	5,849	4,631
28,100	**28,150**	5,464	4,219	5,863	4,645
28,150	**28,200**	5,478	4,226	5,877	4,659
28,200	**28,250**	5,492	4,234	5,891	4,673
28,250	**28,300**	5,506	4,241	5,905	4,687
28,300	**28,350**	5,520	4,249	5,919	4,701
28,350	**28,400**	5,534	4,256	5,933	4,715
28,400	**28,450**	5,548	4,264	5,947	4,729
28,450	**28,500**	5,562	4,271	5,961	4,743
28,500	**28,550**	5,576	4,279	5,975	4,757
28,550	**28,600**	5,590	4,286	5,989	4,771
28,600	**28,650**	5,604	4,294	6,003	4,785
28,650	**28,700**	5,618	4,301	6,017	4,799
28,700	**28,750**	5,632	4,309	6,031	4,813
28,750	**28,800**	5,646	4,316	6,045	4,827
28,800	**28,850**	5,660	4,324	6,059	4,841
28,850	**28,900**	5,674	4,331	6,073	4,855
28,900	**28,950**	5,688	4,339	6,087	4,869
28,950	**29,000**	5,702	4,346	6,101	4,883

If line 37 (taxable income) is— At least	But less than	And you are— Single	Married filing jointly *	arried filing separately	Head of a household
		Your tax is—			
29,000					
29,000	**29,050**	5,716	4,354	6,115	4,897
29,050	**29,100**	5,730	4,361	6,129	4,911
29,100	**29,150**	5,744	4,369	6,143	4,925
29,150	**29,200**	5,758	4,376	6,157	4,939
29,200	**29,250**	5,772	4,384	6,171	4,953
29,250	**29,300**	5,786	4,391	6,185	4,967
29,300	**29,350**	5,800	4,399	6,199	4,981
29,350	**29,400**	5,814	4,406	6,213	4,995
29,400	**29,450**	5,828	4,414	6,227	5,009
29,450	**29,500**	5,842	4,421	6,241	5,023
29,500	**29,550**	5,856	4,429	6,255	5,037
29,550	**29,600**	5,870	4,436	6,269	5,051
29,600	**29,650**	5,884	4,444	6,283	5,065
29,650	**29,700**	5,898	4,451	6,297	5,079
29,700	**29,750**	5,912	4,459	6,311	5,093
29,750	**29,800**	5,926	4,466	6,325	5,107
29,800	**29,850**	5,940	4,474	6,339	5,121
29,850	**29,900**	5,954	4,481	6,353	5,135
29,900	**29,950**	5,968	4,489	6,367	5,149
29,950	**30,000**	5,982	4,496	6,381	5,163
30,000					
30,000	**30,050**	5,996	4,504	6,395	5,177
30,050	**30,100**	6,010	4,511	6,409	5,191
30,100	**30,150**	6,024	4,519	6,423	5,205
30,150	**30,200**	6,038	4,526	6,437	5,219
30,200	**30,250**	6,052	4,534	6,451	5,233
30,250	**30,300**	6,066	4,541	6,465	5,247
30,300	**30,350**	6,080	4,549	6,479	5,261
30,350	**30,400**	6,094	4,556	6,493	5,275
30,400	**30,450**	6,108	4,564	6,507	5,289
30,450	**30,500**	6,122	4,571	6,521	5,303
30,500	**30,550**	6,136	4,579	6,535	5,317
30,550	**30,600**	6,150	4,586	6,549	5,331
30,600	**30,650**	6,164	4,594	6,563	5,345
30,650	**30,700**	6,178	4,601	6,577	5,359
30,700	**30,750**	6,192	4,609	6,591	5,373
30,750	**30,800**	6,206	4,616	6,605	5,387
30,800	**30,850**	6,220	4,624	6,619	5,401
30,850	**30,900**	6,234	4,631	6,633	5,415
30,900	**30,950**	6,248	4,639	6,647	5,429
30,950	**31,000**	6,262	4,650	6,661	5,443
31,000					
31,000	**31,050**	6,276	4,664	6,675	5,457
31,050	**31,100**	6,290	4,678	6,689	5,471
31,100	**31,150**	6,304	4,692	6,703	5,485
31,150	**31,200**	6,318	4,706	6,717	5,499
31,200	**31,250**	6,332	4,720	6,731	5,513
31,250	**31,300**	6,346	4,734	6,745	5,527
31,300	**31,350**	6,360	4,748	6,759	5,541
31,350	**31,400**	6,374	4,762	6,773	5,555
31,400	**31,450**	6,388	4,776	6,787	5,569
31,450	**31,500**	6,402	4,790	6,801	5,583
31,500	**31,550**	6,416	4,804	6,815	5,597
31,550	**31,600**	6,430	4,818	6,829	5,611
31,600	**31,650**	6,444	4,832	6,843	5,625
31,650	**31,700**	6,458	4,846	6,857	5,639
31,700	**31,750**	6,472	4,860	6,871	5,653
31,750	**31,800**	6,486	4,874	6,885	5,667
31,800	**31,850**	6,500	4,888	6,899	5,681
31,850	**31,900**	6,514	4,902	6,913	5,695
31,900	**31,950**	6,528	4,916	6,927	5,709
31,950	**32,000**	6,542	4,930	6,941	5,723

* This column must also be used by a qualifying widow(er).

Continued on next page

1989 Tax Table—Continued

If line 37 (taxable income) is—		And you are—			
At least	But less than	Single	Married filing jointly *	Married filing separately	Head of a household
		Your tax is—			

32,000

At least	But less than	Single	Married filing jointly	Married filing separately	Head of a household
32,000	32,050	6,556	4,944	6,955	5,737
32,050	32,100	6,570	4,958	6,969	5,751
32,100	32,150	6,584	4,972	6,983	5,765
32,150	32,200	6,598	4,986	6,997	5,779
32,200	32,250	6,612	5,000	7,011	5,793
32,250	32,300	6,626	5,014	7,025	5,807
32,300	32,350	6,640	5,028	7,039	5,821
32,350	32,400	6,654	5,042	7,053	5,835
32,400	32,450	6,668	5,056	7,067	5,849
32,450	32,500	6,682	5,070	7,081	5,863
32,500	32,550	6,696	5,084	7,095	5,877
32,550	32,600	6,710	5,098	7,109	5,891
32,600	32,650	6,724	5,112	7,123	5,905
32,650	32,700	6,738	5,126	7,137	5,919
32,700	32,750	6,752	5,140	7,151	5,933
32,750	32,800	6,766	5,154	7,165	5,947
32,800	32,850	6,780	5,168	7,179	5,961
32,850	32,900	6,794	5,182	7,193	5,975
32,900	32,950	6,808	5,196	7,207	5,989
32,950	33,000	6,822	5,210	7,221	6,003

33,000

At least	But less than	Single	Married filing jointly	Married filing separately	Head of a household
33,000	33,050	6,836	5,224	7,235	6,017
33,050	33,100	6,850	5,238	7,249	6,031
33,100	33,150	6,864	5,252	7,263	6,045
33,150	33,200	6,878	5,266	7,277	6,059
33,200	33,250	6,892	5,280	7,291	6,073
33,250	33,300	6,906	5,294	7,305	6,087
33,300	33,350	6,920	5,308	7,319	6,101
33,350	33,400	6,934	5,322	7,333	6,115
33,400	33,450	6,948	5,336	7,347	6,129
33,450	33,500	6,962	5,350	7,361	6,143
33,500	33,550	6,976	5,364	7,375	6,157
33,550	33,600	6,990	5,378	7,389	6,171
33,600	33,650	7,004	5,392	7,403	6,185
33,650	33,700	7,018	5,406	7,417	6,199
33,700	33,750	7,032	5,420	7,431	6,213
33,750	33,800	7,046	5,434	7,445	6,227
33,800	33,850	7,060	5,448	7,459	6,241
33,850	33,900	7,074	5,462	7,473	6,255
33,900	33,950	7,088	5,476	7,487	6,269
33,950	34,000	7,102	5,490	7,501	6,283

34,000

At least	But less than	Single	Married filing jointly	Married filing separately	Head of a household
34,000	34,050	7,116	5,504	7,515	6,297
34,050	34,100	7,130	5,518	7,529	6,311
34,100	34,150	7,144	5,532	7,543	6,325
34,150	34,200	7,158	5,546	7,557	6,339
34,200	34,250	7,172	5,560	7,571	6,353
34,250	34,300	7,186	5,574	7,585	6,367
34,300	34,350	7,200	5,588	7,599	6,381
34,350	34,400	7,214	5,602	7,613	6,395
34,400	34,450	7,228	5,616	7,627	6,409
34,450	34,500	7,242	5,630	7,641	6,423
34,500	34,550	7,256	5,644	7,655	6,437
34,550	34,600	7,270	5,658	7,669	6,451
34,600	34,650	7,284	5,672	7,683	6,465
34,650	34,700	7,298	5,686	7,697	6,479
34,700	34,750	7,312	5,700	7,711	6,493
34,750	34,800	7,326	5,714	7,725	6,507
34,800	34,850	7,340	5,728	7,739	6,521
34,850	34,900	7,354	5,742	7,753	6,535
34,900	34,950	7,368	5,756	7,767	6,549
34,950	35,000	7,382	5,770	7,781	6,563

35,000

At least	But less than	Single	Married filing jointly	Married filing separately	Head of a household
35,000	35,050	7,396	5,784	7,795	6,577
35,050	35,100	7,410	5,798	7,809	6,591
35,100	35,150	7,424	5,812	7,823	6,605
35,150	35,200	7,438	5,826	7,837	6,619
35,200	35,250	7,452	5,840	7,851	6,633
35,250	35,300	7,466	5,854	7,865	6,647
35,300	35,350	7,480	5,868	7,879	6,661
35,350	35,400	7,494	5,882	7,893	6,675
35,400	35,450	7,508	5,896	7,907	6,689
35,450	35,500	7,522	5,910	7,921	6,703
35,500	35,550	7,536	5,924	7,935	6,717
35,550	35,600	7,550	5,938	7,949	6,731
35,600	35,650	7,564	5,952	7,963	6,745
35,650	35,700	7,578	5,966	7,977	6,759
35,700	35,750	7,592	5,980	7,991	6,773
35,750	35,800	7,606	5,994	8,005	6,787
35,800	35,850	7,620	6,008	8,019	6,801
35,850	35,900	7,634	6,022	8,033	6,815
35,900	35,950	7,648	6,036	8,047	6,829
35,950	36,000	7,662	6,050	8,061	6,843

36,000

At least	But less than	Single	Married filing jointly	Married filing separately	Head of a household
36,000	36,050	7,676	6,064	8,075	6,857
36,050	36,100	7,690	6,078	8,089	6,871
36,100	36,150	7,704	6,092	8,103	6,885
36,150	36,200	7,718	6,106	8,117	6,899
36,200	36,250	7,732	6,120	8,131	6,913
36,250	36,300	7,746	6,134	8,145	6,927
36,300	36,350	7,760	6,148	8,159	6,941
36,350	36,400	7,774	6,162	8,173	6,955
36,400	36,450	7,788	6,176	8,187	6,969
36,450	36,500	7,802	6,190	8,201	6,983
36,500	36,550	7,816	6,204	8,215	6,997
36,550	36,600	7,830	6,218	8,229	7,011
36,600	36,650	7,844	6,232	8,243	7,025
36,650	36,700	7,858	6,246	8,257	7,039
36,700	36,750	7,872	6,260	8,271	7,053
36,750	36,800	7,886	6,274	8,285	7,067
36,800	36,850	7,900	6,288	8,299	7,081
36,850	36,900	7,914	6,302	8,313	7,095
36,900	36,950	7,928	6,316	8,327	7,109
36,950	37,000	7,942	6,330	8,341	7,123

37,000

At least	But less than	Single	Married filing jointly	Married filing separately	Head of a household
37,000	37,050	7,956	6,344	8,355	7,137
37,050	37,100	7,970	6,358	8,369	7,151
37,100	37,150	7,984	6,372	8,383	7,165
37,150	37,200	7,998	6,386	8,397	7,179
37,200	37,250	8,012	6,400	8,411	7,193
37,250	37,300	8,026	6,414	8,425	7,207
37,300	37,350	8,040	6,428	8,439	7,221
37,350	37,400	8,054	6,442	8,453	7,235
37,400	37,450	8,068	6,456	8,467	7,249
37,450	37,500	8,082	6,470	8,484	7,263
37,500	37,550	8,096	6,484	8,500	7,277
37,550	37,600	8,110	6,498	8,517	7,291
37,600	37,650	8,124	6,512	8,533	7,305
37,650	37,700	8,138	6,526	8,550	7,319
37,700	37,750	8,152	6,540	8,566	7,333
37,750	37,800	8,166	6,554	8,583	7,347
37,800	37,850	8,180	6,568	8,599	7,361
37,850	37,900	8,194	6,582	8,616	7,375
37,900	37,950	8,208	6,596	8,632	7,389
37,950	38,000	8,222	6,610	8,649	7,403

38,000

At least	But less than	Single	Married filing jointly	Married filing separately	Head of a household
38,000	38,050	8,236	6,624	8,665	7,417
38,050	38,100	8,250	6,638	8,682	7,431
38,100	38,150	8,264	6,652	8,698	7,445
38,150	38,200	8,278	6,666	8,715	7,459
38,200	38,250	8,292	6,680	8,731	7,473
38,250	38,300	8,306	6,694	8,748	7,487
38,300	38,350	8,320	6,708	8,764	7,501
38,350	38,400	8,334	6,722	8,781	7,515
38,400	38,450	8,348	6,736	8,797	7,529
38,450	38,500	8,362	6,750	8,814	7,543
38,500	38,550	8,376	6,764	8,830	7,557
38,550	38,600	8,390	6,778	8,847	7,571
38,600	38,650	8,404	6,792	8,863	7,585
38,650	38,700	8,418	6,806	8,880	7,599
38,700	38,750	8,432	6,820	8,896	7,613
38,750	38,800	8,446	6,834	8,913	7,627
38,800	38,850	8,460	6,848	8,929	7,641
38,850	38,900	8,474	6,862	8,946	7,655
38,900	38,950	8,488	6,876	8,962	7,669
38,950	39,000	8,502	6,890	8,979	7,683

39,000

At least	But less than	Single	Married filing jointly	Married filing separately	Head of a household
39,000	39,050	8,516	6,904	8,995	7,697
39,050	39,100	8,530	6,918	9,012	7,711
39,100	39,150	8,544	6,932	9,028	7,725
39,150	39,200	8,558	6,946	9,045	7,739
39,200	39,250	8,572	6,960	9,061	7,753
39,250	39,300	8,586	6,974	9,078	7,767
39,300	39,350	8,600	6,988	9,094	7,781
39,350	39,400	8,614	7,002	9,111	7,795
39,400	39,450	8,628	7,016	9,127	7,809
39,450	39,500	8,642	7,030	9,144	7,823
39,500	39,550	8,656	7,044	9,160	7,837
39,550	39,600	8,670	7,058	9,177	7,851
39,600	39,650	8,684	7,072	9,193	7,865
39,650	39,700	8,698	7,086	9,210	7,879
39,700	39,750	8,712	7,100	9,226	7,893
39,750	39,800	8,726	7,114	9,243	7,907
39,800	39,850	8,740	7,128	9,259	7,921
39,850	39,900	8,754	7,142	9,276	7,935
39,900	39,950	8,768	7,156	9,292	7,949
39,950	40,000	8,782	7,170	9,309	7,963

40,000

At least	But less than	Single	Married filing jointly	Married filing separately	Head of a household
40,000	40,050	8,796	7,184	9,325	7,977
40,050	40,100	8,810	7,198	9,342	7,991
40,100	40,150	8,824	7,212	9,358	8,005
40,150	40,200	8,838	7,226	9,375	8,019
40,200	40,250	8,852	7,240	9,391	8,033
40,250	40,300	8,866	7,254	9,408	8,047
40,300	40,350	8,880	7,268	9,424	8,061
40,350	40,400	8,894	7,282	9,441	8,075
40,400	40,450	8,908	7,296	9,457	8,089
40,450	40,500	8,922	7,310	9,474	8,103
40,500	40,550	8,936	7,324	9,490	8,117
40,550	40,600	8,950	7,338	9,507	8,131
40,600	40,650	8,964	7,352	9,523	8,145
40,650	40,700	8,978	7,366	9,540	8,159
40,700	40,750	8,992	7,380	9,556	8,173
40,750	40,800	9,006	7,394	9,573	8,187
40,800	40,850	9,020	7,408	9,589	8,201
40,850	40,900	9,034	7,422	9,606	8,215
40,900	40,950	9,048	7,436	9,622	8,229
40,950	41,000	9,062	7,450	9,639	8,243

* This column must also be used by a qualifying widow(er).

Continued on next page

1989 Tax Table—Continued

If line 37 (taxable income) is— / And you are— / Your tax is—

Columns: At least | But less than | Single | Married filing jointly * | Married filing separately | Head of a household

41,000

At least	But less than	Single	Married filing jointly	Married filing separately	Head of household
41,000	41,050	9,076	7,464	9,655	8,257
41,050	41,100	9,090	7,478	9,672	8,271
41,100	41,150	9,104	7,492	9,688	8,285
41,150	41,200	9,118	7,506	9,705	8,299
41,200	41,250	9,132	7,520	9,721	8,313
41,250	41,300	9,146	7,534	9,738	8,327
41,300	41,350	9,160	7,548	9,754	8,341
41,350	41,400	9,174	7,562	9,771	8,355
41,400	41,450	9,188	7,576	9,787	8,369
41,450	41,500	9,202	7,590	9,804	8,383
41,500	41,550	9,216	7,604	9,820	8,397
41,550	41,600	9,230	7,618	9,837	8,411
41,600	41,650	9,244	7,632	9,853	8,425
41,650	41,700	9,258	7,646	9,870	8,439
41,700	41,750	9,272	7,660	9,886	8,453
41,750	41,800	9,286	7,674	9,903	8,467
41,800	41,850	9,300	7,688	9,919	8,481
41,850	41,900	9,314	7,702	9,936	8,495
41,900	41,950	9,328	7,716	9,952	8,509
41,950	42,000	9,342	7,730	9,969	8,523

42,000

At least	But less than	Single	Married filing jointly	Married filing separately	Head of household
42,000	42,050	9,356	7,744	9,985	8,537
42,050	42,100	9,370	7,758	10,002	8,551
42,100	42,150	9,384	7,772	10,018	8,565
42,150	42,200	9,398	7,786	10,035	8,579
42,200	42,250	9,412	7,800	10,051	8,593
42,250	42,300	9,426	7,814	10,068	8,607
42,300	42,350	9,440	7,828	10,084	8,621
42,350	42,400	9,454	7,842	10,101	8,635
42,400	42,450	9,468	7,856	10,117	8,649
42,450	42,500	9,482	7,870	10,134	8,663
42,500	42,550	9,496	7,884	10,150	8,677
42,550	42,600	9,510	7,898	10,167	8,691
42,600	42,650	9,524	7,912	10,183	8,705
42,650	42,700	9,538	7,926	10,200	8,719
42,700	42,750	9,552	7,940	10,216	8,733
42,750	42,800	9,566	7,954	10,233	8,747
42,800	42,850	9,580	7,968	10,249	8,761
42,850	42,900	9,594	7,982	10,266	8,775
42,900	42,950	9,608	7,996	10,282	8,789
42,950	43,000	9,622	8,010	10,299	8,803

43,000

At least	But less than	Single	Married filing jointly	Married filing separately	Head of household
43,000	43,050	9,636	8,024	10,315	8,817
43,050	43,100	9,650	8,038	10,332	8,831
43,100	43,150	9,664	8,052	10,348	8,845
43,150	43,200	9,678	8,066	10,365	8,859
43,200	43,250	9,692	8,080	10,381	8,873
43,250	43,300	9,706	8,094	10,398	8,887
43,300	43,350	9,720	8,108	10,414	8,901
43,350	43,400	9,734	8,122	10,431	8,915
43,400	43,450	9,748	8,136	10,447	8,929
43,450	43,500	9,762	8,150	10,464	8,943
43,500	43,550	9,776	8,164	10,480	8,957
43,550	43,600	9,790	8,178	10,497	8,971
43,600	43,650	9,804	8,192	10,513	8,985
43,650	43,700	9,818	8,206	10,530	8,999
43,700	43,750	9,832	8,220	10,546	9,013
43,750	43,800	9,846	8,234	10,563	9,027
43,800	43,850	9,860	8,248	10,579	9,041
43,850	43,900	9,874	8,262	10,596	9,055
43,900	43,950	9,888	8,276	10,612	9,069
43,950	44,000	9,902	8,290	10,629	9,083

44,000

At least	But less than	Single	Married filing jointly	Married filing separately	Head of household
44,000	44,050	9,916	8,304	10,645	9,097
44,050	44,100	9,930	8,318	10,662	9,111
44,100	44,150	9,944	8,332	10,678	9,125
44,150	44,200	9,958	8,346	10,695	9,139
44,200	44,250	9,972	8,360	10,711	9,153
44,250	44,300	9,986	8,374	10,728	9,167
44,300	44,350	10,000	8,388	10,744	9,181
44,350	44,400	10,014	8,402	10,761	9,195
44,400	44,450	10,028	8,416	10,777	9,209
44,450	44,500	10,042	8,430	10,794	9,223
44,500	44,550	10,056	8,444	10,810	9,237
44,550	44,600	10,070	8,458	10,827	9,251
44,600	44,650	10,084	8,472	10,843	9,265
44,650	44,700	10,098	8,486	10,860	9,279
44,700	44,750	10,112	8,500	10,876	9,293
44,750	44,800	10,126	8,514	10,893	9,307
44,800	44,850	10,140	8,528	10,909	9,321
44,850	44,900	10,154	8,542	10,926	9,335
44,900	44,950	10,169	8,556	10,942	9,349
44,950	45,000	10,185	8,570	10,959	9,363

45,000

At least	But less than	Single	Married filing jointly	Married filing separately	Head of household
45,000	45,050	10,202	8,584	10,975	9,377
45,050	45,100	10,218	8,598	10,992	9,391
45,100	45,150	10,235	8,612	11,008	9,405
45,150	45,200	10,251	8,626	11,025	9,419
45,200	45,250	10,268	8,640	11,041	9,433
45,250	45,300	10,284	8,654	11,058	9,447
45,300	45,350	10,301	8,668	11,074	9,461
45,350	45,400	10,317	8,682	11,091	9,475
45,400	45,450	10,334	8,696	11,107	9,489
45,450	45,500	10,350	8,710	11,124	9,503
45,500	45,550	10,367	8,724	11,140	9,517
45,550	45,600	10,383	8,738	11,157	9,531
45,600	45,650	10,400	8,752	11,173	9,545
45,650	45,700	10,416	8,766	11,190	9,559
45,700	45,750	10,433	8,780	11,206	9,573
45,750	45,800	10,449	8,794	11,223	9,587
45,800	45,850	10,466	8,808	11,239	9,601
45,850	45,900	10,482	8,822	11,256	9,615
45,900	45,950	10,499	8,836	11,272	9,629
45,950	46,000	10,515	8,850	11,289	9,643

46,000

At least	But less than	Single	Married filing jointly	Married filing separately	Head of household
46,000	46,050	10,532	8,864	11,305	9,657
46,050	46,100	10,548	8,878	11,322	9,671
46,100	46,150	10,565	8,892	11,338	9,685
46,150	46,200	10,581	8,906	11,355	9,699
46,200	46,250	10,598	8,920	11,371	9,713
46,250	46,300	10,614	8,934	11,388	9,727
46,300	46,350	10,631	8,948	11,404	9,741
46,350	46,400	10,647	8,962	11,421	9,755
46,400	46,450	10,664	8,976	11,437	9,769
46,450	46,500	10,680	8,990	11,454	9,783
46,500	46,550	10,697	9,004	11,470	9,797
46,550	46,600	10,713	9,018	11,487	9,811
46,600	46,650	10,730	9,032	11,503	9,825
46,650	46,700	10,746	9,046	11,520	9,839
46,700	46,750	10,763	9,060	11,536	9,853
46,750	46,800	10,779	9,074	11,553	9,867
46,800	46,850	10,796	9,088	11,569	9,881
46,850	46,900	10,812	9,102	11,586	9,895
46,900	46,950	10,829	9,116	11,602	9,909
46,950	47,000	10,845	9,130	11,619	9,923

47,000

At least	But less than	Single	Married filing jointly	Married filing separately	Head of household
47,000	47,050	10,862	9,144	11,635	9,937
47,050	47,100	10,878	9,158	11,652	9,951
47,100	47,150	10,895	9,172	11,668	9,965
47,150	47,200	10,911	9,186	11,685	9,979
47,200	47,250	10,928	9,200	11,701	9,993
47,250	47,300	10,944	9,214	11,718	10,007
47,300	47,350	10,961	9,228	11,734	10,021
47,350	47,400	10,977	9,242	11,751	10,035
47,400	47,450	10,994	9,256	11,767	10,049
47,450	47,500	11,010	9,270	11,784	10,063
47,500	47,550	11,027	9,284	11,800	10,077
47,550	47,600	11,043	9,298	11,817	10,091
47,600	47,650	11,060	9,312	11,833	10,105
47,650	47,700	11,076	9,326	11,850	10,119
47,700	47,750	11,093	9,340	11,866	10,133
47,750	47,800	11,109	9,354	11,883	10,147
47,800	47,850	11,126	9,368	11,899	10,161
47,850	47,900	11,142	9,382	11,916	10,175
47,900	47,950	11,159	9,396	11,932	10,189
47,950	48,000	11,175	9,410	11,949	10,203

48,000

At least	But less than	Single	Married filing jointly	Married filing separately	Head of household
48,000	48,050	11,192	9,424	11,965	10,217
48,050	48,100	11,208	9,438	11,982	10,231
48,100	48,150	11,225	9,452	11,998	10,245
48,150	48,200	11,241	9,466	12,015	10,259
48,200	48,250	11,258	9,480	12,031	10,273
48,250	48,300	11,274	9,494	12,048	10,287
48,300	48,350	11,291	9,508	12,064	10,301
48,350	48,400	11,307	9,522	12,081	10,315
48,400	48,450	11,324	9,536	12,097	10,329
48,450	48,500	11,340	9,550	12,114	10,343
48,500	48,550	11,357	9,564	12,130	10,357
48,550	48,600	11,373	9,578	12,147	10,371
48,600	48,650	11,390	9,592	12,163	10,385
48,650	48,700	11,406	9,606	12,180	10,399
48,700	48,750	11,423	9,620	12,196	10,413
48,750	48,800	11,439	9,634	12,213	10,427
48,800	48,850	11,456	9,648	12,229	10,441
48,850	48,900	11,472	9,662	12,246	10,455
48,900	48,950	11,489	9,676	12,262	10,469
48,950	49,000	11,505	9,690	12,279	10,483

49,000

At least	But less than	Single	Married filing jointly	Married filing separately	Head of household
49,000	49,050	11,522	9,704	12,295	10,497
49,050	49,100	11,538	9,718	12,312	10,511
49,100	49,150	11,555	9,732	12,328	10,525
49,150	49,200	11,571	9,746	12,345	10,539
49,200	49,250	11,588	9,760	12,361	10,553
49,250	49,300	11,604	9,774	12,378	10,567
49,300	49,350	11,621	9,788	12,394	10,581
49,350	49,400	11,637	9,802	12,411	10,595
49,400	49,450	11,654	9,816	12,427	10,609
49,450	49,500	11,670	9,830	12,444	10,623
49,500	49,550	11,687	9,844	12,460	10,637
49,550	49,600	11,703	9,858	12,477	10,651
49,600	49,650	11,720	9,872	12,493	10,665
49,650	49,700	11,736	9,886	12,510	10,679
49,700	49,750	11,753	9,900	12,526	10,693
49,750	49,800	11,769	9,914	12,543	10,707
49,800	49,850	11,786	9,928	12,559	10,721
49,850	49,900	11,802	9,942	12,576	10,735
49,900	49,950	11,819	9,956	12,592	10,749
49,950	50,000	11,835	9,970	12,609	10,763

* This column must also be used by a qualifying widow(er).

50,000 or over—use tax rate schedules

TABLE 47. MARGINAL FEDERAL INDIVIDUAL INCOME TAX RATES—1988*

	NUMBER OF DEPENDENTS	TAXABLE INCOME	RATE (PERCENT)
Single		$ 0–17,850	15
		17,850–43,150	28
	None	43,150–100,000	33†
	1	43,150–111,400	33
	2	43,150–122,320	33
	3	43,150–133,240	33
	4	43,150–144,160	33
Married		$ 0–29,750	15
filing		29,750–71,900	28
jointly‡	None	71,900–171,090	33
	1	71,900–182,010	33
	2	71,900–192,930	33
	3	71,900–203,850	33
	4	71,900–214,770	33
Head of		$ 0–23,900	15
household		23,900–61,650	28
	None	61,650–134,710	33
	1	61,650–145,630	33
	2	61,650–156,550	33
	3	61,650–167,470	33
	4	61,650–178,390	33

Note: All additional income, regardless of category, is taxed at 28 percent.

*As of this writing these brackets were scheduled to be in effect from 1988 on, but to reflect inflation, the taxable income bracket at which the 28 percent rate begins will be subject to adjustment.

†The 33 percent bracket is designed to lessen the value of the personal exemption for high earners; therefore, it applies differently for those with greater exemptions.

‡Married, filing separately, divide by half.

Source: Brad J. Sherman, Esq.

TABLE 48.   CORPORATE TAX RATES*

TAXABLE INCOME	RATE
Under $50,000	15 percent
Over $50,000 but not over $75,000	25 percent
Over $75,000 but not over $100,000	34 percent
Over $100,000 but not over $335,000	39 percent†
Over $335,000——	34 percent

*Tax year beginning July 1, 1987.
†The 39 percent rate includes 5 percent added tax to phase out the benefits of graduated rates between $100,000 but not over $335,000 of taxable income for years beginning after June 30, 1987.

TABLE 49.   STANDARD DEDUCTIONS 1989*

Joint return filers and surviving spouses	$5,200
Married filing separately	2,600
Head of household filers	4,550
Single filers	3,100

Personal Exemptions†

1988	$1,950
1989	2,000

*For years after 1988, the standard deduction will be subject to an adjustment for inflation.
†Beginning after tax year 1989, the $2,000 exemption amount will annually be subject to adjustment for inflation.

CHILD-CARE TAX TREATMENT

Both the child-care tax credit and the Dependent Care Assistance Plan (DCAP), a salary reduction, have an earnings requirement. In the case of a married couple, both must show earned income to qualify.

The maximum child-care expenditure that can be used for child- or dependent-care *credit* is limited to $4,800 in the case of two qualifying children. The credit is scaled according to taxable income with a maximum credit of 30 percent of the $4,800 for income at $10,000. The credit cannot exceed the amount of income earned.

The sliding scale is shown in table 50, page 256.

The child-care tax credit is a valuable tool for working parents who must pay large expenses, provided their incomes meet the test. (A homemaker cannot obtain the credit unless she is actively engaged in seeking employment.)

A disadvantage to this credit will be obvious to anyone who has had to pay for child care in an urban area. The figure against which the credit is issued and the income limits are unrealistically low. Quality child care for children from two and a half to

TABLE 50.

FAMILY ADJUSTED ($4,800)† GROSS INCOME	PERCENT*	1 CHILD ($2,400)†	2+ CHILDREN
0–$10,000	30	$700	$1,440
$10,001–$12,000	29	696	1,392
$12,001–$14,000	28	672	1,334
$14,001–$16,000	27	648	1,296
$16,001–$18,000	26	624	1,248
$18,001–$20,000	25	600	1,200
$20,001–$22,000	24	576	1,152
$22,001–$24,000	23	552	1,104
$24,001–$26,000	22	528	1,056
$26,001–$28,000	21	504	1,008
$28,001 and above	20	480	960

*Percent of employment related dependent care expenses permitted as credit.
†Maximum amount to which credit percent can apply.

five years of age runs approximately $400 a month in many areas. This is $4,800 a year for one child.

During the tax reform process, the Women and Tax Coalition, a Washington, D.C., lobbying group, pointed out that because of the phaseout feature, very few families can actually qualify for the maximum credit because no one earning $10,000 a year would spend $4,800 for child care. In practice, the credit has limited value to middle-income families.

Another option is the Dependent Care Assistance Plan (DCAP), which allows for either employer-paid, nontaxable care (or other benefits) or a voluntary salary reduction very much like the 401(k) plan, except that it is for child-care purposes. The money comes off the top before the salary is paid. The amount that can be spent is limited to $5,000 or the earned income of you or your spouse, whichever is lower.

THE TIME VALUE OF MONEY

TABLE 51.   PRESENT VALUE OF $1.00

YEAR	DISCOUNT RATE 10 PERCENT
1	.909
2	.826
3	.751
4	.683
5	.621
6	.564
7	.513
8	.466
9	.424
10	.385
11	.350
12	.318
13	.289
14	.263
15	.239
16	.217
17	.197
18	.179
19	.163
20	.148

SPECIAL TIPS

ON MARRIAGE

AND MONEY

Marriage historically meant total financial and legal subordination for women; even with the enormous changes in American law and custom, women today still very often bring less economic clout to the marital partnership. It is now possible for a married woman to maintain a separate financial identity and enjoy the benefits of her partnership in an economic unit. To do so, however, she has to be aware of her financial rights and responsibilities as an individual and as a spouse.

Despite the advent of "palimony," the legal distinction between being married and just living together remains intact. Marriage creates specific property rights and financial responsibilities, such that even if you and your spouse choose not to commingle your assets and financial affairs totally, you must still pay attention to the legal implications of marriage.

Many married couples simply fall into the "most convenient" system of decision making and operating the family budget given their resources and circumstances. Often these arrangements result in the woman's being a less-than-equal partner.

Prenuptial Financial Planning

People who discuss money management issues before they marry probably find it easier to develop a money management plan that squares with the value systems of both partners and ensures that each has a full say in the family finances. Just as many couples seek premarital counseling with their minister or a therapist in preparation for the emotional responsibilities of marriage, they may also find it extremely useful to have a premarital session with an attorney—not only to discuss their material rights and responsibilities but also to prepare a prenuptial agreement reflecting their financial intentions. It is my feeling that if an engaged couple cannot agree on property and money matters, they should postpone the wedding—perhaps indefinitely.

Prenuptial agreements, formerly the preserve of the rich, are now becoming popular in the middle class, especially with people who have been married before, or who marry for the first time later in life. One reason is that partners who bring a good deal of prior experience to marriage often bring material assets that they want to keep separate from material property for children or other heirs.

For a prenuptial agreement to have validity, it is imperative that both partners fully disclose all assets and specify those that are to be included in—or excluded from—the assets of the marriage. If one spouse hides a real estate fortune, for example, any prenuptial agreement made under these circumstances would not be binding, and the other spouse could have a legal claim on the hidden asset.

The only way to restrict your spouse's legal claim on assets is to list all your assets and specifically state in a prenuptial agreement which assets your spouse is to have no claim on. A prenuptial agreement should also address what will happen at the end of the marriage—whether through the death of one or both of you, or through divorce. Think of this section of the agreement as "marriage insurance." Each of you should prepare or update your will pursuant to the prenuptial agreement.

Don't forget to talk about how you would handle the custody of your children. If you have any children from a previous relationship or other dependents (parents you support, for example), you may want to declare some previously acquired major assets separate from marital property so that they can clearly be reserved for your children. This move has benefits beyond purely financial considerations: children who might fear being displaced by a new marriage could be somewhat reassured knowing you have taken special care to protect their financial interests in your estate.

How you will handle your credit matters during the course of the marriage, and also in the event of its termination, should also be spelled out. I strongly advise a woman to keep credit in her own name to avoid loss of her credit identity.

If you want, your prenuptial agreement can even specify who will perform which housekeeping tasks and state the religion in which future children will be raised. However, specialists in marital and property law note that since "quality of life" agreements are ordinarily not enforceable (except for children's religion) the way property agreements are, quality of life clauses can serve as little more than a personal statement of intent.

For a complete checklist of what you need to have on hand for a prenuptial consultation with your lawyer, it may be helpful to consult the Prenuptial Checklist on pages 262–65 at the end of this appendix.

What if later you want to change your prenuptial agreement? A prenuptial agreement is a legal contract, and like any other contract, it can be revised with the agreement of both parties. If only one partner wants changes, she or he would have to pursue the matter in court.

Warning: If you are planning to be a full-time homemaker for an extended period, make sure your prenuptial agreement spells out the financial terms on which your at-home contribution to the household economy is to be recognized. For example, even if you live in a separate-property state, you may want to emulate the California community-property model in which the homemaker-spouse automatically owns half of everything. Conversely, if you live in a community-property state and expect to be a full-time homemaker, be sure you do not sign away your community-property rights.

For the Already Married: Revising Your Economic Partnership

If you are married now, you may be thinking, All this prenuptial stuff is great, but it's a little late for me. Whenever I talk with women in traditional marriages, they most frequently want to know how they can readjust the financial power imbalance without alarming their husbands. Because sitting down to rework ongoing financial arrangements has traditionally been a first step to separation, the suggestion can put an otherwise reasonable spouse on the defensive. Even professional women who are married to other professionals sometimes have difficulties here. It is never too late to change your financial arrangements, but you must proceed with logic.

If you are not sure that you want to become a full "managing partner" in your joint economic interests, you should still have a complete, accurate, up-to-date picture of your financial position. The spouse who functions in the managing partner role should provide the other with monthly or quarterly reports. In any event, you both should strive to avoid the kind of dependency that frequently arises when a husband dies and leaves money in trust for his surviving spouse (that is, under the management of financial advisers or bankers in her behalf—an arrangement I do not recommend). A widow in that situation often discovers that no matter how little financial expertise she has previously acquired, she nonetheless must become capable of overseeing her trustee. This is another argument for both spouses learning the financial basics.

Separate Is Not Equal

Having observed or experienced the effects of lopsided economic partnerships, many women and men seek complete financial autonomy, even when they are married. Organizing your financial affairs by what is "yours," "mine," and "ours" usually results in the most equitable arrangements.

For most couples, it is virtually impossible to keep finances completely separate. Money is often too tight and time too scarce to keep income and expenses strictly divided between "hers" and "his." It is more practical for both to contribute from her or his income into a joint household account from which all the family bills are paid. But you should always, if possible, also have separate, individual accounts as well.

There is no escaping the fact that once you tie the marital knot, your finances are joined in a unique way. It is up to the two of you to make sure that your finances are organized in such a way that gives you both security and independence.

Prenuptial Checklist

ASSETS

Bring a complete list and full documentation. For example, if you own real estate, bring the trust deed; if stocks or bonds, the identifying information; if a car, the license plate number and registration; if jewelry, an official appraisal. Be prepared to specify which assets are to be excluded from marital property.

DEBTS

Bring a list of all debts and clarify how these will be paid. Generally, each of you is solely responsible for liabilities incurred before the marriage ceremony, but you should both know the debt load that each partner carries. Specify which credit cards you intend to keep separate and which accounts you will share both during the marriage and thereafter, should you divorce.

WILL

Know what you want to leave to your children and what you want done with your possessions when you die. You should both make wills if you have any assets, personal property, or children. To protect your children, be sure to specify the individual you want as guardian of the children themselves *and* the individual you want as guardian of their estate. The two can be the same individual or two different individuals.

MONEY MANAGEMENT

Specify how you intend to set up your bank accounts and clarify to whom the money belongs—hers, his, or ours. In some states simply keeping the money in a separate account does not obliterate your partner's interest—unless you specifically agree in writing. Use the meeting to clear up all points of money management that concern you.

QUALITY OF LIFE

If there are issues that concern you, such as housekeeping responsibilities, religious practices, and so on, you can include a statement of intent in your prenuptial agreement.

PROPERTY TITLE

Ask your attorney about the property laws of your state with specific reference to control of property during marriage and disposition of property on dissolution of the marriage.

Who Owns What According to State Law

Our states follow two different types of property law, one deriving from English common law and the other from Roman law and the Napoleonic code or civil law. Write your state attorney general for a booklet on marital property rights.

COMMON-LAW OR SEPARATE-PROPERTY STATES

If you live in a separate-property state, the general rule is that your earnings are yours and his are his. Each of you has the right to manage and dispose of your own earnings. The property each of you brought into the marriage belongs to you individually, as does any subsequent inheritance.

If one spouse dies and does not leave a will, the surviving spouse would be entitled to between a third and a half of the property of the deceased, depending on state law. Your right to continue to live in the family home would depend on how title is held.

If you divorce, you cannot count on being awarded half of marital assets. Most separate-property states have moved to a system of equitable distribution, under which the assets are divided proportionately according to the ages of the two spouses, their individual earning capacities, the number and ages of their children, and other criteria set by law in various states. This system is usually better for women than the old common law, under which the wife's claim to any property not specifically in her name was limited.

COMMUNITY-PROPERTY STATES

In the eight community-property states (California, Texas, Arizona, Nevada, New Mexico, Louisiana, Idaho, and Washington) each spouse owns an undivided 50 percent interest in the community—for example, all earnings and property acquired during the marriage, excluding individual inheritances and property each brought into the marriage. In general, even if you keep all your earnings separate, your spouse is entitled to half of them, as long as you are entitled to his. If you buy property, your spouse will have half-interest unless you make a specific written exception. The control of community assets, including your individual salaries, varies from state to state. Traditionally, although the wife owned half, management of the community was vested in the husband. Since the early 1970s, community-property laws have been changed to allow equal-management rights in most states. California went one step further and gave either spouse the right to commit 100 percent of the community. In theory, if you lived in California and your husband earned $100,000 a year, you would have the right to spend all of it down to the last penny—and he would have equivalent rights over your earnings, too.

In community-property states, each spouse also has the right to will her or his half of community property to any heir of her/his choosing. Thus, if you want to protect your tenancy in the family home (which is usually community property), you had better make sure that your spouse does not will an interest in it to someone else.

Upon the dissolution of a marriage in community-property states, half of the community property and assets goes to each spouse unless there is a legal agreement to another arrangement.

Wisconsin has adopted a uniform marital-property act that gives rights which are a hybrid between the two predominant systems.

Once You're Married: A Postnuptial Financial Inventory

BANK ACCOUNTS

Your banker should know you as an individual as well as part of a couple, and only through having separate bank accounts can you ensure separate financial identities. (You may even wish to have your personal accounts at different banks or branches.) Separate accounts also ensure that in the case of death or incapacitation of one partner, the other would have immediate access to cash, unhampered by red tape.

YOUR HOME AND OTHER REAL PROPERTY

You both need to understand the difference between jointly and separately owned assets. The United States Constitution leaves property laws for the states to define, so the first step is to learn how your own state handles property ownership. In most states, if your name is not on the title you do not have an interest in the property, but there are some states that recognize both spouses' interest in property even when only one name is listed on the title—as long as there is no written agreement to the contrary.

You may encounter four ways of owning property with someone else, and you should know the basic differences between them:

1. *Joint Tenancy.* You both own half, but you cannot will your half to anyone other than your partner, who automatically inherits your portion when you die.

2. *Tenancy in Common.* You own half and you can will your portion to whomever you like.

3. *Tenancy by Entirety.* In separate-property states only, this form of ownership works like joint tenancy, but is reserved for married people exclusively.

4. *Community Property.* This is a special form of ownership for married persons in community-property states. You each own an undivided half-interest, but at death you can will your portion to whomever you want.

Which of these forms of ownership you choose for assets shared between you and your spouse would depend on whether either of you has other heirs to whom you would like to leave your property interest, and on state law. Estate tax considerations also come into play here. Although dying intestate—that is, without a will—imposes burdens on your survivors and/or heirs that you should avoid, a surviving spouse can inherit property held in joint tenancy (all states) or tenancy by the entirety (separate-property states) without a formal will. (*Note:* The 1981 Economic Recovery Tax Act eliminated federal inheritance taxes between spouses.)

CREDIT

A married woman should be sure to have at least a bank card (Visa or MasterCard) in her own name—that is, Elizabeth Thomas or Elizabeth Thomas Scott, or even Elizabeth Scott, but not Mrs. John Scott. For credit purposes, Mrs. John Scott is persona non grata.

The Equal Credit Opportunity Act of 1974 provides that a married woman has the right to claim the credit records on joint accounts or accounts she uses with her husband when she applies for credit on her own. However, married women still frequently have trouble securing individual credit because so many creditors fail to report joint-account performance on the married woman's individual credit record. Although the law requires such reporting for accounts opened after 1977, the only way you can be sure it happens is to write your local credit reporting agency and obtain a copy of your credit report. To learn more about credit rights, see my book *Staying Solvent: A Comprehen-*

sive Guide to Equal Credit for Women (New York: Holt, Rinehart and Winston, 1985).

RETIREMENT

Retirement is another area in which separate is not equal. There was federal legislation in the 1970s to upgrade and protect women's rights in this area. Now, a two-earner married couple can contribute $2,000 each to separate tax-free Individual Retirement Accounts (IRAs), for a total of $4,000 annually, provided you meet the earnings limits if you have a pension. A one-earner couple (in which one spouse is a homemaker or has a small earned income) also has the option to establish a "Spousal-IRA" for each partner, provided they file a joint return. However, the combined annual contribution to both accounts cannot exceed $2,250. No more than $2,000 a year can be paid to either account, but equal payments can be made to both. Full-time homemakers should also remember that in the case of divorce or, in some cases, your spouse's death, you could lose some or all of your interest in your spouse's employer-paid pension fund. Check all the facts of the plan and be sure to include pension disposition in your financial review.

INSURANCE

If you are both wage earners and both incomes are essential to the family, then both of you need to review insurance options— health, life, and disability. You want to make sure that the face amount of any life insurance coverage is enough to replace the annual income of the deceased for as many years as you anticipate the surviving partner would need it. If one partner is a full-time homemaker, and you have small children, you may want to insure the homemaker's life so that the surviving partner could purchase home and child-care services should the homemaker die. (You can *discount,* that is, purchase life insurance bearing a lower face amount to reflect the fact the lump-sum death benefit could be accumulating interest in the bank at the same time the surviving spouse and dependents slowly consume it.) Conversely, do not overinsure yourselves. Put the money to work in investments.

You both should consider purchasing disability coverage beyond what would ordinarily be provided by state worker's compensation. Unfortunately, extra disability coverage—if the cost is not paid or at least shared by your employer—is prohibitively expensive for many. Full-time homemakers, in most cases, cannot obtain this coverage at all.

RESOURCES

FOR

ENTREPRENEURS

AMERICAN WOMAN'S ECONOMIC DEVELOPMENT COR-
PORATION (AWED), 60 East Forty-second Street, New
York, NY 10165; telephone 1-800-442-AWED; New York
City, Alaska, or Hawaii: 212-692-9100. Offers workshops,
training programs, counseling. Members have access to low-
cost insurance, product discounts, newsletter, and referrals:
annual fee. Four specialized training and support groups
offered for women at different stages of business development, plus counseling programs, including a fee-based hot
line.

BUSINESS PLANNING WORKSHEET, Office of Small Business Development Center, 400 Commercial Street, University of New Hampshire, Manchester, NH 03103; telephone
603-625-4522. These worksheets are helpful organizational
aids that include topics such as marketing strategy, financial projections, and business plans. They can be purchased
in a set with Dr. William Osgood's *Business Planning Guide*
(Black Diamond, Inc.): $21.50 as a set, $16.50 for the book,
or $9.00 for the worksheets (includes postage).

EMILY CARD, Ph.D., J.D., Attorney at Law and Consultant, P.O. Box 3725, Santa Monica, CA 90403; telephone 213-461-3622. Business and strategic planning, financial projections, and fund-raising for businesses and individuals. Hourly rates and fee-based telephone consultations. Call or write for further information.

ENTERPRISE ASSOCIATES, Rural Route 1, Box 238A, South Street, Cummington, MA 01026; telephone 413-268-3697. Offers financial planning, cash-flow analysis, and strategy on marketing, organizational, and employee issues. Hourly rates.

INDUSTRY ORGANIZATIONS. Locate organizations within your industry by using the *Encyclopedia of Associations* (Gale Research Company, Detroit, MI), updated annually and available at most libraries.

NATIONAL ASSOCIATION OF WOMEN BUSINESS OWNERS (NAWBO), 645 North Michigan Avenue, Chicago, IL 60611; telephone 312-951-9110. Offers networking, lobbying, and educational programs: initial fee, annual fee, and variable local fee. Sole proprietors, partners, and corporate owners with day-to-day responsibility are eligible to join.

NATIONAL FEDERATION OF BUSINESS AND PROFESSIONAL WOMEN'S CLUBS (BPW), 2012 Massachusetts Avenue, N.W., Washington, D.C. 20036; telephone 202-293-1100. Offers a credit card program, a national magazine, insurance programs, training programs, lobbying, legislative updates, a financial newsletter, and investment programs: local annual fee for members; annual fee for inactive "members at large."

SMALL BUSINESS ADMINISTRATION (SBA), 1441 L Street, N.W., Washington, D.C. 20416; telephone 1-800-368-5855. Offers "prebusiness" workshops, free and for-sale publications, and assistance programs—including SCORE program; ACE (Active Corps of Executives); SBI (Small Business Institute); and SB development centers at selected universities. For more information about these services in your area, call the toll-free number above for a referral to your local office. Two useful SBA publications: "Women's Handbook: How SBA Can Help You Go into Business" and "Women Business Owners: Selling to the Federal Government."

U.S. CHAMBER OF COMMERCE, 4940 Nicholson Court, Kensington, MD 20895; telephone 1-800-638-6582. Offers subscriptions to *Business Advocate* (newspaper) and *Nation's Business* (magazine), brochures, pamphlets, lobbying, and legislative updates: $125 annual fee. Call the toll-free number listed for more information or contact the chamber of commerce in your city for services specific to your area.

ANNUAL

TAX

UPDATE

The tax information in this book is current as we went to press in late 1989 and should be accurate for filing 1989 taxes. However, the tax laws are subject to legislative change and constant interpretation in the courts.

For the tax year 1990 and after, stay current by checking in your library for current information.

To receive the annual *Tax Alert for Women,* write Women's Credit and Finance Project, P.O. Box 3725, Santa Monica, CA 90403. Enclose a self-addressed stamped envelope for price list. Specify year(s) required.

ESTATE

PLANNING

If your investments are sizable, if you have dependents, or if you care about the disposition of your hard-earned money, you should do two kinds of planning for after your death: examine your will (along with tax planning for your estate) and life insurance (see Appendix 9 for insurance).

Your Will

You should draw up a will if you have any assets, personal property, or children. If you are married, both you and your spouse should have separate wills. Be sure to specify a guardian for your children (if any), as well as a guardian for your estate (the two may be the same person if you so choose).

Another protective measure that you can take for your children is to start estate tax planning. Many estate taxes are easily avoidable, thus leaving behind more money for your loved ones. If your assets, your spouse's assets, and your life insurance add up to around $600,000, it will probably be worth it for you to obtain tax-oriented estate advice.

INSURANCE

Life and disability insurance protect your income for yourself or your family. You take out a policy against your ability to provide for yourself, your spouse, and your children. Generally, though (and this is true for most kinds of insurance), people buy too much insurance or the wrong kind of insurance plan for their needs. You usually cannot entrust insurance agents with all your decisions; remember, they work on commission. When purchasing insurance, the best way to protect yourself is to do some basic research and to shop around.

Life Insurance

If you are single and have sufficient assets to cover funeral expenses or are married without children and both you and your spouse earn good wages, forgo life insurance. The same thing goes if your family is very wealthy, wealthy enough to do without the income that you provide. Everyone else, though, should purchase some form of life insurance.

The tricks to life insurance, as with any other type of insurance, are trying to determine how much coverage and what type of plan to acquire. This is no simple matter. However, the following information should serve as a starting point.

When you buy life insurance, you seek to keep your family at about the same financial level after your death as when you were alive. Thus, your insurance should cover your income minus the money you take up when alive. Most experts estimate that figure to be around 75 percent of your take-home pay. So, if you make $24,000 per year after taxes, you should insure yourself for about $18,000 per year. However, you should subtract from the 75 percent figure other sources of income that you have now or that will kick into effect should you die, such as Social Security survivor benefits, pension and profit-sharing plans, savings, and investments.

Unfortunately, all too often people assume that because the homemaker doesn't contribute tangible income, she or he does not need to be insured. If you or your spouse is a homemaker and you have children, the homemaker should definitely insure herself or himself at an amount that would compensate for child care and the many other vital tasks a homemaker carries out.

In choosing an insurance company, check out its "Best" rating. A. M. Best & Co. rates insurance companies on their financial strength. Because there are so many insurance companies with A+ ratings (the best possible), you should probably deal only with them.

Now, let us turn to the different kinds of life insurance offered. There are two rather loose categories of life insurance: term and whole life.

Term insurance gives coverage for a set amount of time, usually one year. You can get renewable or nonrenewable term insurance. Nonrenewable is cheaper and can actually be renewed. However, to renew you must requalify for the policy by taking a physical or filling out a health questionnaire. This means that the insurance company can refuse to renew your term insurance if you are less healthy (when you need it most). Renewable insurance is more expensive by 25 to 60 cents per $1,000 of coverage—but it is worth it. When your policy expires, the company must renew it at your request unless you have not paid your premium.

Term insurance is the most flexible and inexpensive of the two categories of life insurance. However, the disadvantage is that your premiums increase as you go along. In many instances, term insurance may be the best to buy, particularly if you and your spouse do not have a lot of money to spend on insurance.

The second category of life insurance is *whole life* insurance. With whole life, you give your insurance company premiums, part of which go to your insurance policy (which is basically the same as term insurance). The company then invests the rest of your premium (minus the administrative expenses of the company) on your behalf. This accumulating cash value belongs to you. You can cash in your policy or take it out in the form of policy loans. The advantage of whole life insurance over other investments is that the interest you earn from the investment is tax-free until you withdraw it. You also have fixed premiums. The catch is that these premiums are much higher than those of term insurance. In addition, you are paying for more commission. Another disadvantage is that during the initial years you hold the policy, most of your money goes to cover commissions and fees. Thus, you must hang on to whole life for at least five years (and even longer is better) for it to pay off.

Traditional whole life is usually not a good investment because it invests in very long-term instruments such as mortgages, which as we have seen can become less valuable over time. Other types of whole life insurance such as universal (which invests in money-market funds) and variable (you pick your own investments) whole life are better choices if you are going to buy whole life insurance.

In the end, some experts recommend buying term insurance and investing your own money, but you need to check around and see what is the best for your own situation.

Disability

Disability coverage is key. Unfortunately many people do not realize this. In fact, people between the ages of thirty-five and sixty-five are much more likely to become disabled than to die. Insurance companies allow only up to a certain percentage of your salary to be insured, generally 60 to 70 percent.

The costs of disability differ because of such variables as your age, gender, or occupation, and the waiting period you choose. A policy with a longer waiting period (that is, the time you must wait when disabled until your insurance kicks in) is less expensive than a policy with a shorter waiting period. Weigh the amount you save on these policies against your income loss for the waiting period of the policy.

Be careful when buying disability to buy "guaranteed renewal." This way, the company can cancel you only for not paying your premiums. Also, look for the word *noncancellable*, meaning that your premiums are set for the entire life of the policy.

INDEX

Table references are indicated by a T following the page number, for example, 235T.

279